Routledge Revivals

Introduction to Proust

This book, first published in 1940, provides an introduction to the life and work of the French novelist, critic, and essayist Marcel Proust, who is considered by many to be one of the greatest authors of all time. This book will be of interest to students of literature.

Introduction to Proust
His Life, His Circle and His Work

Derrick Leon

First published in 1940
by Kegan Paul, Trench, Trubner & Co., Ltd.

This edition first published in 2015 by Routledge
2 Park Square, Milton Park, Abingdon, Oxon, OX14 4RN
and by Routledge
711 Third Avenue, New York, NY 10017

Routledge is an imprint of the Taylor & Francis Group, an informa business

© 1940 Derrick Leon

All rights reserved. No part of this book may be reprinted or reproduced or utilised in any form or by any electronic, mechanical, or other means, now known or hereafter invented, including photocopying and recording, or in any information storage or retrieval system, without permission in writing from the publishers.

Publisher's Note
The publisher has gone to great lengths to ensure the quality of this reprint but points out that some imperfections in the original copies may be apparent.

Disclaimer
The publisher has made every effort to trace copyright holders and welcomes correspondence from those they have been unable to contact.

ISBN 13: 978-1-138-90802-4 (hbk)
ISBN 13: 978-1-315-69481-8 (ebk)

INTRODUCTION TO PROUST
HIS LIFE, HIS CIRCLE AND HIS WORK

DERRICK LEON

LONDON
KEGAN PAUL, TRENCH, TRUBNER & CO., LTD.
BROADWAY HOUSE, 68-74 CARTER LANE, E.C.4.

First published 1940

Printed in Great Britain by
Lowe and Brydone Printers Limited, London, N.W.10

To
VIRGINIA AND LEONARD
WOOLF

AUTHOR'S NOTE

For biographical facts and other material regarding my subject, I have gone first to Proust's own works, and then to his collected letters. Material has been derived also from the books which are to be found listed at the end of this volume. To all of these I am indebted; but most of all am I indebted to the writers of those vivid and expressive essays, monographs and memories of Proust, who not only admired the author, but both knew and loved the man.

The passages quoted from *A la Recherche du Temps Perdu* come from the fine English translation by C. K. Scott-Moncrieff, which was concluded, after his death, by Stephen Hudson, and is now published in its entirety by Messrs. Chatto & Windus.

CONTENTS

PART ONE

	PAGE
CHAPTER I.	15

Childhood and adolescence: Illiers, the Champs Élysées and the Lycée Condorcet: early friendships and first literary efforts

CHAPTER II. 29

Entrance into Society: the drawing-room of Mme Strauss: portrait of the young author: the literary coteries of Mme Aubernon, Mme Arman de Caillavet and Mme de Loynes

CHAPTER III. 44

Military service: new friendships: Anatole France: choosing a career: the Sorbonne: *Le Banquet*: Mme Laure Hayman and the receptions of Mme Lemaire

CHAPTER IV. 57

Robert de Montesquiou

CHAPTER V. 64

The invalid about Town: the "imitations": the Princesse Mathilde: supper at Weber's and nocturnal discussions

CHAPTER VI. 77

The Honorary Attaché to the Mazarine Library: *Les Plaisirs et les Jours*: *Les Lauriers sont Coupés*: the duel

CHAPTER VII. 88

The Dreyfus Case

CHAPTER VIII. 96

First journalistic pieces: the invalid at home: more new friendships: the Gothic Cathedrals: the family circle: death of Professor Proust

CONTENTS

	PAGE
CHAPTER IX.	107

The *Bible of Amiens*: *Figaro* sketches: death of Mme Proust

CHAPTER X. 113

Sesame and Lilies: imprisonment at Versailles: preparation for *À la Recherche du Temps Perdu*

CHAPTER XI. 120

Years of work: more *Figaro* sketches: holidays at Cabourg: the search for a publisher: the choice of titles: the appearance of *Swann*

CHAPTER XII. 139

War: the amplification of the novel: Céleste: the change of publishers: more new friends: the armistice

CHAPTER XIII. 149

The appearance of *Pastiches et Mélanges* and *À l'Ombre des Jeunes Filles en Fleur*: the move from the Boulevard Hausmann: the *Prix Goncourt*: success at last: *Le Côté de Guermantes* and *Sodome et Gomorrhe*: friendship with the critics: last days

PART TWO

CHAPTER I. 169

Posthumous publications: an outline of *À la Recherche du Temps Perdu*

CHAPTER II. 213

The effects of Time and the world of Society

CHAPTER III. 228

The chief characters of the book, their derivations and development. Swann: Odette: Mme Verdurin: the Guermantes: Françoise

CHAPTER IV. 264

The world of Art: Berma, Vinteuil, Elstir and Bergotte

CHAPTER V. 271

Gilberte and Albertine: desire, jealousy and love

CONTENTS

	PAGE
CHAPTER VI.	281
Memory and the unconscious: imagination and habit	
CHAPTER VII.	288
Time Regained: consciousness and reality: the inspiration and the function of creative art	
CHAPTER VIII.	297
Critical survey and conclusion	
BIBLIOGRAPHY	310
INDEX	313

PART ONE

CHAPTER I

In the autumn of that dramatic and disastrous year, 1870, there was conceived the child who, half a century later, was to be generally recognized as the greatest novelist of his time. The months preceding his birth were deeply shadowed with uncertainty and gloom. Gone, now, were the courtly splendours, the pomp, the pride, of but a year before. The brilliance of the Exhibition of 1867 was but a memory, and tales of the princely throng that had filled the capital, a legend and a dream. That apogee of gaiety and luxurious ease was now remote as Troy. The arrogance that had entered upon a war with aggressive triumph, was eclipsed by all the humiliation of defeat. The Second Empire crushed and fallen, the emperor exiled and the army vanquished, Paris was in mourning alike for her departed glory and for her slain. The tragic failure at Sedan and the revolution of the fourth of September had so weakened the resistance of the nation that it desired now nothing but peace. But the peace that followed was bitter to the heart of a stubborn, conquered nation; a peace that brought with it little but the silent determination for revenge.

Such was the state of affairs when Marcel Proust opened his eyes for the first time on the 10th of July, in 1871. He was born in his father's spacious apartment at 9, boulevard Malesherbes; but though it was here that he passed most of his childhood and youth, his most vivid early memories were to be of the holidays which he spent on his aunt Amiot's estate at Illiers.

His father, Dr. Adrien Proust, was already eminent in his profession, not only as a private practitioner and a hospital physician, but as a professor of the faculty of medicine in the University of Paris. Descended from a staunch Catholic family for long established at Chartres, he had recently married an educated and beautiful young Jewess from the prosperous family of Weil: but despite this difference of religion, the atmosphere pervading their home was one of unusual harmony and devotion.

Two years later their second son, Robert, was born; and soon afterwards Marcel was often to be found leaning over his brother's pram and watching him with an alert and affectionate interest. All his impressions of these early summer holidays were of a richness which was seldom to be equalled later. Their little village, but a few miles from Chartres, was set in the beautiful countryside of Eure et Loire, almost equidistant from Normandy and Touraine; a countryside through which flow the sleepy, winding tributaries of the Loire, bordered by rows of poplars; a countryside of green fields and sweeping plains, dominated by the towers of the most noble of all the Gothic cathedrals of France.

Every year, when the streets of Paris became hot and dusty, and the leaves of the trees seemed to have grown old before their time, there was all the excitement of watching the preparations for the journey—country clothes being got out from cupboards and boxes packed. And then the rapture of the journey itself, with the crowded station and the whistling of engines, until finally the train steamed away and the boy could settle down to anticipate the pleasure of arrival. Every year, as they alighted from the train, he looked about him with the same exquisite delight in which the shock of recaptured familiarity was blended with surprise. He waited with intent anticipation for the sudden silence after the train had stopped, for the shouts of the porters; and, during the drive to the house, drank in with quiet appreciation the scent of the air, the shadows on the road, the shapes and colours of his favourite trees. Everything was bathed in the celestial light of childhood; and this was his seventh heaven, the paradise to which in after life he was to long so often and so poignantly to return.

Life, for the next few weeks would be full of simple and idyllic pleasures. Waking up to find the sky a singing blue and the sun pouring through the stiff white muslin curtains; going to Mass on Sunday mornings in the village church; coming out after the service to see the shadows of the shops and houses slanting across the dusty square; rushing into the kitchen as soon as they got home, to find out what there was for lunch; and going upstairs, as soon as the meal was over, to rest on his little white bed, while the sun, streaming through the fluttering curtains, made shadows on the floor like flowing water, and voices from the street below drifted up in an indistinct and drowsy murmur.

And then, just when he had almost fallen asleep, he would hear his mother calling to him to get ready to go out; and immediately the absorbing problem occupied him as to which direction they would take. Passionately devoted to her, the most customary walk upon which she accompanies them fills him with blissful satisfaction. Each small incident of the afternoon is imbued with wonder: the moments when his father pauses to talk to some passing neighbour; the friendly greetings exchanged with the village postman; the flowers that he finds unexpectedly growing beneath a hedge, or the glimpse of some church spire through a clump of trees. Often during these walks, he would pause to stare, with an almost rapt intensity, into the water of the stream beside him; or, gazing up at the sky, would watch, as though entranced, the transient formation of some drifting clouds; at other times, kneeling on the grass, he would examine a cluster of flowers with so intent and prolonged a scrutiny that his parents had to pause and call to him.

Sometimes, too, the family would come to Illiers for the

Easter holidays, when the apple orchards and the hawthorn trees in blossom aroused in him a sense of deep and poignant beauty which haunted him long afterwards.

And then, as soon as he had learned to read, there was born in him a new interest that was to become the abiding passion of his life—his love of books. No longer, in his rest hour after lunch, would he lie staring at the ceiling, while a train of thoughts and images passed vaguely through his mind, in a state of dreamy satisfaction heightened by his anticipation of the moment of release. But, completely absorbed in the tale he was reading, he could scarcely wait for the meal to be over in order to run up to his little room and continue in peace the strange and enthralling new existence into which it plunged him. In these long, drowsy summer afternoons, he made a series of stimulating and great discoveries—the novels of Georges Sand, Théophile Gautier and Dickens, the poems of Mallarmé: while the exotic and ever new Arabian Nights wove around him a fresh spell of wonder. Looking up, from time to time, to stare at the antiquated clock on the mantelpiece, or the old-fashioned, friendly furniture; to sniff the familiar, comfortable smell of beeswax, or listen to the peaceful, resonant chimes of the old church clock chiming the hour in the distance, these moments became indelibly printed in his memory, and for ever associated with the charm of the passage he had been reading. Nor could he lay aside his book even when it was time for him to go the accustomed walk. Whether at Illiers, now, or at home in Paris, a book was always his inseparable companion, and games, conversations and meals so many distractions which kept him away from this perfect friendship.

At Auteuil, where he went often at Easter to spend the holidays with an uncle of his mother, in his large and comfortable house in the rue la Fontaine, near the beautiful gardens of the old Convent of the Assumption, this passion still dominated his existence. He read in the mornings, while the rest of the family were out walking or writing letters, grudging even the time he must devote to meals: he read, whenever there was an opportunity after lunch; he read in bed at night, furtively, with the delicious pleasure of defying all laws, by the light of an extra candle carefully smuggled upstairs beforehand.

His uncle's house, despite its air of comfort, was rather more pretentious than imposing. The furniture, though impressive, was heavy and overcarved, and the walls decorated with large panels of imitation tapestry. The whole environment, indeed, though prosperous, was scarcely one of distinguished taste: but there was a large garden, and here, on state occasions, the boy was allowed to invite his friends. As he grew older these parties became a source of considerable pride and satisfaction. He dropped the habit of asking boys and girls to tea simply because they happened to be neighbours or the children of old family friends, and insisted upon choosing his guests from among his personal favourites. Some of the friendships he made on these visits to Auteuil, notably with Jacques-Émile Blanche, Gabriel de la Rochefoucauld and Fernand Gregh, were to endure for many years: and very soon he became the leader of a small circle with whom he could share his enthusiasm for literature and to whom he spouted resounding passages from his favourite poets.

Yet despite his great and early appreciation for nature and for literature; despite his affection for his brother Robert and his passionate devotion to his mother, his childhood was far from being entirely happy. His extraordinary sweetness of disposition, his bursts of unexpected gaiety, were always accompanied by an abnormal sensitiveness. The slightest thing would excite him unduly, or move him to a fit of weeping: added to which the general frailty of his constitution was soon to show itself in the malady which was never to leave him completely for the rest of his life.

In Paris it was the custom for the two boys to go for walks with their governess every afternoon in the Champs Élysées, sometimes accompanied by one or another of their young friends. One afternoon, when he was ten years old, and his brother had been in one of his customary moods of effervescent exuberance, Marcel was brought home hurriedly with a terrible attack of coughing. Although he was immediately put to bed, nothing could stop the frightful spasms which shook his delicate frame. Having tried every remedy she knew, his mother then sent an urgent message to Dr. Proust to come home without delay. By the time he arrived, the boy could scarcely breathe. Propped up on his pillows, he was coughing and choking with such violence that it seemed that he would never survive.

At last, however, the attack abated, and far into the night Mme Proust sat up at her son's bedside. But though her presence with him at this unwonted hour was a momentous event that should have caused him only the deepest bliss, it brought him little save a great sadness. For he understood then that her hopes that he should grow up healthy and strong as other children were now finally extinguished, and that the loving tenderness which she bestowed on him so freely was an open acknowledgment both of his own weakness and of the abiding sorrow it must cause her.

So many times in the past, after his last good-night kiss, he had begged in vain for her to remain with him, that now he realized that what would, in any other circumstances, have been his greatest pleasure, could no longer rejoice his heart, since it meant only defeat for her. But though not unmixed with pain, it brought him, at least, a long respite from the intermittent misery of torturing himself by thinking, when, on account of some naughtiness of his own, she was forced to mask her devotion for him with assumed indifference, that perhaps she had ceased to love him.

"Only give me your love" he had been wont to say, when,

in the past, his mother had asked him what he would like, as a present from her, for his birthday. "But of course, you little silly, you have that always," she would reply. "I mean what books or toys." Henceforward he was never again to doubt her word. But never again, in payment, except on very rare occasions, was he able to delight in the scent of his favourite flowers; and the joy of each new spring was always to be spoiled for him by violent attacks of hay fever and terrifying spasms of asthma.

The following year, nevertheless, he began his schooldays at the Lycée Condorcet; but his health was so uncertain that for a long time his attendance was most erratic, and interspersed with long and gloomy intervals spent in bed. Only several years later did he begin to pursue his studies with any vigour and enthusiasm. In the meantime, when he was well enough to go out, there were always his afternoons in the Champs Élysées. Here he already had a band of friends, similar to that of Auteuil, which he initiated by degrees into the delights of literature. His amazing precocity of taste must at first have been somewhat startling; but his sweetness of nature and lively good humour soon dissipated any suspicions as to the benefit to be derived from his friendship; and to several future writers—Robert Dreyfus, one of his earliest friends, the witty and sensitive Jean de Tinan, the gruff, sympathetic and passionate Louis de la Salle—to the embryo philosopher, Léon Brunschwicq and the daughters of the future President, Antoinette and Lucie Félix-Faure, he quoted from time to time verses from the latest poets to arouse his admiration—Racine, Hugo, de Musset, or Leconte de Lisle.

These, and a small host of other children, had a special meeting place where they collected almost every afternoon: a large grass plot with a fountain in the centre, near the Restaurant des Ambassadeurs; and here there were many and vigorous games of hide and seek and prisoners' base. In spite of this, however, Marcel had small compunction about deserting when some little girl appeared to whom he was particularly attracted, and at the ripe age of twelve he had already lost his heart, and went through all the frenzied ecstasies, the hopes, the pains and disappointments of a first love affair. At home, in the mornings, no matter if he was confined to bed or reading in the dining-room before lunch, all he could really think about was whether it would be fine enough in the afternoon for him to meet this little girl. If it was sunny, he was joyful: if it was misty or overcast, he was depressed; and the barometer in the hall at which he continually ran to look, foretold, no less than the weather, the state of his emotions for the day. Now, more than ever, the first necessity of his nature was to love and to be loved; and the grief he experienced was the more keen by reason of his complete ignorance of those laws which govern the emotions, and which later he was to discover for himself only after much suffering.

Often when he was confined to bed for a long period at a time, he would dream of these afternoons of comradeship with a wistful pleasure, and seek to console himself with intent and repeated glances at a photograph which one of his friends had given him. Having gazed for a long time at the portrait, he would turn it over to read again the inscription on the back—"To my best friend but one." He knew by now the formation of every word so well that he could copy it accurately, letter for letter, with his eyes closed. But how that little phrase "but one" disturbed him. Who, he wondered, was the fortunate mortal loved better than himself? Wistfully he brooded over the rapturous happiness his rival must enjoy. Some time later, however, when he was well enough once more to have visitors, his friend came to tea. The whole afternoon they talked together with the unclouded intimacy that always gave Marcel so much pleasure. When it was time for his companion to go, he pointed to the photograph in order to show him how much he treasured it. His friend took it up and turned it over. With a smile he glanced at his young host and then again at the inscription. At last, taking a pencil from his pocket, he obliterated the last two words and handed the photograph back. Marcel read the single remaining phrase, "To my best friend" with the greatest joy. It was one of the happiest moments of his life.

These periods of illness, alas, did more than interrupt his education. They prevented him from going in future to Illiers for his summer holidays. The pollen from the flowers, even the scent of his beloved hawthorn trees, was found to aggravate his asthma: and though sometimes, still, he went to stay with the uncle at Auteuil, his vacations henceforward were usually spent at Trouville or Cabourg, both, now, at the height of their glory, where it was hoped that the sea air would fortify his constitution.

The Lycée Condorcet, situated in the rue Havre, was one of the oldest and most famous schools in Paris. Beneath the various names it had worn through the decades—Lycée Bonaparte, Lycée Condorcet, Lycée Fontanes, then Lycée Condorcet again—it had been the training ground of many distinguished statesmen, diplomats, journalists and poets. Far from being strict, the discipline, indeed, was considered by many of the parents to be too lax; and in the senior forms, the professors and their more promising pupils adopted a relationship that was rather more one of mutual friendship than is usually to be found in English schools. There were other major differences. Many of the pupils were day boys, whose status in the school was considered in no way derogatory: and though these might remain in the same division for many years without exchanging a word, when they did make friends, their friendships were usually based upon mutual sympathy rather than a common proficiency at football, and, instead of being drawn together because they happened to be in the same House, they were far more likely to become acquainted through a shared passion for history or science. Moreover, such relations had the additional advantage of being augmented at each other's homes, so that in time they naturally included most of the civilities of ordinary social life. The friends who, as small boys, went to tea with each other or played together in the afternoon in the Champs Élysées, later on became guests at each other's parents' dinner parties or receptions. But besides this, intelligence and originality were far more respected than at any English Public School. Therefore, instead of Proust being miserable and misunderstood during his school life, we find him, on the contrary, especially as he approached manhood, surrounded by a host of brilliant and admiring friends.

As soon as his health improved sufficiently to enable his attendance at lessons to become fairly regular, his interests began to deepen and increase. Literature was always to remain for him an absorbing passion, and he soon developed a precocious taste for the classics, which was based on an unusual appreciation of their worth. The enthusiasm with which he discovered in turn the Latin poets and the Greek tragedians was equalled only by the extraordinary spell which was cast over his imagination by great historic names. His history professor, M. Jallifier, author of several standard educational works, was a man who warmed to the faintest suggestion of genuine interest, and Proust knew well how to draw him out. But what distinguished the youth most, even at this early age, was his conversation and his writing, both of which were sufficiently extraordinary to arouse the curiosity and good-humoured jibes of his fellows. For at school, no less than at Auteuil or in the Champs Élysées, he was quick to seize any opportunity for delivering a dissertation on some newly discovered masterpiece. His appreciation of language was exceptional and his conversation reflected engagingly from term to term a series of special words he had but lately added to his vocabulary. He employed many recondite and literary phrases, and rolled upon his tongue with luxurious enjoyment a string of picturesque and pungent adjectives. His speech, already, was characteristic in the long and complex structure of its sentences: and this novel and involved discursiveness soon became apparent in his literary style. He always devoted the utmost care and attention to the preparation of his essays, and later they became monuments of skill and preciosity, full of unusual observations and original reflections. Of these the dry and pedantic M. Cauchval was not at all appreciative. He regarded them with the utmost suspicion and even with some distaste. The other professor of literature, however, M. Gaucher, a man of exceptional culture, and one of the literary critics on the *Revue Bleue*, was interested in them from the first, and did his utmost both to understand and to encourage their precocious author. Sometimes he read out his pupil's essays to the class, praising his sound judgment and criticizing with indulgent humour his intricate and elaborate style. Although this aroused for their author a considerable admiration among those of his fellows who shared his literary aspirations, and was even responsible for a wave of emulation among several of his class mates, who took, without success, to cultivating a florid and affected style, there were others who endured these performances with the glummest of disgust and put down the youthful writer to be both a *poseur* and a prig.

M. Gaucher, however, continued his encouragement, and considered Proust by far the most interesting and promising boy in his division. When an inspector from the university came one day to visit the class, the master instructed Proust to read aloud his last week's composition. The inspector, however, was anything but impressed by this extraordinary achievement. The reading finished, Proust sat down, while the inspector caustically inquired of M. Gaucher whether there was not, among the lower boys in the class, some pupil who wrote with greater clarity and correctness. "Sir," replied the indignant master, "none of my pupils are taught to write like copy books."

Second only to Proust's passionate love of literature was his love, almost as passionate, for philosophy. He listened to Professor Darlu's dissertations with a rapt attention, and discussed them later in enthusiastic detail with both his brother and his friends. His master's manner of discourse made a great appeal to him and he developed a friendly affection for him that was to endure for many years. The great systems of thought filled him with increasing excitement, and a thousand problems of time and space, of reality and consciousness, aroused his extraordinary genius for abstract thought and speculation. Plato's *Dialogues*, in particular, influenced him deeply,[1] and he tried to adopt the Socratic method of approach when discoursing with his companions. But though his arguments were long and tenacious, Proust was never dogmatic in his assertions, or anxious to convert anyone to his way of thought. It was of greater interest to him, by forcing his friends to express themselves with the utmost clarity, to try to enlarge his point of view and enrich his own understanding.

The circle of his friends, meanwhile, was steadily widening. There were now among his schoolfellows Pierre Lavallée, Louis de la Salle and Gabriel Trariaux from the old group of the Champs Élysées, and in addition others, such as the charming and intelligent Robert de Flers, the witty and high-spirited Jacques Bizet, with his talented cousin, Daniel Halévy; Léon Brunschwicq and Jacques Baignères. Proust, however, was still extremely sensitive, and subject to moods of painful doubt and depression when he felt that his friend-

---

[1] The influence of Plato is very apparent in the philosophical aspect of Proust's later work. Much of this, no doubt, came direct from Plato himself; but, indirectly, much also came from Ruskin, who himself averred that all the philosophy that he taught was Plato.

ship was not sufficiently reciprocated. If one of his companions omitted to say good morning to him, he would ponder for a week as to what he could possibly have done to offend him. This intense susceptibility was inclined to become a little wearisome to his companions. His almost ingenuous demonstrations of friendliness, while simply the spontaneous expression of an affectionate and generous nature, were frequently misunderstood and taken for a sign of affectation. His extravagant sympathy was considered weakness; just as his delight in dwelling upon historic names, a form of snobbery. On the other hand, his intense and passionate devotion to the things of the mind won him a very real respect. Moreover, in his lively and exuberant moods nobody could be more amusing: and often he was the first to laugh at his own exaggerated enthusiasms, his succulent adjectives and his passionate attachments.

Now it was the theatre that was his great topic of conversation, now some pretty little Viennese girl whom he had met in the holidays and with whom he went everywhere. He would expatiate with equal vigour on the wonderful performance Bernhardt had just given in *Hamlet*: the extraordinary grace and beauty of the famous courtesan Closmenil whom he had seen walking in the Bois, and with whom he had just exchanged photographs and a letter: or the great misfortune of not having been able to make use of an opportunity he was once offered, because his parents considered that he was too young to go out at night, of being taken to see Lemaître.

With those of his friends who shared his interest in letters, there were various attempts at producing a magazine. *La Revue Lilas* was one of these early efforts, a production with a rather sickly-looking mauve cover, and articles in manuscript, which was handed round from one to another of the band in turn. There were also the *Revue de Seconde*, *Lundi* and *La Revue Verte*, all pamphlets of a similar order, to which Daniel Halévy, Robert de Flers and Proust all contributed with the highest seriousness. Juvenile productions, certainly, and only of interest in retrospect: but there was nevertheless a sketch by Proust in the first named of these which is startlingly like a memorable passage which, a quarter of a century later, was to be found in *Swann*!

The constricted and narrow world of school, however, began at last to seem inexpressibly wearisome. A dozen conflicting desires were at work within him. He had days in which life was so rich and his vitality so great that he longed to do innumerable different things at once. He would like to give a tremendous party for all his friends, and delight and amuse them by some astonishing display of brilliance. He would like to set out, completely alone, to make a tour of all the Gothic cathedrals in Europe. He would like to have a series of tremendous and passionate affairs with half a dozen different beautiful and brilliant women. He would like to visit Italy and Spain: to bury himself alone in the heart of the country. He would like to retire from the world and write a masterpiece: to go into the world and cut a figure. He would like to see a thousand pictures, listen to a thousand symphonies, and read a thousand books.

His prizes for French composition, his honourable mentions in Latin and Greek, his prize of honour for dissertation, all these seemed to him now completely bereft of interest and value: as childish and remote as the toys he used to play with in the nursery. He wanted to meet new people, to make new friends. Already he had been invited to the receptions of his friend Bizet's mother, Mme Strauss, and to intimate dinner parties with Mme Baignères. He was well aware that they had found him amusing and intelligent; and the world of fashion exerted upon his imagination a persistent and compelling fascination. Let his friends consider him a snob and warn him that he would become nothing but a futile dilettante. Why should he care? He was seventeen and stood on the fringe of the great world!

CHAPTER II

As young as fifteen Proust had been taken to see Mme Strauss by her son, and had astonished her by his intelligent conversation and his curiously ceremonious manners. Now, entering her drawing-room again, he became, for the next few years, a habitual visitor; and thus began one of the most valued friendships of his life.

The drawing-room of Mme Strauss, already famous, was shortly to become one of the most entertaining and one of the most brilliant in Paris. A woman of remarkable beauty and intelligence, the daughter of Halévy, the composer of *La Juive*, Mme Strauss had been formerly the wife of the musician Bizet, and was now married to a talented barrister of great wealth and reputation. Although soon to be at the height of her success, she was nevertheless no stranger to the most poignant stings of failure and disappointment. She had been present at that terrible first night of *L'Arlésienne*, the work upon which her first husband had set all his hopes and had lavished so much care, when the majority of the audience had got up and walked out in the middle of the second act. She had seen him die, broken-hearted at his failure; and then witnessed after his death, when he could no longer profit by it, the spectacular success both of *Les Pêcheurs des Perles* and of *Carmen*; all of which had left deep traces on her character.

Of distinguished elegance in attire and address, her face was marked with both wistfulness and humour. Pale and oval, with large, dark pensive eyes, a sensitive and passionate mouth, its expression could convey tender sympathy or the most ironic wit. She had little taste for the usual insipid insincerities of society, however, and a positive horror of being bored.

Although a close friend of the Princesse Mathilde, and received by all the Faubourg St. Germain, she preferred to entertain in her own drawing-room people of intellect and humour. Her apartment in the boulevard Hausmann was beautifully furnished with a careful mixture of antique furniture and modern paintings. Her circle in the earlier days was comparatively small: it was considered an honour to be of it; and every newcomer was regarded by the longer favoured with a veiled resentment. For many years the English Ambassador, Lord Lytton, had been a constant visitor: while the glass of fashion, Arthur Meyer, and Forain, were also frequent guests. Her intimate receptions were held on Sunday evenings after dinner: but sometimes there would be vast "at homes" in which to work off the less welcome of her set. Renowned not only for wit and charm, but also for unerring taste in art and literature, she nevertheless laughed at all intellectual pretentions, and was careful that her house should never smack predominantly of the literary or pedantic. People were invited because they amused her, because she liked them, and not because she wished them to cast any indirect lustre upon herself.

Unfortunately, she suffered with nerves, and was extremely delicate: but, when she was confined to bed, many of the most fashionable duchesses would call simply for the pleasure of exchanging a few words with her through the door of her room. Stories of her wit were famous throughout Paris, and were passed on eagerly by all her friends. Of these is her retort at a large luncheon party, to some pertinacious and exasperating neighbour who would insist, despite all discouragement, in maligning one of her oldest friends. "I have already told you, he is a friend of mine," Mme Strauss was obliged to repeat at each fresh onslaught. Her neighbour was not in the least abashed. "Never mind," she replied, "you can have your revenge by talking about mine." Mme Strauss's reply was delivered with a superb and disarming suavity. "You have got friends, then?" Her victim routed, she could turn her attention to the acquaintance at her other side.

Such was the woman and the drawing-room that were to give the young aspirant his first impressions of society. His success was almost immediate. Who was this extraordinary youth, people wished to know, who would approach any one who interested him with the same sort of engaging candour as an affectionate puppy? Certainly there was much about him to arouse curiosity.

Already his appearance was distinguished by remarkable good looks. Though his build was but slender, and it was evident that he was not robust, his figure was lithe and graceful, and his face expressive of unusual intelligence and sensibility. Long and thin, with firm, full cheeks, his head was crowned with a splendid crop of fine, wiry, thick, well-brushed jet black hair. His nose was well modelled, but firmly arched—a fact which caused him much humorous consternation—and his rather full, sensitive mouth outlined with a small moustache. His most remarkable feature was his eyes. Large and black, with heavy drooping lids and long eyelashes, they would reflect instantaneously all that was in his mind. Just as his smile, which displayed so white a row of teeth, could be sympathetic, wistful or extraordinarily lively and infectious, so they would flash at one moment with gaiety or sarcasm, and at the next, stare pensively in front of him as though absorbed by some inner vision. His reactions were so vivid and spontaneous that often he had the greatest difficulty in concealing them, and frequently his hand would be raised to his mouth in order to hide the irrepressible smile some trivial incident had evoked. When his friends told him that he reminded them of some Neapolitan or Persian prince, he would give a low, complacent chuckle of appreciation; but he was never studiously concerned with his appearance. His voice, striking by reason of its faintly childish quality of candour and enthusiasm, could be as expressive of his thoughts and feelings as was his face. Low and gentle, with a wide range of inflections, its tone varied constantly from the gracious and deferential to the acidly sarcastic. Just as the slightest gesture of friendship would arouse his warm response, so the merest suspicion of dislike would cause a cloud to quench his accustomed buoyancy.

His manners, though inclined to ceremoniousness, were always natural, and he was as pleased to listen as to talk. People would unfold themselves to him quite simply on a first meeting, because this capacity for listening was the manifestation of an interest that combined both tolerance and understanding. His great desire was to know people as they were, and he was never tired of absorbing information. When he himself spoke, it was with an ease and an authority above his years. Scholars were amazed by the penetration of his intellect and the erudition of his learning just as writers were astonished by the breadth and certainty of his literary taste. Almost deliberately modest, he would seldom take the initiative in general discussions, but when he did express his views, it was with an earnestness and an originality that aroused an almost passionate attention. During the ensuing years he was to display, in the world of fashion and the world of literary cliques, the same enthusiasm and respect for music, art, poetry and philosophy that characterized his early youth; and his friends were to develop an increasing respect for his opinions.

To assume that he was universally admired and liked, however, would be quite erroneous. There were always people who took his intelligence for precocity, his enthusiasms for affectation, his exaggerated appreciation of his friends for flattery, his interest in the aristocracy for snobbery, and could see nothing but a form of distasteful sycophancy in the extraordinary gratitude he was always to evince for anyone who did him the slightest service.

Such then was the youth who was now to be seen leaning negligently over the antique gilt *bergère* in which Mme Strauss was usually seated, and fast discovering for himself the characters and idiosyncrasies of her friends.

Shortly afterwards, also, just before his departure for military service, Proust entered one of the literary coteries that was later to become as famous, in its way, as was already that of Mme Strauss in the world of fashion.

At this period, it was customary for eminent writers to gather in the drawing-rooms of such women as Mme Aubernon, Mme Arman de Caillavet and Mme de Loynes,[1] just as, in a previous epoch, they had been attracted to the circles of Mlle de Lespinasse, Mme Récamier and Mme du Deffand. And although it was to Mme de Caillavet that Proust was first introduced, in order fully to understand the social life of the period, and the better later to appreciate its portrayal in his work, it is necessary to pause for a moment and take a short survey of the literary scene.

The drawing-room of Mme Aubernon was already famous. Although it was not to reach the perihelion of its course for another few years, it had been steadily increasing in brilliance and importance during the past decade.

The niece of a fabulously rich banker, Mme Aubernon was a wealthy woman of the middle class, with a passionate devotion to literature and a tremendous taste for conversation. Although often wont to remark upon her glorious body, it must be admitted that she was somewhat stout. But if her looks were plain, they were usually forgotten in the vivacity of her smile and the infectious exuberance of her

[1] There were also the distinguished. if less famous, literary drawing-rooms of Mme Greffulhe and the Baronne Aimery de Pierrebourg. Although unnecessary to describe them here, it may be observed that there is evidence to show that later Proust became acquainted with them both.

manner. "You are never bored!" a lady one day remarked to her gushingly. "Sometimes," Mme Aubernon admitted, "during the night." Living apart from her husband, she was often referred to by her acquaintances as "*La Veuve*," while she herself was frequently heard to exclaim that she hoped one day to celebrate a golden wedding of blissful marital separation. With her mother, Mme de Nerville, she used to give huge receptions at her mansion in the square de Messina, which by their flavour had soon earned for both of them the title of "*Les précieuses radicales.*" Although there was always much vague reference to their intense republicanism, this phrase seems scarcely very apt, since they were very little precious, and radical not at all. The jibe of being blue-stockings, which also clung to them, certainly had a shred more justification, since their table was dedicated formally to literature and philosophy; and women remarkable only for their beauty or their smartness were rigorously excluded. "I am given to conversation," Mme Aubernon was wont to say, "and not to making love."

The atmosphere of her house was opulent but tasteless. A collection of old chasubles adorned the walls, and pieces of antique embroidery hung over the backs of comfortable but clumsy arm-chairs. The furniture was cumbersome and pretentious, and upon mantelpieces heavily festooned, there stood monumental dishes of wax fruit under glass. Not unlike this style of decoration was the cooking offered to her guests at dinners, where, apart from a formidable and famous spinach, renowned for the unpleasantness of its flavour, the courses were many and substantial, but remarkable only for their extreme banality.

It is to be presumed, however, that the visitors came to talk rather than to eat, for the conversation was considered to be remarkable both for its interest and its brilliance. Discussions were invariably general, and all intimate asides strictly forbidden. Mme Aubernon kept a bell beside her plate, and regulated the proceedings with a vigilant and indefatigable zest. At the slightest sign of rebellion, a terrific tintinnabulation would immediately reduce the offender to silence.

In her earlier days Mme Aubernon had tried to write. Her efforts, it must be admitted, were so lamentable that they proved a considerable source of embarrassment to the friends who had been called upon to offer criticism. Since then, the whole of her creative energies were directed towards debate. She would prepare a subject for discussion at the next dinner, studiously collecting her material so that she could shine at the subsequent engagement, which she would propose with a carefully dissimulated spontaneity. But the sudden questions she was accustomed to hurl at unsuspecting guests of honour could be extremely disconcerting. "What is your opinion of love?"[1] she once inquired of the completely unprepared d'Annunzio, who had been brought to lunch with her. "Madame," he replied, "pray read my books and let me eat." A more amusing retort was once made by a lady whose views upon adultery had been as unexpectedly asked. Casting down her eyes with affected demureness, the guest responded: "But, madame, I came this evening prepared only to talk of incest."

Gifted with a certain natural wit, Mme Aubernon studiously augmented her somewhat limited powers by carefully collecting in a special book the epigrams that she came across in her reading, learning them by heart and proudly quoting them later whenever a suitable opportunity arose. "Often, but a little at a time"[2] was one of these phrases she was particularly fond of repeating.

[1] "Love? I make it, constantly, but I never talk about it," is the retort that Mme Leroi makes to this question in *Le Côté de Guermantes*; another reply that may well have been made once to Mme Aubernon.
[2] This remark is to be found in *Du Côté de chez Swann*, where it is attributed by Marcel's grandfather, who frequently quotes it, to Swann's father, who is said first to have used it.

Her circle, including Renan, Dumas fils, Becque, Lemaître, Sardou and Ludovic Halévy (a cousin of Mme Strauss), was also composed of a number of unattractive and formidable old dowagers, friends of her mother, to whom she was accustomed to allude as her "sacred monsters." But the real importance of her influence was due to the theatrical performances which she staged in her house especially for her friends, many of which were subsequently shown in the more progressive repertory theatres of the day. She had her own private company, and, first in the huge hall of her mansion in the square de Messina and later, when she moved, in the rue d'Astorg and finally in the rue Montchanin, organized ambitious productions, not only of the works of her "chosen," but also of hitherto unknown pieces from abroad. She was first to produce Becque's *Parisienne*, with Antoine and Réjane; and the comedy *Village*, by Octave Feuillet. It is also to her eternal credit that it was at her house that there were played for the first time in Paris Ibsen's *Doll's House* and *John Gabriel Borkman*.

The production of these plays, however, was more successful when the "mistress" took no direct part in it. For a long time Dumas fils was the brightest star in her constellation of celebrities, and her admiration of him was unbounded. At the performance of his play, *Diane de Lys*, there was a sort of prologue in which she herself suddenly appeared as the presiding deity of drama, in a costume specially created to exhibit the depth of her homage to the author. Her vast form was swathed in a wide band the colour of the Legion of Honour, on which was inscribed in letters of gold the titles of all his other works. On her head, slightly askew, there was perched a gilded bust of her distinguished idol. It was a moment of acute embarrassment for all her guests; and even Dumas found it a little difficult to accept this apparition with seemly enthusiasm. To the further discomfort of her friends, she later appeared in an even more fantastic version of this attire at a costume ball. On this occasion, the same shining effigy crowned her head, but the names of the immortal works were inscribed on fluttering streamers which all but concealed the "glorious" figure of which the wearer was so proud.

Passionately devoted to her "faithful," Mme Aubernon would continue to entertain them during the summer at her country house, Cœur Volant, in Louveciennes; but her almost possessive patronage did not always procure for her the undivided allegiance that she desired.

For a long time, in this drawing-room where women were regarded by the hostess with but little favour, one of the most brilliant and attractive visitors had been the young Mme Arman de Caillavet, whose brother had married the daughter of Dumas fils. When people remarked her surrounded by an appreciative group, or talking intimately with Jules Lemaître or the young and but slightly known Anatole France, Mme Aubernon would give a little nod in her direction, and remark with benevolent approbation, "Isn't she charming? I discovered her." Alas, relations were not to remain in this state of blissful cordiality for very long.

Mme de Caillavet, *née* Lipmann, had married, as a young girl, a rich but unstable landowner, whose father, rejoicing in the name of Arman, had added the de Caillavet as a form of easy snobbery.[1] While M. de Caillavet was always to possess an open admiration for the nobility, his wife was indeed republican, even though her wedding had taken place in the chapel of the Tuileries in the presence of the Emperor and Empress. From her earliest years her character had been marked by great vigour and originality. "Give me back my tears," she had demanded, as a child, of the nursemaid who had taken a handkerchief into which she had been crying in a fit of rage. On another occasion, at the age of three, she had conceived the delightfully practical idea of throwing her

[1] It is interesting to note that the title of Mme de Villeparisis, the famous Guermantes aunt of *A la Recherche du Temps Perdu* was acquired in a similar manner.

baby brother out of the window because his incessant grizzling bored her. In order to make her understand the depravity of her desires, and the tragedy that might have ensued from her succumbing to them, her parents staged a demonstration in which they cast out of the same window one of her favourite dolls. Rather than being impressed by the enormity of her own wickedness, however, she merely replied, when they brought her the broken pieces, "It wasn't my *doll* that made all the row."

Her marriage, one of convenience, which, as a girl, she had accepted, almost as a matter of course, was but indifferently successful. If she laughed at her husband for his zeal in continually displaying the documents which proved his ownership of their country house of Capion since the seventeenth century, his gambling losses and extravagance were nevertheless a continual source of anxiety.

He was a keen yachtsman, however, and under a pseudonym wrote the yachting news for the *Figaro*. An indulgent, easy-going mortal, with a piercing voice and a curious predilection for exaggerated white bows, he would nevertheless assert his authority in all their differences by making violent scenes.

Mme Arman herself was a woman of exceptional culture and erudition. Without the slightest affectation or preparation, she could converse and argue upon almost any subject. Her knowledge of literature was immense, and she would quote from memory long passages of prose or poetry with equal ease. More successful in her literary aspirations than Mme Aubernon, she had published, under a pseudonym, a novel that had been well received. Although by nature of a retiring disposition, she had, after continual perseverance, cultivated an easy and somewhat ironic manner; and she would express her views and feelings with a frankness that could be almost embarrassing. Far from beautiful, she nevertheless had a pleasant, expressive face, with deep blue eyes.

Her dark hair was worn brushed down over her forehead and curling loosely about her face: though in later years she was to dye it with henna and part it in the centre.

To her apartment in the avénue Hoche, Mme Arman de Caillavet was accustomed to invite many of the eminent men she had met first at Mme Aubernon's. Foremost of these was Anatole France, who had originally been discovered by Lemaître, and taken to the square de Messina while he was still a gauche and struggling young man. Mme Arman had immediately discovered his subtle charm and talent, and made him a welcome visitor to her home. There were small dinner parties where several of the *habitués* of the Aubernon drawing-room were gathered in an atmosphere of friendly intimacy far different from that of the formal and famous banquets of the "mistress," where all personal conversations were severely discouraged and you were continually being interrupted by the tinkling of that annoying bell. When Mme Aubernon learnt of this, however, she was far from pleased. Her distress was aggravated by the fact that France, becoming increasingly popular with Mme de Caillavet, scarcely ever came to see her now at all. He had even been heard one day to hold up her famous dinners to ridicule. "Is it true, M. France," she asked him brusquely when next they met, "that you go about telling people that my parties bore you to distraction?" "I may have said so, Madame," replied the candid but embarrassed novelist, "but I certainly never intended that the remark should be passed on to you."

There was a bitter display of grief and indignation when Lemaître refused one of Mme Aubernon's invitations, to dine instead with her former "discovery"; and henceforward the two women became rivals rather than friends. The final rupture was effected by the startling defection of Dumas fils from the mansion where so long he had been held in veneration. The incident which caused this was ludicrous in the extreme. Having discovered his son making declarations of love to Mme Aubernon's daughter, in the ensuing fracas he gave out that Mme Aubernon had quarrelled with his entire family. In actual fact, Mme Aubernon had considered the drama devoted to the affair grossly disproportionate to so trivial an offence; but Dumas had evidently tired of so much persistent adulation, and was glad to find an opportunity to escape. As Mme de Caillavet was allied to the Dumas by marriage through her brother, she also seized this chance of making a definite break. But though most of Mme Aubernon's favourites pretended to ignore the schism and continued to visit both houses, Anatole France remained exclusively faithful to Mme Arman.

After this, the influence which she exerted upon his work became increasingly marked. He spent the greater part of his days at her house, where she had to struggle with him continually to make him write regularly. As time passed and his books began to attract a wider circle of readers, the position he occupied in her drawing-room grew more and more like that recently held by Dumas in Mme Aubernon's. He was employed as a sort of bait to attract fresh visitors, and invitations to lunch or dinner were invariably accompanied by that alluring phrase "you will meet Anatole France." Her Wednesday dinners, at which he was always present, became famous, and both the rare and complicated dishes served, and any visitors of particular distinction, were announced at the beginning of the evening with befitting clarity and zeal. There is no suggestion, however, that Mme Arman's devotion to France was anything but passionate and sincere. Indeed, she was to become so absorbed in his success that at last she could scarcely bear to hear praise given to any other novelist. By then, indeed, France had become not only the chief attraction of her drawing-room, but the most important attachment in her life. And to anticipate, since there will be no occasion to return to the subject later, the same sorrow that Mme Aubernon had known over the loss of Dumas was to be hers. The same? No. A sorrow even deeper. When, after many years, France, too, was to chafe over her too passionate domination, and they became estranged, it was a blow from which she never recovered.

She, too, like Mme Aubernon, finally became a slave to the position of her drawing-room, and was prepared to defend its brilliance with any weapons that were available. "Look at that woman, in ambush behind my door like a poacher in a wood," she cried one evening, of a guest who was exerting all her charms in order to inveigle a famous politician into visiting her. "She pretends that she comes here because she likes me. She comes only because of the people she hopes to meet!"

Now just as Mme Arman had annexed France from Mme Aubernon, so had Mme de Loynes[1] shortly afterwards annexed Lemaître from the avénue Hoche; an act of war to which Mme de Caillavet retaliated by refusing to permit France to accept any further invitations from Mme de Loynes.

The origin of Mme de Loynes is somewhat mysterious. She was the daughter of a contractor of Rheims, whose father had died while she was a child, confiding her to the care of friends. Some say that she had been educated by Sainte-Beuve; others that she had been introduced to him by Dumas fils while she was still a girl. To him, anyhow, she is said to have announced her ambition to have all Paris at her feet. Changing her name from Détourbet to Mme de Tourbey, when scarcely out of her teens, she regularly entertained a large circle of admirers. Though not beautiful, she had dark red hair and greenish eyes which she knew how to use with great advantage. Her husband, the Comte de Loynes, had been bequeathed to her, together with a large fortune, by an admirer who had been killed in the war of

---

[1] There is no direct evidence that Proust visited Mme de Loynes. Several of his friends did, however; and certainly he knew all about her.

1870. He was an inept young man, however, who soon began to spend her money, but otherwise played a part of no importance in her life. His parents had frowned upon the match, and the couple soon parted, Mme de Loynes continuing to receive her friends from five to seven every afternoon, conveniently relieved of his presence. She particularly encouraged writers, and for years had a deep passion for Jules Lemaître, whom she had first met at a masked ball and on whom she exerted an influence similar to that which Mme Arman de Caillavet exerted upon France.

Unlike Mme Aubernon and Mme de Caillavet, however, Mme de Loynes preferred to listen rather than to talk. She would sit for hours with her dog in her lap and watch the speakers with an enigmatic expression of approval; and instead of the chairs in her drawing-room being disposed in a circle, they were arranged in separate groups, so that her guests could talk informally among themselves. She welcomed artists and politicians no less than writers; and it was she who had introduced to Paris both Burne-Jones and Æstheticism. Her dinners, famous over a long period, were of a celebrated grandeur. Here she played the Aubernon, and permitted only general conversation. She emulated even the famous bell; but gave it up after a few abortive trials. The visitors were invariably limited to ten in number, and the ritual was of great formality and distinction. The food was choice, elaborate and rare; the flowers superb and the service faultless. The hostess, however, would sometimes assemble a somewhat incongruous selection of guests, as when, at one of her parties, Mata-Hari was invited to dance and the Curies to give a lecture on radium.

Always ambitious, Mme de Loynes prided herself on the fact that she could procure for an aspirant more votes for the Academy than any other woman in Paris. Despite her liaison with Lemaître, she gladly received anyone who might cast upon her drawing-room a further lustre; and at different periods of her career de Maupassant, Flaubert, Coppée, Forain, Detaille and Barrès were all her frequent visitors.

To the end of their lives, Mme de Caillavet and Mme de Loynes loathed each other. They broke up, between them, the old friendship between Lemaître and France, and each strove her utmost to discredit the position of the other. When Mme de Loynes died, Mme de Caillavet never ceased to quote the famous witticism she heard had been made to Lemaître at her rival's funeral: "My friend, you will meet her again in a better demi-monde."

Such were some of the dramas, the comedies and the passions of the literary drawing-rooms. To these women who sought expression in a period before they could enter the professions or achieve success as dressmakers and decorators, their drawing-rooms were their very lives. To what purpose the young Proust observed them, questioning his friends as to their origins, their quarrels, their gradual rise from comparative obscurity to brilliance, was to become apparent only when these luminaries shone no longer.

CHAPTER III

IN his eighteenth year Proust was called up for military service and joined the 76th Infantry at Orleans. His health now seemed to have taken a turn for the better, and he was able to participate in the normal life of the regiment. His year of training was, on the whole, one of unusual and unexpected contentment. With his intensely impressionable and emotional temperament, it was a relief to him to be thus removed from the wild oscillation of his moods. Life in barracks, with its daily routine in which everything was pre-ordained, its scheduled hours for rising, for eating, for exercise, for drill and for relaxation, its necessary submission to authority, brought him an unusual calm that he was often to remember later with satisfaction. He loved the serenity of the countryside and the gradual changes which came over it with the movement of the sun and the progress of the seasons. There were times when his heart would leap, as in his childhood, at the sight of an orchard of fruit trees in flower, or a field of ripening grain; and relaxation after a day's hard exercise had a savour of peace he had never experienced before. To his lively intelligence, the theory of military tactics was of enormous interest, and there would be endless conversations with his fellows over the various classical forms of strategy. He was delighted, too, by the friendliness and spontaneity of his peasant comrades. Always deeply responsive to simple goodness, he loved these lads from the farms and the villages who displayed a continual cheerfulness and humour, whose manners were completely natural and unaffected, and whose minds had remained original and unspoilt. The freshness of their ideas and opinions pleased him no less than the supple ease and strength which their bodies had acquired from toiling in the fields. Just as at Illiers he had enjoyed visiting the kitchen and had very soon become good friends with the servants, so now he was delighted by the opportunity afforded him of becoming acquainted with a type so completely different from any that he had met before.

At Orleans, too, he found once more all the charm and satisfaction of new friendship. Here he met, for the first time, Robert de Billy, and at once a deep sympathy sprang up between them which was to last for over thirty years. They had long and frequent discussions together on literature, on philosophy, on every conceivable subject that could possibly attract the still developing mind; and for many months the two were inseparable. Gaston de Caillavet, too, one of his other most recent friends, used to come down to Orleans from time to time to pay him a visit in barracks, and Proust would introduce him to his companions in arms with great delight.

It is very probable that Gaston de Caillavet had been Proust's contemporary at the Lycée Condorcet, for there is a letter extant in which his mother, Mme Arman, writes to him reproachfully that while Halévy and Brunschwicq have carried off respectively the first and second prizes, he has not received even an honourable mention. But if this were so, strangely enough Proust had never met him there. They had become acquainted, rather, in Mme Arman's drawing-room, and immediately had been greatly attracted to each other. Gaston de Caillavet, who had been brought up by his mother to respect and admire both culture and intelligence, had been enormously impressed by this young man who was at once so brilliant and so friendly; and had taken an immense pleasure in writing him long and studious letters almost as soon as his new friend had joined his regiment.

Every week-end, when Proust went on leave to Paris, he used to leave his home on Sunday afternoon to call at the avénue Hoche, where Mme Arman received from five till eight.

At his first meeting with the master, his feelings had been a mixture of trepidation and delight. France had been standing before the fire, his hair brushed back from his forehead, his moustache and beard both characteristically awry, talking to a circle of admirers who were grouped about him. His voice, now gentle and resonant, now booming with resentment, lapsed frequently into silence, when he would glance round apprehensively as though he were disappointed in the effect he had made and scarcely knew how to proceed. When this pause became noticeable, Mme Arman would coax him into going on; and each time, only after several exhortations, would the novelist be persuaded to continue.

Since he had become a habitual visitor, all Proust's diffidence had left him, and he spent many afternoons discussing with France literature, politics and art, and anything else which happened, at the moment, to occupy his attention. A willing disciple at the feet of the great man, he listened to him rapturously by the hour, his expressive face reflecting interest, astonishment, humour and agreement by turns.

In his cadet's uniform, which always looked too big, Proust would seem even slighter than ever, and lying back in unsoldierly luxury against a pile of cushions, would engage in argument until he became completely oblivious to his imminent return to barracks. As time wore on, and the room began to fill, Gaston would glance across at him meaningly from the sofa on which he was still seated next to the beautiful young woman with whom he had been conversing intimately most of the afternoon. With a smile and a shrug Proust would at last finish his talk, rise languidly to his feet, and, with his habitual punctilious politeness, make a formal round of the drawing-room, shaking hands with everyone he knew and exchanging ceremonious good-byes, while his friend hung upon his heels, urging him on with good-humoured impatience lest he should miss the train. Next, Proust must take leave of Mme Arman herself, who would insist upon seeing that he was supplied with sandwiches and cakes to eat during his journey. At last, after a final lingering glance about the room, he would precede his companion downstairs to the waiting carriage.

For every Sunday, with persistent regularity, de Caillavet insisted upon accompanying him to the station, even although it meant he could not possibly get home again in time for dinner. In these long drives together they would feel very much in sympathy. Sometimes they would talk, sometimes they would remain silent. Sometimes they would discuss their mutual friend, Robert de Flers, for whom both of them had the greatest affection. Only one subject, heavy in Proust's heart, he never dared venture to approach. That tall and beautiful young woman, with her slow and graceful movements, to whom his friend had confined his attentions for most of the afternoon, had completely captured his own imagination. But he knew that Gaston also adored her; and since it was whispered that they were secretly betrothed, he dared not even admit to himself his feelings. Poor Proust, the susceptible, the affectionate, always losing his heart, always, intermittently, from the age of twelve, suffering the pangs of unreciprocated love!

At last they would reach their destination. The train, invariably, would be about to go. In the bustle of the station the two young men would shake hands. Then, having jumped into a carriage as the whistle blew, Proust would lean out of the window to raise his hand in a last salute.

Both these friendships continued when Proust's year of service was over. Robert de Billy he was to meet again at the Sorbonne; and meanwhile he continued his frequent visits to the avénue Hoche. Sometimes Gaston be Caillavet, Robert de Flers and himself would dine out together in a restaurant, where they spent long evenings discussing together the subject of most absorbing interest to them all—literature. On other occasions, he would meet de Caillavet and his fiancée at the tennis club at Neuilly, of which they and many of their mutual friends were members. The game was too strenuous for Proust to play himself, but he loved to sit in a deck chair in the sun watching his friends' white-clad figures moving about the court, while waiting for the set to finish so that they could join him. Sometimes when the courts were crowded and there were other spectators, he would become the centre of a band of young girls waiting their opportunity for a game, and of the mothers who had come to watch them. Fascinated by his conversation, when the time came for them to take the court, one of them would exclaim that it was much too hot for tennis, and they would all continue to listen to him with rapt attention.

Sometimes, too, he would come armed with a huge supply of strawberries or chocolates, and frequently he would repair to the refreshment room, to emerge, a few minutes later, staggering beneath an enormous tray of ices and cold drinks. As the afternoon drew on, other players would drift along to join the group. And when play was finally over, they would linger on, long into the dusk, until the memory of some engagement for which it was already very late, would cause someone suddenly to jump up, and so start the break-up of the party.

In all this tranquil summer comradeship, there must have been, for Proust, much latent sadness: for, although renouncing all claims upon the young woman whom he and his friend both admired, he once tried, with wistful persistence, to obtain her photograph. When de Caillavet discovered this, he was furious. There was a sudden quarrel; but it lasted only for a few days. Very soon they were again on the best of terms, and when, a few years later, his friend's dramatization of the *Red Lily* was produced for the first time, Proust was among the small party of friends who gathered to celebrate the occasion.

As soon as his military service was over, Proust was faced with that exacting and inevitable problem, the choice of a career. In his own mind, he was already determined to be a writer; but, for a young man, this is the one profession usually most difficult of achievement. Parents who are convinced that their sons will attain the highest rank in medicine, diplomacy or the law, are rarely found to look with an equal eye upon the determined desire to become a novelist.

Although Proust's parents, partly on account of the precarious state of his health, always treated him with the utmost affection and indulgence, in this his most cherished wish he was not, for some time, to get his way. His father remained tolerant but firm. Truth to tell, he could not understand this extraordinary son of his; and while not unsympathetic towards his desire to be a writer, was fully determined that it should accompany, and not supplant, the practice of some more orthodox profession. The young man, therefore, gave the matter his earnest consideration and discussed it from every possible angle, both with his family and his friends. One by one the vocations of doctor, barrister, solicitor and priest were carefully reviewed, debated upon, and finally discarded. His health would scarcely permit of medicine; he had no interest or inclination for the law, and could scarcely see himself in the capacity of a father confessor. As time passed, and still he remained undecided, his father became more pressing. At last the idea of the Diplomatic Service was put forward, and, as it seemed to be more tolerable than any alternative he had yet considered, Proust decided in its favour. It would require a long and not unattractive course of preparation; and would, at least, put an end to the interminable debates upon the subject which had become so tiresome; even although it remained very doubtful as to whether he would ever be sufficiently well to be sent abroad.

He therefore entered the Sorbonne in the faculty of Political Science, reading law under M. Monnot and history with

M. Albert Sorel. History had always interested him, and continued still to do so: but to the former he was willing to devote only the least amount of energy and attention that would enable him finally to succeed in his examinations. Gone were the days when Proust was the studious young prodigy sitting with rapt attention at the feet of his professors. If now, a subject interested him, no one could devote himself to it with greater application: but if he were bored, he would display his state of mind with disconcerting frankness, and make not the slightest pretence of taking notes. With an amused smile, his eyes would wander over the ranks of his more industrious companions, their heads bent so studiously over their notebooks: until, moving his hand towards his mouth to conceal a splutter of laughter, he would set himself to produce some pungent lampoon on the innocent professor.

Meanwhile, encouraged both by Mme de Caillavet and by Mme Strauss, he was writing, from time to time, short essays and sketches, and longing fervently for an opportunity of seeing himself in print. As it happened, he was not alone in this desire. By now, many of his old companions from the Condorcet were also undergraduates in different faculties of the university; and with few of them had the passion for literature abated. At the end of 1891, therefore, they determined to pool their resources and produce a literary review. A whip round was made to collect any of their acquaintances who wished to collaborate, and eventually a group gathered in the drawing-room of Mme Strauss to discuss ways and means, among whom were Robert de Flers, Gaston de Caillavet, the cousins Daniel Halévy and Jacques Bizet, Robert Dreyfus, Fernand Gregh, Henri Barbusse, Léon Blum, Louis de la Salle and Marcel Proust.

Several times the group met, first at one house and then at another, before any definite plans could be agreed upon; but finally it was decided that by each contributing ten francs a month, they might produce a magazine that would be not unworthy of their united talents. This review was to appear once a month and to be limited to not more than 400 copies of each number. To agree upon a title, however, was far less easy, as everyone had his own ideas and was not backward in expressing them. One man suggested *Varia*, another *l'Indépendance*. After innumerable other proposals, *Le Chaos* and *Les Divergences* were also considered. At length Fernand Gregh, the originator of the affair, suggested, in honour of Plato, *Le Banquet*: and after the further discussion necessary for so many young men of determined views to agree, this title was finally selected.

Eight numbers of *Le Banquet* appeared in all, in 1892. It was printed by Eugène Reiter, a friend of Jacques Bizet, in the presses of *le Temps*, and finally petered out owing to financial difficulties. In the meantime it published many essays and sketches of considerable interest. The general tone of the magazine, as might be expected, was literary in the extreme—in fact it was probably its excessive literariness that led to its somewhat premature extinction—and there appeared a series of advanced and earnest articles on Swinburne, Ibsen, Nietzsche and Schopenhauer.

Several contributions to this review by Proust have been collected subsequently in his miscellaneous works. The article, *Conte de Noël*, upon a Christmas story by Ganderax that had appeared two months before in the *Revue des Deux Mondes*, and which was published in the first number, is to be found in *Chroniques*. The *Esquisse après Madame . . .* which appeared in a following issue, was included in his first published volume, *Les Plaisirs et les Jours*, and is significant because it displays already his intense admiration for Mme Adheaume de Chevigné, whom he had first met at Mme Strauss's, and who was later to serve as one of his models for Oriane de Guermantes. *Violante, ou la Mondanité*, which appeared in No. 7, was also included in the same volume, and will be considered later; but it is interesting to note in passing that both these pieces were written when their author was but twenty-one.

In the third number, Proust had an article entitled *l'Irreligion d'État*, attacking atheism and demonstrating that godlessness invariably produces an intolerance and persecution as violent as any of the worst excesses of the Church. Another essay, *La Conférence Parlementaire de la rue Serpente*, is revealing because its tone of affectionate politeness is so characteristic of the author's personal address. For some reason, however, his colleagues considered that this pleasant little report of a college debate was far too flattering in tone to some of the participants, and the editor added a note to say that of course the views expressed did not necessarily represent the considered opinion of the review. Proust, the susceptible, was very hurt. He felt, indeed, that the attitude of many of his fellow contributors towards him was both prejudiced and unfair. Now, more than ever, they criticized his intense interest in fashionable society, and were indefatigable in warning him that his desire to extract the utmost from two worlds could only lead to his ultimate failure as a writer. But Proust was not convinced. The horizon of life was still widening before him, and he intended to explore it in all directions to the utmost of his capacity.

The idea that his interest in society was in any way a predominant one was, indeed, quite erroneous. His passionate interest in literature was still deepening, and he was reading with the greatest appreciation the works of Saint-Simon and Montaigne, of La Rochefoucauld, Pascal and La Bruyère. But as soon as he sensed the slightest cloud between himself and one of his comrades, he no longer felt able to express himself with complete freedom, and so explain his views; and therefore this false idea of him persisted. Other contacts that he made at the time, however, fortunately make it possible to trace the inner development of his character. How high was his ideal of friendship is illustrated in a revealing passage from one of his letters to Robert de Billy, who was away from Paris, in which he speaks with affectionate enthusiasm of the many virtues of Robert de Flers. "Return soon to Paris," he concludes, "and learn for yourself how a man should love his friends."

During his morning walks, too, with his young English friend, Willy Heath, he would show a very different side of his nature. Describing to him, once, an evening that he had spent drinking beer with a group of companions in a brothel, he admitted that he felt as if he had left there a part of his moral being.

Sometimes the two would walk together in the Tuileries Gardens, where sunshine sprinkled through the foliage of the trees and dappled the path below; while the breeze was filled with the scent of lilac and the fountains threw streams of glittering water into the air. In the rue de Rivoli, the grey façades of the houses would be gay with orange sunblinds, and in the stone urns of the gardens there would be red geraniums. From time to time Proust would suddenly grow silent, and, pausing in their walk, stare, long and intently, at some object that had attracted his attention. Then, without remarking upon this unexpected abstraction, he would just as suddenly walk on again with another abrupt change of expression, and resume their conversation as if there has been no interruption.

More often, however, during the vacations, he would take himself to the Bois, where his friend would be waiting for him beneath a clump of trees, with the "pensive elegance" that recalled to the impressionable Proust one of his favourite portraits by Van Dyck. At last he felt that he could express freely his most intimate ideals, and was never tired of explaining his belief that by means of kindness all things should be possible. Agreed upon the falseness, the stupidity, the vulgarity, and the viciousness of the world, the two friends would then determine to isolate themselves as far as possible from all its follies, to spend more of their time together, and to live only among a chosen circle of men and women who had both cultured and intelligent minds, and fine and sympathetic natures.

It was to the Bois, too, that Proust frequently repaired to admire the beauty and the elegance of the fashionable women of the day, as, from their carriages, they bowed with gracious condescension to the men who, strolling on the paths, had paused to raise, with expressive flourishes of admiration, their grey top hats. Many were the times that he waited, with a suppressed thrill of anticipation, for the beautiful Mme Laure Hayman to appear, so that he could offer her a similar courtesy with the ceremonious exaggeration that never ceased to elicit from her a benevolent smile of gratification. Just as his imagination was captured by the elegant and beautiful Mme de Chevigné in the world of fashion, so too he adored with a somewhat naïve and excessive enthusiasm this lovely and exquisitely dressed woman, who, described by Paul Bourget as Gladys Harvey, represented for him all the glamour and distinction of the famous courtesans of the Second Empire. For her he ran up formidable bills with florists and hotels, dispatching her enormous bouquets of flowers and delighting to be seen lunching with her in fashionable restaurants. The amused grace and friendliness with which she accepted these attentions aroused his most ardent devotion, and for a few months he bathed unstintedly in her atmosphere of luxurious femininity. In addition to her coterie of distinguished and elegant admirers, Mme Hayman possessed also a treasured collection of antique porcelain, and the name "*mon petit saxe psychologique*" with which she included him in her train, at once won his affectionate and rapturous appreciation.

Much of his leisure, too, at this period, was spent in the studio of Mme Lemaire, whose receptions then represented the peak of the fashionable and artistic worlds. Madeleine

Lemaire was a successful painter of considerable distinction. Her portrait of the Prince Imperial hung in the famous long gallery of the Princesse Mathilde: her charming flower groups were often bought before she had even completed them. She inhabited a small but pleasant house in the rue Monceau, with a studio built out into a courtyard gay with lilac trees. Her huge receptions had grown from small "at homes" given for her personal friends. She had for long been intimate with many celebrities of the musical and theatrical worlds, and, in earlier days, it would have been no unusual event, on calling upon her to find Saint-Saens or Massenet seated at the piano, Réjane and Coquelin playing together some impromptu little sketch, or Bernhardt and Mounet-Sully giving an informal recitation.

Mme Lemaire had also taken a few pupils of exalted social position who had served unconsciously to noise her fame abroad. When foreign royalties came to Paris, they would therefore request to be allowed to see her studio; and she had received there at different times the Princess of Wales, the Empress of Germany, the Queen of Belgium and the King of Sweden. Her vast receptions were held in the early summer, on the first Mondays of the month; and throughout such evenings the surrounding streets would be filled with the carriages of her guests. Eminent politicians would attend these functions, together with writers, musicians, editors and diplomats. There would be celebrated actresses and equally celebrated society beauties; and in the closely packed rooms one might meet the Comtesse Adheaume de Chevigné, the Comtesse d'Hausonville, the Duchesse d'Uzès, or Mme Strauss. Anatole France would be there, and probably Lemaître and Forain; and Proust himself might have been seen with such favourite companions as Reynaldo Hahn, Gaston de Caillavet or Robert de Flers. Each of these guests would be treated by their hostess with the same simple friendliness; and if all the chairs were full, a president or a princess might equally have to stroll out into the courtyard to find a place under the lilac trees. In the crowded studio, where the more observant could find traces of her afternoon's work—here a posy in a glass, that she had just been painting, there a canvas, still damp, which had been pushed hurriedly into the darkest corner of the room—Mme Lemaire and her guests would wait expectantly for the programme to begin. For, if, in the drawing-room of Mme Aubernon, the "mistress" was a passionate devotee of drama, here the presiding deity of music was worshipped with an ardour no less fine. At every function some work was given which it was considered an honour to be permitted to hear. One evening it would be the sonata of some famous pianist, played by himself in public for the first time; another, the brilliant performance of a celebrated Polish violinist in Paris only for a few days. Now some talented society woman would sing, who could rarely be persuaded to perform before so large an audience; now some celebrated poet would recite his verses; and here, on many occasions, Reynaldo Hahn had finished the evening by singing lyrics of his own composition.

The attitude of the audience was perforce one of the most attentive appreciation, for woe to the offender of sufficient temerity to raise his voice in the middle of a piece! More humiliating even than the famous bell of Mme Aubernon, would be the stern rebuke administered publicly by the mistress of the house.

It was here, one evening when some of that poet's verses were being recited by Bartet, that Proust met for the first time the celebrated Comte Robert de Montesquiou-Fézensac.

CHAPTER IV

IT was 1893, and Robert de Montesquiou had recently published his *Chauve-Souris* and his *Chef des Odeurs Suaves*. Of an arrogance and an insensate pride beyond belief, and a strange exotic culture that had already been portrayed by Huysmans in the des Esseintes of *À Rebours*, he could display, when he chose to exercise it, a courtly charm of manner that was flattering even to the most fêted women of the day. Tyrannizing over a certain group of the fashionable world with an implacable snobbery, expressing himself in terms of an extraordinary sensitiveness or ferocity, surrounding himself with famous poets, actresses and professional beauties; the friend of Bernhardt, Duse, Rostand, Loti, Mallarmé and Verlaine, it was the fashion for people, not only to imitate his exaggerated manner of speech, but even to extend to him a homage that amounted almost to idolatry.

Consumed with pride of ancestry, and eternally proclaiming his descent from that Blaise de Montluc, whose *Commentaire* had been named by Henry IV of France, the *Soldiers' Bible*; from the François de Montesquiou, whose exploits under his adopted name of d'Artagnan had been immortalized in Dumas' *Three Musketeers*—that d'Artagnan whose two sons had been godfathered, one by the Dauphin and one by Louis XIV himself; from the Abbé de Montesquiou who had been for years the friend and protector of the Gautiers, and whose natural son, indeed, the talented Théophile was claimed to be; he could recite every reference to his family in the pages of Saint-Simon, and knew each slender and intricate link which allied him to many of the most princely houses of Europe. "I cannot bear that man who is always talking to me about his ancestors," Anatole France was once heard to remark, precipitately leaving one of Montesquiou's parties to which he had been lured only with the greatest difficulty.

Second only to this pride of race was the Count's personal vanity. Despite his tendency to tuberculosis, he had an impressive figure; and his handsome face was crowned by magnificent waving hair. But his small mouth was artificially reddened, and his skin always coated with a faint layer of powder. Such was his colossal conceit, however, that he got his portrait painted successively by Helleu, La Gandara, Boldini, Whistler and de Laszlo. Troubetskoy sculptured a bust of him; and he was in a continual passion to see his head done in bronze by Rodin. But Rodin demanded 25,000 francs, while Montesquiou expected to get his features immortalized for the mere sake of the reflected glory he insisted that the work would cast upon the sculptor. Rodin preferred cash to this dubious honour, alas, so the desire was not fulfilled.

During the course of his life Montesquiou was photographed very nearly two hundred times. These photographs were collected carefully in a series of albums, as carefully labelled, and brought out, whenever an opportunity occurred, with a ritual of the most ceremonious condescension.

Antiquary, gourmet, connoisseur, essayist, and poet, he had lived for years in a setting of the most fantastic luxury: and in a succession of mansions, each more magnificent than the last, gave an unending series of parties at which poems were recited or lyrics sung, and the richness and splendour of the women's dresses were rivalled only by the ornate but exquisite decoration of the rooms. Fondly imagining himself as a glamorous survival from the Second Empire, he aped the manners of a ruling prince with an assiduity that amounted almost to frenzy. His dress was elegant, and the most trivial detail selected with an exaggerated care: his clothes were always deeply impregnated with the scent of lilac. His conversation, although mannered, was full of polished phrases and succinct and witty observations that displayed a shrewd, original and cultured mind. Delivered with smiling eyes and an unctuous appreciation for his own ingenuity, his remarks could be ingratiating, insolent or malicious with equal facility and zest. Accompanied by expressive movements of his hands, his forehead and his eyebrows, his voice would mount stridently to the shrill notes of a peacock, or fall, wistful and plangent, to the most mournful notes of grief.

Incessantly involved in quarrels with relations and acquaintances, his wit was as feared by his enemies as it was applauded by his friends. At one moment generous and even affectionate, his mood would change, for no apparent reason, to the most vitriolic malice. When he disliked anyone, he pursued him with a remorseless hatred; and far better than Whistler might he have written *The Gentle Art of Making Enemies*.

Desiring one day to go to a fancy dress ball in a costume that required many jewels, he wrote to a great lady begging her to lend him something suitable for the occasion. Misunderstanding his needs, she sent him one ring alone, selected, so she told him, because it was a family heirloom. "I had no idea that you had a family," he wrote, returning the ring, "but I thought that you at least had jewels." He had composed portraits in verse on some of his circle that were of a monstrous and unparalleled malignancy. Entrapping Mme Gaston de Caillavet one evening in a corner, during a reception given in his honour by Madeleine Lemaire, Montesquiou recited to her some of these odious lines upon their hostess, and proceeded to follow them with others even more vile upon Mme Arman. At last perceiving the young woman's expression of shocked indignation, he remarked with triumphant relish: "Don't you know that, however amusing it may be to slander your enemies, it is infinitely more delightful to slander your friends?"

His wit, however, could be both spontaneous and pungent;

and listening to his remarks at a costume ball, a source of unending entertainment. On one such occasion he was talking to a friend when there passed two young women, one dressed in orange and the other in a gown adorned with garlands of cherries. "In orange," he murmured, "in order to show her quarters, I suppose." And then, glancing at her companion: "I had yet to learn that young girls bore fruit."

His habitual likening of himself to King Solomon or King David often became a little wearisome and his sudden grievances were the cause of continual scenes. On one occasion when he had arranged to appear at a Greek Ball as Orpheus, clad in purple and with a golden lute, a number of young admirers had agreed to accompany him as attendants. At the last moment, however, he took offence and would not go; so that a forlorn troupe arrived without their lord. "The excessive only is supportable" was his family motto, and certainly he did his utmost to live up to it.

It was he who had composed the verses which were offered publicly to Edmond de Goncourt at the huge garden party given in his honour by his publisher Charpentier; and his poems were recited frequently by Sarah Bernhardt at the exclusive receptions of the Duchesse de Rohan.

These poems, though of no little merit, never became well known. Published at the expense of the author, in limited editions of unusual luxury, they would be glanced at but cursorily even by his intimate friends, who would usually display the book in a conspicuous position without having read more than the first few pages. This fact evoked from Montesquiou many envenomed diatribes against the public's abysmal lack of taste.

It was inevitable that such a personality should exert a considerable influence on the young and impressionable Proust. His conversation, his whims, his talent, his idiosyncrasies never ceased to fascinate and astonish him. And this new disciple's naïve and somewhat excessive admiration aroused Montesquiou to some of his most memorable displays. For him Montesquiou engaged in arguments of astonishing erudition and complexity; for him he would offer dazzling displays of wit, epigram following epigram with amazing facility. For him he entered into long dissertations upon his family tree, and its ramifications; discoursed incessantly on every subtle problem of æsthetics. For him he produced his albums of photographs, his famous family documents, his collections of historic manuscripts. "I should like to be your Eckermann," Proust told him in one of his early letters. How, and to what extent he was to be so, neither of them had yet guessed.

Some time after this first meeting Proust made the acquaintance of a young musician named de la Fosse. This young man, who had been a slave to the piano from his earliest youth, had conceived a wild admiration for Montesquiou, to the extent of having even set several of his verses to music. Touched by so ardent an enthusiasm, Proust offered to introduce him to the master, whom he hoped might be persuaded to take an interest in the young pianist's work. The introduction having been arranged, and Montesquiou duly impressed, he agreed that de la Fosse should be given his *début* at one of his forthcoming parties. Delighted, in fact, at an opportunity to play his favourite role of the benevolent patron prince, he organized the affair with a magnificent extravagance. In the garden of the Pavillon des Muses, his mansion at Versailles, a huge temporary theatre was erected for this one performance. Invitations were sent out, in his usual style. only to the most influential and important of the social world, and on the prescribed evening a gathering of historic brilliance thronged the grounds. Mme Barrès came dressed in a costume copied from a picture by David, and the famous and beautiful Comtesse Greffulhe in a wonderful dress of orchid tulle, with her face veiled, and orchids in her hair, which aroused in Proust the most ardent admiration.

INTRODUCTION TO PROUST

The evening was a memorable one. Sarah Bernhardt recited for the first time *Le Coucher de la Mort*; and later, with Bartet and Reichenberg, as a trio, Chénier's *Ode to Versailles*. Finally de la Fosse played. Bending over his piano with a passionate seriousness which created an effect of noble beauty that caused him subsequently to be nicknamed "the Angel," he drew from it tones now of thundering triumph now of exquisite pathos. The ovation he received was terrific; Montesquiou was radiant with delight, and his rhapsodies even more extravagant than usual. His affection for his *protégé* grew with each new success. But his friendship was followed by one of his characteristic wild oscillations of feeling. De la Fosse had won the admiration and protection of an elderly Swiss lady who was also highly enthusiastic over his talent. Montesquiou was furious, and, relinquishing his *protégé*, "I won't say into her arms, because I don't believe she has any, but at her feet, which are very large," as he made haste to publish to his friends, refused ever to speak to him again.

For the next few years, Montesquiou's star was at its highest. His poems were slowly winning a certain success of esteem, and the huge fêtes that he continued to give at the Pavillon des Muses brought him no little fame. At last he had found, in the person of his secretary Ytturi, a disciple who worshipped him with an ardour as constant as it was whole-hearted. Ytturi was a rather too beautiful young Spaniard from South America, who, at the early age of fifteen, had left his native village to seek adventure in Buenos Aires. Since this city also was unable to offer all the beauty and sophistication that his nature craved, he determined to go from there to Paris. He had a pale, expressive face, with blazing brown eyes, and hair that had too soon grown thin. Already he exuded a strong odour, now of chloroform, now of apples; symptoms of the diabetes which was speedily ravaging his constitution. He had met Montesquiou first at an exhibition of Whistler's paintings, and had been immediately enchanted by his elegance, his intellectual distinction and the glamour of his reputation. Thenceforward he offered him an unstinted admiration in which his idol never failed to find both gratification and consolation. When, eventually, the young man died, thanking Montesquiou for showing him "all the beauty that had so much delighted him," his patron was inconsolable, gave up the Pavillon des Muses and offered the furnishings to anyone who would take the trouble to remove them.

All this Proust observed with studious attention. When Montesquiou was friendly, he reciprocated with his usual unaffected spontaneity; when he was morose, and even insulting, he bore it with patient good humour, accepting it from whence it came. Until almost the end of his life, he remained practically the one man with whom Montesquiou never succeeded in quarrelling. That the reflections and observations for which he offered the material were eventually to flower in the portrayal of one of the most colossal, the most pathetic, the most monstrous and the most tragic characters ever depicted in fiction was not to be fully realized until after both men themselves were dead.

CHAPTER V

By the time Proust was twenty-five, he had penetrated into almost every stratum of the social sphere. Although he had now obtained his degrees and left the university, his health still made it impossible for him to settle down to any regular profession, so that his time was divided principally between his excursions into society and his bed. Like his future master, Ruskin, he had by now evidently quite decided that "to be a first-rate artist you mustn't be pious, but rather a little wicked, and entirely a man of the world."

His attacks were of an irregular frequency, but an appalling violence, and sometimes lasted for a whole day and night. He never knew either when they would come on, or when they would end. In a crisis of asthma, the diameter of the small air passages which lead from the bronchial tubes to the lungs are diminished by a spasm of the muscular coat, and clogged by excessive secretions from the mucous membrane. In breathing in, these small bronchi are opened, so that the obstruction is reduced. In breathing out, however, the ends of the tubes become compressed, and it is difficult for the patient to expel even a little air. The lungs, consequently, gradually become inflated to their fullest extent, and the violent efforts required to breathe result in fits of choking. Very often, if the crisis is prolonged, the patient becomes exhausted in his struggle for air, and it seems that inevitably he must expire through lack of breath. The ordeal is an alarming one and, not unnaturally, produces a latent but abiding fear of the terrible fight in which it may be necessary to engage at any moment.

There were often nights when, in order to breathe, it was

necessary for Proust to remain for many hours propped up against his pillows so that sleep became impossible until the morning. Thus these periods of illness, which often must have brought with them a very vivid realization of death, made it possible for him to assimilate and to reflect upon the impressions he received during his evenings of release, with a maturity and detachment unusual for his years.

He had met now, at the Princesse de Wagram's, that much admired cousin of Montesquiou, the Comtesse Greffulhe, who, with all the beauty and distinction of a Récamier, affected to despise the stupidity of people in society, and surrounded herself only with the most intelligent men.[1] He had been enchanted again, both by the beauty of her face and the mystery in her brilliant eyes: had watched her gestures, listened to her conversation, and, on arriving home, made notes upon the originality and distinction of her clothes, and the gorgeous manner in which she dressed her hair. He had been invited to the famous musical parties of the Princesse de Polignac, and discussed literature, art, and politics with the Prince. He had been taken to see the Comtesse d'Haussonville at her beautiful country house, Coppet, and had admired the antique and historic furniture for which it was so famous. He had listened, enraptured, to the lovely voice of the Com-

---

[1] The Comtesse Greffulhe, because of her wealth, her beauty and her exalted social position seems to have adopted an attitude of Olympian superiority towards most of her fellow creatures that was only slightly less insolent than that of Montesquiou.

One day she gave a garden party, at which a specially trained choir was to sing the waltzes of Strauss which had never before been heard in Paris. An imposing trellis was erected, painted gold and covered with roses, behind which the musicians were duly assembled. But just as the concert was about to begin the hostess flew into a rage, and, turning to the guests who stood waiting in silence, cried out in a loud voice that they could all talk, in consequence of which a hubbub arose which completely drowned the voices of the singers.

On another occasion, years later, she is said to have remarked, with an expression of morose and arrogant disdain, to M. Poiret who had returned from the country specially to supervise the final fitting of a magnificent gown of cloth of gold bordered with sable, that he had designed for her to wear at her daughter's wedding in the Madeleine: "I imagined that you knew how to dress midinettes and chorus girls, but I had no idea that you were really capable of making a dress for a great lady."

tesse de Guerne, and been invited to receptions by the most exclusive duchesses; he had been introduced to Mme Alphonse Daudet at a dinner party given by Mme Baignères, and had been received also at the table of the eminent novelist himself, both of whose sons he had added to the number of his friends. His portrait had been painted by Jacques-Émile Blanche, and he had spent afternoons escorting Mme Daudet or the Baronne Alphonse de Rothschild on their visits to their dressmakers and milliners. He had even penetrated to the famous precincts of the rue de Berri.

Proust had probably first met the Princesse Mathilde in the drawing-room of Mme Strauss, where she was frequently a visitor. Being a woman who never bothered to disguise her love affairs, when she broke off her relationship, because she found him unfaithful, with the famous master enameller whose mistress she had been for many years, it was to Mme Strauss that the Princess used to go for consolation. In the late afternoon, when her lover had been wont to visit her, she often found it impossible to bear the solitary formality of her own apartments; and if she had been paying calls, Mme Strauss would frequently arrive home to find her sitting in a corner of her drawing-room, vainly pretending to be interested in the pages of some periodical.

The mansion of the Princess was reached through a vast courtyard. In the formal entrance hall there were imposing busts of the late Emperor Napoleon and the Empress Eugénie. Her drawing-room, which had regained an almost imperial splendour soon after Sedan, had retained a supreme position ever since. As her guests entered the Princess would be seated upon a huge and comfortable chair, which gave the vague impression of being a throne, placed in a slanting position almost opposite the door. She was an imperious-looking woman, and, though long past middle age, would be dressed in a ceremonious evening gown that exposed much of her breast and shoulders. Round her throat she wore invariably a magnificent rope of black pearls. These were her only jewels.

Her natural brusqueness was softened by a smile of unusual sweetness; a slight stiffness in her movements being the only indication of her age. Her guests were all received with the same rigid formality. The women would first curtsey very low; then, raising them up, she would kiss them on the forehead, and exchange a few words on some topic of general interest. If she ever thought one of them was about to kiss her hand, however, she would prevent her by unobtrusively concealing it behind her back. Her conversation was of a robust frankness, and very little adorned with graces. When some asinine woman once asked her, with unabashed but sycophantic curiosity, if she were heir to the same ills of the flesh as others of her sex, the Princess replied sharply: "My good lady, if you want to know things like that you must ask someone of noble birth." Yet, in spite of this, she considered the blood of Napoleon which flowed in her veins infinitely superior to that of any royal house. Nor did she ever conceal her gratitude to that great adventurer. "If it had not been for him," she was accustomed to remark, "I should doubtless be selling oranges in the harbour of Ajaccio." With her maids of honour, however, she was not always so sweet as with her guests. One in particular, who often irritated her, frequently evoked the public rebuke: "Really, you are too stupid for words." When Prince Louis Napoleon wished to join the army, the Princess lamented to her friends: "Just because there has been one soldier in the family, it doesn't mean there is any reason why he should do the same."[1]

When the drawing-room became full it was usual for the more recent arrivals to be directed into the adjoining gallery, where the habitual guests would be showing round such visitors as had been invited for the first time, and pointing

---

[1] This remark the Princess also makes to the Swanns, in *À la Recherche du Temps Perdu* when she meets them, with Marcel, one day out walking.

out to them the objects of particular historic interest. Meanwhile the Princess would move from group to group and exchange a few words with everyone, perhaps remembering sadly the old days when her favourite guests used to be such writers as the Goncourts, Mérimée, Flaubert, and Sainte-Beuve.

As usual, Proust observed everything with close attention. He had many conversations with the old Comtesse de Baulaincourt, questioning her in his customary polite but persistent manner on many details of the social and political drawing-rooms of the past. He knew already that one day he would settle down seriously to write, and was beginning to collect material that later would be useful in his work.

At this period it was Proust's habit to get up late, shaving and dressing very slowly, and with the utmost care lest he should bring on an attack of coughing. Since he had come under the influence of Montesquiou, he took rather more trouble than formerly with his clothes. But his interest was never sufficiently deep for him to become a dandy. In a fit of sudden enthusiasm, he might put himself to some trouble to try and find a smart unusual material for a suit; but if he could not get what he wanted without delay he would invariably allow his tailor to put him off with something readily available, even when he fully realized that it would not turn out particularly well. The affair simply did not seem of sufficient importance for him to waste his time in continuing his search elsewhere. His suits indeed, although obviously expensive, never seemed to fit him properly, and his jackets hung loosely from his narrow shoulders. His linen, however, was invariably of the finest quality, while the thick silk ties he affected rather loosely and carelessly knotted, gave him a faintly Bohemian air. Out of doors he would wear an orchid in his buttonhole and carry a smart cane; but the whole of the effect would be ruined by a pair of creased and dirty gloves that he had snatched up at the last moment, because he was in a hurry and could not be bothered to find clean ones. In the evening, no matter how hot the weather, he would wear a light overcoat unbuttoned rather deliberately to display his white shirt-front. If the weather was cold, or even fresh, he put on a heavy cloak.

His deep and passionate love for his mother had never changed; and she continued to watch over him with the same tenderness as if he were still a child. If the family had finished their meal by the time he was ready, he always knew that something special would be prepared for him the moment he was at the table, and that his mother would remain with him while he ate. When he was going out to dinner, he usually had something to eat at home first, so that later he would be able to talk more freely. Despite his extraordinary social success he had remained completely unspoiled, and was as simple, as charming, as affectionate in his manner as he had been at seventeen. Certainly he had acquired an ease and assurance that were foreign to him in his youth; and his natural courtesy had received a more worldly polish; but in spite of the facility with which he could get himself introduced to anyone he wished to know, he had never lost the almost childlike candour of his manner, and was still absurdly sensitive over the small lies and deceits of social intercourse. If one of his friends had been invited to some social function, but did not mention the fact because he was not sure whether Proust had had a card, and the latter found out, he would invariably meet the friend concerned, at their next engagement, in a mood of ill-concealed reproach. He could not rest until he had received a full admission. "Why couldn't you have told me?" he would ask, in a sad but gentle tone. "I can't see that there was any necessity for deceit."

Nor could he understand the half good-humoured, half malicious banter which so many of his comrades adopted towards each other. One day, when he had invited two young men to dine with him in a restaurant, one of them told a story which made the other appear a considerable fool. Proust was amazed. He knew them to be fond of each other and could not believe that such behaviour could be reconciled with genuine good feeling. It did not at all agree with his own ideas of how a man should treat his friends. On the other hand, there was no trouble to which he would not go to perform some trivial service for anyone he liked. "Politeness," said Macaulay, "has been well defined as benevolence in small things." Such politeness was always an essential feature of Proust's character. The excessive gratitude that he would unaffectedly evince for the slightest kindness, was only equalled by the dismay he felt if he learned that anyone had been spiteful about him. His manners were the expression of a sincere and gentle nature; his attitude of courtesy never varied, and he would be as charming to a barmaid as to a duchess.

His great desire in all things was to reach the truth, and to this end his curiosity would appear insatiable. He would not only ply his friends with the most searching questions about anything and everything; but if once he wanted to know something, he would never rest until his object had been attained. One day when he was travelling with a companion in a public tram, he saw a beautiful woman deep in conversation with the conductor. Becoming wildly interested to know what they could have been discussing, when the woman got out he offered the man a large tip to tell him. This curiosity was equalled only by his lavish generosity. His parents gave him an ample allowance, which he loved to spend on giving pleasure to his friends. The enormous bouquets which he sent to the women who entertained him had become a byword. For this extravagance he was often gently reprimanded. When he invited his comrades out to dinner, nothing was too good for them. Waving aside the menu, he would hold a long consultation with the head waiter and order, without a thought of the expense, the most rare delicacies and the finest wines. But there was never any ostentation in his generosity. He gave his friends the best he could afford, just as he poured out to them unstintedly all his ideas and feelings. To a young man less well off than himself, no one could display a more charming delicacy. When a new acquaintance remarked to him one day that he found it embarrassing to have friends much richer than himself, Proust replied that he understood exactly how his companion felt. "Please don't imagine I am well off," he added. "I have nothing but the small allowance my parents give me; and that I always squander far more quickly than I should." His tips were of a proverbial generosity. "We shall never dare to dine here again," his companions would remark, seeing the magnitude of the sums which the waiters slipped into their pockets after they had served him. He would tip with the same extravagance in a restaurant where he was well known, or at a station buffet where he would probably never return; and if anyone who served him seemed at all tired or nervous, he would give them even more than usual. His reward was the genuine, half-embarrassed smile with which they thanked him. One evening in a restaurant, after Proust had settled his bill a friend was amazed to see him beckon to a boy who had not been near their table the whole evening, and slip into his hand the accustomed generous tip. "But, Marcel," his companion protested, "he hasn't so much as poured you out a glass of water." "I know," Proust replied. "But didn't you see how sad he looked standing over there by himself, watching, with envious and wistful eyes while I tipped the others? Only," he added a moment later, "you must promise me never to mention at home that I did it. I'm afraid my parents are obsessed with the idea that I can't be trusted to look after myself as it is."

A pleasant period of his life this; a period of leisurely visits to the Louvre with Pierre Lavallée or Lucien Daudet, during which he would stand before some favourite picture for a quarter of an hour at a time, in order to collect material for the *Portraits de Peintres* on which he was at work: of friendly walks in the Jardins d'Acclimatation with Reynaldo Hahn; of visits to the opera and the theatre with Jacques Bizet and Jacques Baignères; of working late at night in bed, his table piled high with newspapers, books, and reviews; of reading with prodigious zest the novels of Stendhal, Balzac, Tolstoy, and Dostoievsky.

When he went to Trouville for the summer, he continued to visit such friends as were also in the neighbourhood, and to write to others from whom he was separated, about the life he was leading and the development of his taste in literature and music. Such diversions, however, were frequently interrupted by the precarious state of his health. One summer, when he went to Segrez to spend a few weeks with Pierre Lavallée, he was taken so ill on the evening of his arrival that he had to go away the next day. In Paris the same unhappy fate frequently overtook him. Now it was some concert at Mme Lemaire's that he must leave in the middle, for fear lest his sudden attack of coughing should disturb the audience: now some play at Mme Aubernon's, because he had unexpectedly developed a temperature almost as soon as he had left home. Even if a party had been arranged specially in his honour, no one was ever quite sure whether he would arrive at the last moment, or a note to say that he had just been seized with one of his attacks.

Whenever he left the flat in the evening, his mother, if she were at home, would go to the door with him to kiss him good night. Out in the street he would drink in impressions of the evening sky with an almost deliberate relish, or else leaning back in his cab, would finger the camellia or the orchid in his buttonhole, sadly resisting the temptation to smell it lest its scent should bring on a fit of coughing.

When he arrived at his destination it would probably be

very late. Proust had little idea of time and had never been known to be punctual for anything. Frequently he was the last guest to arrive. His presence usually was soon noticed, and one or another of his friends would join him eagerly. If the party was nearly over, a circle would form round him in a corner, clamouring for him to do some of his imitations; for, to the immense delight of his companions, he had cultivated an extraordinary talent for mimicry. "Come on, Marcel," someone would cry, "do Montesquiou." At first he would refuse and make his friends tell him, instead, all that had happened before his arrival. Had Mme de Chevigné been? Or Mme Greffulhe? And how were they dressed? In detail they must satisfy his curiosity. "What a pity," he would remark, if he had missed them. "I should so like to have seen how they looked." As soon as he was satisfied, however, one of them would try again. "Come on, Marcel. Do Montesquiou. Be a good fellow." Again Proust would hesitate, glancing carefully round the room. "Well, are you sure he's gone?" Too well he knew Montesquiou's disapproval of these performances. His friends would emphatically reassure him. "Quite sure, Marcel. He left nearly an hour ago. Come on."

In a moment the whole expression of his face would alter. His lips would be drawn over his fine white teeth, as he assumed the Count's well-known smile. Suddenly he would break into a laugh. It might have been Montesquiou himself. Then he would hurl himself into some impassioned declamation. The words, the phrasing, the intonation and the facial expressions, all were exact. He even copied his model's gestures with his hands. There were the same high notes like the shrill, strident cry of a peacock: the same sudden drops to an almost lachrymose tenderness. Nothing would be exaggerated, nothing altered. The little circle about him would be overjoyed. But Proust would cease as abruptly as he had begun, smiling suddenly with his own customary charm. His friends would laugh and applaud. Some of them would pat him on the back. Proust would be delighted at his success. Still they would not be satisfied. "Come on, Marcel, do another. Do Madeleine Lemaire." Without replying, his face would now assume a different mask. How he did it, no one knew, but they could see her, standing near the door of her studio, saying farewell to a group of departing guests. "Dear friend, you played so beautifully this evening. I was almost in tears." A smile, a nod. "Just look at that woman. Isn't she astonishing? A positive vision of youth. You wouldn't take her for a day over twenty." Another smile. "Au revoir, Montesquiou, dear, clever, wonderful man. How I adored your new book. . . . Now, Marcel, mind you don't catch cold. . . . Take care of him, Reynaldo. And don't be late next Tuesday, either of you. Mme de Guerne is going to sing. . . ." A pause for the door to close, then, turning to an imaginary companion, the voice would become completely different: "It is time you were in bed, Suzette." With vigorous frankness, it would then express the hostess's real feelings about her guests.

Once more Proust would pause abruptly. There would be the same laughter, the same enthusiasm. Again his companions would demand more. This time he would shake his head. "I see M. Barrès is still here. I must go and speak to him."

He would then seek out one or two other acquaintances, and having parted from them with his usual ceremonious politeness, catch the eye of some more intimate friend across the room. Waiting until he had finished his conversation he would slip across and take his arm. "Come along, let's go," he would say. "You've been here quite long enough for one evening." They would probably go together for supper to Weber's in the rue Royale. Proust would talk and talk. At first their conversation would be frivolous. They would discuss the party they had just left, their acquaintances, their friends. But gradually their mood would change. They would talk of music, and Proust deplore the affectation of those people who at one moment admire only Wagner, at another only Beethoven, at a third, only Bach. From music they would turn to literature, to the theatre, to art.

His companion would suddenly glance at his watch. "Good lord, Marcel, it's nearly one o'clock. I must get along." Proust would call for the bill. If his friend put his hand in his pocket, immediately Proust would restrain him. "Don't be so absurd. You are my guest." The bill paid and the waiter lavishly tipped, with much smirking and bowing they would be escorted to the door. Proust would sniff the air. "Good, it's fine. Let's walk. I'll see you home."

Ordering his carriage to follow, he would take his friend's arm. When they reached their destination, they would probably be deeply absorbed in conversation. "Are you tired?" Proust would inquire. His companion would give an emphatic denial. "All right. Come back to my place then." Once more they would march along the empty streets, still talking, while the carriage crawled behind. By now they would have become very grave. Perhaps they discussed some abstruse question of philosophy, slowly working towards their conclusion from many different points. When it seemed that at last the topic had been exhausted, Proust would suddenly come out with some startling new approach of his own. Reaching his door, once more they both would be engrossed. "All right," Proust would offer, "I'll come back with you."

Their perambulations might continue for another hour. At last all barriers had been lowered between them, and Proust could express himself with the complete freedom which alone gave him any satisfaction. He would display once more his disgust for the vulgarity, the stupidity and the insincerity rampant in society. "It's tragic, really, how very few people are nice when you get to know them," he says gravely. His friend, glancing at him in sudden surprise, is amazed by the wistful quality in his voice. "Tell me, Marcel, how do you think one should try to live?" Proust pauses in his stride. They face one another. From a street lamp, the light falls across his face, emphasizing its pallor and the intense earnestness of his expression. "I know it sounds banal." he replies, "but to be completely tolerant of others, and severe with oneself, seems to me to be the only rule to follow." And as they are about to part, he adds: "Do you know that passage from the *Imitation*? 'The desires of the senses draw us hither and thither, but, when the hour is past, what do they bring us but remorse of conscience and dissipation of spirit?'" There is a long pause, and he continues in a low voice, "I often feel that."

But if Proust was sometimes now thus grave, he could also be hilarious to the point of boisterousness; and was particularly prone to embarrassing fits of uncontrollable laughter when in the presence of Montesquiou. One day Count Robert invited Proust to bring his friend Lucien Daudet to a party. Since it was this young man, more than any other, who seemed to provoke and to share these outbursts, they wrote a joint letter explaining that, as whenever they were together, they could never restrain themselves from giving way to excruciating fits of mirth, it might be better if they stayed away. It was merely a kind of harmless disease, but he might possibly take it for a form of mockery. Although duly warned, Montesquiou insisted, with characteristic lordliness, upon their presence. When they arrived, however, he greeted them both with an air of suspicion and disapproval so ill concealed that they both succumbed at once, and had to flee, vainly trying to stifle their shrieks of merriment, to the sanctuary of the buffet, where, doubled up with mirth, they remained convulsed until the room gradually began to fill with other guests. Count Robert, it must be added, was not amused.

CHAPTER VI

PROFESSOR PROUST was still dissatisfied with his eldest son. Robert, his younger boy, was proving himself far more worthy. He had now graduated from his medical school and was walking the wards of a hospital with exemplary efficiency. With Marcel, alas, it was very different. People spoke of his brilliance, it was true; and there was still this desire of being a writer. But apart from a few little sketches in *Le Banquet*, which probably would never have seen the light at all if the contributors had not financed the magazine themselves, what had he to show? Certainly there was much talk of a book he was writing at the moment; and it must be allowed that the boy's health was a great handicap: but all those parties he went to could be good for no one, and it was high time that he settled down to a career.

He therefore approached the subject once more, tentatively at first, and then, as he felt that his son did not prove sufficiently responsive, with increasing emphasis. Now that there could be no longer any question of diplomacy, Proust cast about once more to decide upon something else. But this was not so easy, since, whatever position he chose, he must be able to absent himself without complications from it when he was ill, and it must also leave him adequate free time in which to write. Once more there were discussions and consultations with relatives and friends. Eventually he was informed that the Mazarine Library was advertising for three assistants. The positions to be filled were honorary, but the duties were comparatively slight; and this, together with the fact that the environment would be as literary as even he could wish, prompted him to offer himself for one of the posts. His application, the last, was duly received by the authorities and soon accepted. Everyone was pleased. Proust was delighted to style himself honorary attaché to the Mazarine, and his father was gratified to feel that his son was settling down seriously at last. But not for long was the situation to remain so satisfactory. It soon transpired that only two assistants were required at the library itself, and that the third was intended for the Legal Department of the Ministry of Public Education. To this position, therefore, Proust, as the last applicant, was duly relegated. When he received the news, he was filled with consternation. Had he known this beforehand he would never have proposed himself for the position. He had imagined spending his days in the cool and scholarly atmosphere of the Mazarine Library, among cool and scholarly colleagues. The idea of the Legal Department of the Ministry of Public Education, on the other hand, was repulsive. Nor had he the faintest intention of spending his rare days of good health in any office. Now, however, that his father's concern had abated, he could not very well refuse to fulfil his duties. The matter called for a more diplomatic method of negotiation.

His first move, therefore, was to enlist the help of his intended Chief at the library. Granted an interview, he politely explained his disappointment and begged his superior to write to the authorities, and, pleading in excuse the precariousness of his new attaché's health, to try to effect his transference back to the Mazarine. This, with obliging good humour, his Chief consented to do: but without success. The reply of the authorities was both curt and caustic. If the health of the young man was really so bad that he could not work five hours on two days a week, then he had no right to propose himself for the position in the first place. Proust therefore set out to relieve himself of his duties with a determined subtlety.

Excusing himself to his father by explaining that he must

at all costs finish the book on which he was at work, he wrote to the authorities requesting the official grant of a short holiday until the end of the year. This was duly acceded.

Never, during the next five years in which he was nominally attached to the Legal Department of the Ministry of Public Education, did Proust once, in his official capacity, set foot within its doors. As soon as the year was over, he applied for a further twelve months' leave. This application, somewhat surprisingly, was granted without demur, and Proust dispatched a polite and charming note to his Chief, thanking the authorities, through him, for this year's respite, and deploring the circumstances which had deprived him of working in an environment in which he knew he would have been happy.

A few months later he paid a visit to his Chief in person, to perform the pleasant attention of offering him a copy of his book. No sooner was the year over than he used this as an excuse for requesting a further leave, explaining, now, not only that the state of his health was getting worse, but that his literary work demanded the whole of his leisure. He hoped, however, that he might be permitted not only to call sometimes to see his colleagues, but to work in the library as an ordinary reader. It might have seemed strange, otherwise, for an attaché sadly prevented from fulfilling his duties, to be discovered assiduously engaged in study within its precincts.

For instead of his position facilitating his visits to the Mazarine, it merely filled him with such embarrassment that he scarcely dared to put his feet inside the door! The more so, as, at the end of the year, he applied again, with polite and brazen effrontery, for a further extension to his leave. This time he offered as an excuse the serious illness of his mother, which alas! made it necessary for him to spend much of his time visiting her at her nursing-home. More amazing to relate, this further leave of a year's absence was immediately succeeded by a fourth. One begins to wonder now, whether, by continuing this unique method of procedure, Proust will not remain a tragically incapacitated honorary attaché to the Mazarine Library all his life. This time, however, the authorities protested. There was an official inspection of the library, and an examination into the habits of this curious M. Proust. A polite but curt note was dispatched to him requesting him to take up his duties without delay. At last, as he was just about to leave Paris with his mother and Reynaldo Hahn to pay a long-deferred visit to Venice, there was adequate cause for him to offer his resignation; and thus ended the illustrious career of Marcel Proust, librarian.

In the meantime, his first book, *Les Plaisirs et les Jours*, had appeared in 1896. It was a precious-looking volume with a pale green cover, and published at the then high price of 13·50 francs. Besides containing a collection of all the sketches in prose and verse he had written since he was seventeen, it included a preface by Anatole France, illustrations by Madeleine Lemaire and musical settings for four of his poems by Reynaldo Hahn. These had already been sung at Mme Lemaire's musical parties, and were, in addition, published as songs, separately, and also collected together in a handsome portfolio.

The book received but little attention and had only a very small sale. It was generally taken to be the production of a precocious society amateur and unworthy of serious consideration. Yet for many reasons it deserves an attentive examination.

Prefaced by a charming dedication to his friend Willy Heath who had died of dysentery a short while before, it was written in a pure and lucid style, but with a distinct leaning to preciosity; the prose being reminiscent of the less flamboyant works of Wilde, as the verse recalls the somewhat finicking grace and polish of Austin Dobson. "Young with the youth of the author, but old with the age of the world," as France wrote in his introduction, it contained already a foreshadowing of several of the major themes which were to be developed with such persistent power during Proust's maturity. It has been said that the great works of the world, even when they have not actually been produced until old age, have all been conceived before the age of twenty-five, and a reading of these sketches certainly leads one to wonder how much of *Swann* already existed in the author's mind, though it was not to be begun for another decade.

Certainly it was an astonishing book for a young man to have published. "When I was still a child," Proust wrote in his dedication, "the plight of no other character in the Bible seemed to me so sad as that of Noah, on account of the flood, which kept him shut up in the ark for forty days. Later, I was often ill, and for long days at a time also had to rest in 'the ark.' Then I understood that from no other place could he have seen the world so well. . . ." It is these days of illness alone that can explain the maturity and detachment with which the whole of the volume is imbued and which is combined so curiously with an almost childish naïveté and candour. As the man, so the book.

Already there are signs of the philosopher, and even stronger indications of the moralist. "A book produced in my youth, although much better written than *Swann*" was the phrase with which the author was to refer to it years later; and yet precisely what one most misses is the richness and variety, the impelling fascination and complexity of the style that is one of the greatest triumphs of his later work.

The idea running through *La Mort de Baldassare Silvande* was to form, later, one of the principal motifs that precipitates the tragedy of Marcel's great love affair in *La Prisonnière*—the realization that only when a man is alone can he really come to himself, and that the pleasures of love, like the pleasures of social life, are both of them, equally, distractions from the true life of the spirit.

The same idea, but even more powerfully, is expressed in the parable *L'Étranger*. The young, charming, rich and talented Dominique surrounds himself perpetually with a circle of admiring friends. One day, while he is alone, there appears to him a grave yet familiar stranger, who reproaches him sadly because the young man entertains everyone he has ever known, save himself alone. Dominique, charmed by his presence, promises to include him. "If you have me, you must send away your usual companions," the stranger warns him. "I cannot," Dominique replies, "I cannot be alone." Even as he speaks he feels himself to be sacrificing his greatest happiness for an imperious but vulgar habit. "Choose quickly," the stranger warns him. But Dominique's guests are already arriving. "Who are you?" the young man cries, as he sees the stranger already about to depart. In deep dejection he hears the reply. "I am your soul. I am yourself."

Through *Violante, ou la Mondanité* is woven the theme of habit: habit which deadens the perceptions, kills the emotions and blinds the soul alike to satiety and to loss. Violante has left the peace and seclusion of her Styrian castle for a brilliant and flattering life at the court of Vienna. One by one she exhausts the pleasures of admiration, of ambition, of love. But even when she is old and disillusioned, still she does not return to the life of peace and charity she knew in her youth. Though pleasure is dead, passion extinct, every moment sterile, she is enchained by the force which "nourished by vanity, finally succeeds in overcoming disgust, scorn and boredom itself—the force of habit." "Be seldom in the company of young people and strangers, nor love to be seen in the presence of the great. Lean not upon a reed which is blown by the wind, nor put your trust in it: for all flesh is as grass, and its glory passes as the flower of the fields" is the text placed below the heading of this tale; and, worn already in the author's heart, is later to resound, with an ever-deepening note, through all the pages of *Le Temps Retrouvé*.

The series of sketches entitled *Fragments de Comédie Italienne*, and *Mondanité et Mélomanie de Bouvard et Pécuchet*, on the other hand, all display first signs of the shrewd observation and incisive irony that are later to be employed in the pictures of social life that run through the whole series of the novels. *Les Regrets, Rêveries Couleur du Temps*, is a charming collection of sensitive pastels; *Un Dîner en Ville*, a first sketch for the later elaborate dinner party with Oriane de Guermantes, just as *Mélancolique Villégiature de Mme de Breyves* and *La Fin de la Jalousie* foreshadow the two great themes of love and jealousy both of *Swann* and *La Prisonnière*.

In the former of these two, Proust records the crystallization of the love of a cultured young woman of birth for a perfectly commonplace young man whom at first she does not even admire.

Françoise de Breyves sees M. de Laleande at an evening party, where the first impression that he makes upon her is one of such nullity that she refuses even to permit him to be introduced to her. Glancing at him again later, she is struck by the depth and beauty of his eyes, though her second impression of him merely confirms her opinion that, apart from this he is both plain and vulgar. In sheer idleness, however, she permits her eyes to fall on him from time to time in a series of long and tender glances, with the result that, when she meets him later in the hall where he is trying to find his walking-stick, he brushes her arm with his elbow, and in a low voice murmurs his address in her ear. Her interest, already aroused, is immeasurably increased by the fact that, catching sight of him in the distance at another party, she now requests someone to present him to her, but does not meet him because he leaves the house before her wish can be gratified. Intent, at last, upon making his acquaintance, she begs a mutual friend to write to him on her behalf; only to learn that he has gone away for several months. The news fills her with anguish. Her desire to see him again deepens to an unquenchable passion. She is painfully aware that the object of her affections is completely mediocre, yet she lives now only for him. His name mentioned in conversation, a phrase from the *Meistersingers* heard at a party when she is thinking of him, both woke the sensation of his presence with a terrible power. Completely infatuated, nothing can make her forget his face or alleviate her suffering until he returns.

La Fin de la Jalousie, on the other hand, anticipates the terrible pangs of jealousy that, in the novels, are to cause such intense misery both to Marcel and to Swann. Honoré, here, however, has a serious accident and becomes a dying man. Then, for the first time, he realizes that the ideal state of love is comprehensive, that the emotion he feels now, empty alike of anguish and desire, includes, no less than the woman for whom he has tortured himself so vainly, the doctor who is attending him in his last hour and the servants who are standing with tear-stained faces about his bed.

In *Scénario*, too, appears for the first time another of the fundamental Proustian theories on love: the idea that a passionate affection has only to be offered freely, for it to arouse inevitably in its object the reciprocal emotions both of boredom and contempt. A young man, reflecting while he waits for his beloved to arrive, upon the transience of passion, is ardently desirous that their love shall last for ever. Only can it do so, his good fairy informs him, if he professes to disdain the one who loves him, and refuses to permit himself to weary her with perpetual protestations of adoration. If he will but follow this advice, he will obtain his heart's desire. He promises to do so, but alas! his resolution is soon broken, for when his beloved appears, he cannot restrain himself, and at once throws himself precipitately into her arms. This immediately extinguishes all her desire for him, and causes her to regard him henceforward with a torturing indifference.

Yet curiously enough, in spite of the ideas contained in his book, there were many people in whom it deepened rather than lessened the legend that the author was merely a pretentious snob. Particularly was this the case among some of his old friends from the Lycée Condorcet.

Jacques Bizet, recently qualified as a physician, now rented a studio flat on the top floor of an old house not far from his hospital. Here, once a week, there were meetings of the former contributors to *Le Banquet*, besides several other young literary aspirants that they had since added to their number. The only one of the old band who was habitually absent from these gatherings was Proust. As Jacques Bizet knew well, there were plenty of times when Marcel was neither too ill nor too busy to visit Mme Strauss; and if he never came to his own studio, there seemed but one explanation. He clearly preferred to his old companions, the society of the social celebrities who visited her drawing-room. In consequence, the publication of *Les Plaisirs et les Jours* was greeted by the group with an ironic and reluctant admiration that was not without effect: for they had decided to launch an amateur theatre, starting production with a revue called *Les Lauriers sont Coupés*, for which Bizet and Robert Dreyfus wrote the words, Jacques-Émile Blanche, Paul Baignères and Forain designed the scenery and costumes, and in which the following short sketch on Marcel Proust won from the audience tumultuous applause.

PROUST: "Have you read my book?"
A YOUTH: "No, sir. It is too dear."
PROUST: "Alas! That is what everyone says. And you, Gregh, have you read it?"
GREGH: "I had to read it in order to review it."
PROUST: "And did you find it too dear as well?"
GREGH: "Not at all. There is a lot for the money."

PROUST: "Isn't there? A preface by M. France, 4 francs. Pictures by Madeleine Lemaire, 4 francs. Music by Reynaldo Hahn, 4 francs. Prose by me, 1 franc. Verse by me, 50 centimes. Total, 13 francs 50. Surely not too much?"

THE YOUTH: "But, sir, there is much more than that in the *Almanack Hachette*, and that costs only 25 sous."

As the revue was performed three times, it was inevitable that details of the scene should eventually get back to Proust, probably not without a certain amount of malicious distortion. When he heard it, he was rather more pained than indignant. Apparently it never occurred to him to be amused. He simply could not understand how young men who called themselves his friends could do such a thing. He had always been fond of them and had never lost an opportunity of speaking well of them whenever an occasion offered: and that they should reciprocate in this manner was quite beyond him. "I don't understand it," he remarked, with sad bewilderment. "I simply don't understand it."

The supposition, still current, that he was a snob, however, caused him to make in one of his letters of this period this very revealing and significant statement: "The idea that you seem to have that snobbery directs the choice of my goings out astonishes even more than it humiliates me. The revaluation of our pleasures during illness, when we are deprived of almost all of them, is so exact and so genuine that it seems certain to us that everyone else can see what is so clear to ourselves, and directs all our actions to noble and disinterested ends."

Otherwise he gave no sign of his feelings, and as soon as the offenders made renewed overtures of friendship to him, replied to them with all his old cordiality. Shortly afterwards, in fact, he fought a duel, and when subsequently Robert Dreyfus called to leave a card of congratulation upon his safe survival, accepted this civility with habitual warmth. Writing to thank him, however, he did not omit to inform him how surprised he had been to hear of his "treacherous behaviour" and to reproach him frankly for the unfriendliness of his general conduct.

This duel was fought, the year following the publication of his book, at the Tour de Villebon. Feeling deeply insulted by some remarks that had appeared about him in a press notice, Proust immediately decided to avenge his honour, and despatched a challenge to the writer, Jean Lorrain. His seconds were Gustave de Borda, celebrated throughout Paris both for his swordsmanship and the number of his encounters, and his inseparable friend, the painter, Jean Beraud. Fortunately, neither of the participants were particularly good marksmen, or else they fired deliberately into the air. For both of them escaped unscathed, and although the young writer behaved with coolness and courage, once he considered the matter closed, it was only with difficulty that he could be restrained from making characteristic overtures of friendship to his adversary.

Both these episodes illustrate aspects of Proust's nature which were never to change. Inordinately sensitive and susceptible he remained to the end of his days; but he never nursed his grievances nor failed to welcome the first sign of a reconciliation from anyone who had grieved or injured him. His estrangements with his comrades were nearly always transient. When their activities were crowned with success, invariably he would be the first to express his pleasure: and even when illness prevented him from seeing them, his letters show that once a man had been his friend, he continued to think of him with affection until the end of his days.

CHAPTER VII

TOWARDS the end of the decade, Proust was to be found becoming steadily more concerned over the affair that was gradually dividing France into two hostile camps—the Dreyfus Case. In 1894, the French Secret Service had come into possession of a memorandum concerning a series of military secrets that had been divulged to the German Embassy. On the strength of a scrap of paper bearing the initial D, and a certain similarity in handwriting, suspicion had immediately fastened upon Captain Dreyfus, who was known to be in a position where he could have betrayed such information. Despite the fact that Hanotaux, the Minister for Foreign Affairs, when consulted by General Mercier, had said that it was impossible to institute proceedings on such slight evidence, the army took matters into its own hands and charged Dreyfus with high treason. The case was tried by court martial and the evidence upon which he was indicted shown neither to Captain Dreyfus nor to his counsel. The accused was unanimously found guilty, sentenced to official degradation, and imprisoned in solitary confinement on Devil's Island. The fact that he was a Jew immediately provoked a wild outburst of anti-Semitism throughout the country, which had repercussions in every stratum of society.

Although Dreyfus himself had never ceased to protest his innocence, reports were spread abroad that after his trial he had confessed his guilt. Despite the efforts which were being made by the prisoner's family to establish his innocence, the affair would doubtless soon have been forgotten had it not been for the fact that, a year or so later, Colonel Sandherr was obliged to give up his position in the Secret Service, and the vacant place was taken by Colonel Picquart. As no possible motive had ever been discovered for Dreyfus's alleged crime, and both the German and Italian Embassy had gone out of their way to announce publicly that never at any time had either of their respective governments had any relations with the condemned man, Picquart considered it his duty to assure himself of the validity of the evidence which had convicted him. He had never before been at all doubtful, because his senior officers had continually referred to secret documents which they said proved Dreyfus's guilt beyond all question; but now he discovered that not only was the original evidence quite insufficient, but also that the famous secret dossier contained papers which were obvious forgeries.

Finally convinced that there had been a miscarriage of justice, Picquart demanded an interview with General Gonse. "What does it matter to you," he was asked, when he had stated his case, "if this Jew is kept on Devil's Island?" "But, General, he is innocent." "Well then, don't say anything about it," he was told, "and no one will be any the wiser." High words followed, and Picquart ended the discussion by retorting: "I am not going to take this secret with me to my grave."

The result of this episode was that his superiors found it convenient to relieve Picquart of his position, and sent him on some trumped-up expedition to Tunis. Not, however, before he had had time to collect his various proofs and deposit them, in case of accidents, in a sealed envelope with his solicitor. At Tunis, Picquart happened to meet an old friend, the barrister Leblois, and told him that he had very grave reasons for believing that a mistake had been made, and was being upheld, even though it could be proved that the real culprit had been a penniless Hungarian officer of dubious reputation, by the name of Esterhazy. Returning to Paris, Leblois determined to place the matter before Scheurer Kestner, vice-president of the Chamber, who, in turn demanded an interview with the President of the Army Council and the Minister for War. Official notes were issued to this effect, and the Press and the Chamber were suddenly agitated by a series of sensational rumours. Public feeling was revived, racial hatred reinflamed, and the case occupied a position of foremost importance in the minds both of cabinet ministers and of the public. The *Figaro* came out with an article which stated that M. Scheurer Kestner had definite proof that the famous memorandum had not been written by Dreyfus but by Esterhazy: *Le Journal* protested that this was some new plot concocted by the Dreyfus family, who had already appealed to William of Hohenzollern: *Le Temps* published an article by Scheurer Kestner implicating the War Minister; and the Jews were accused of offering prodigious bribes to anyone who helped in obtaining a reversal of judgment. Fresh incidents took place overnight. The nationalists, who bitterly resented that the army should fall under suspicion, were stirred to an unprecedented fury against the Jews, while the small but growing band of Dreyfusards, passionately convinced of the prisoner's innocence, spared itself neither shame nor humiliation in order to establish it. New facts were offered to the public and the most fantastic rumours accepted as truth. The fever spread to schools, clubs, and private families. The same conflicts of opinion which caused riots in the streets, effected wide changes in the fashionable world, where Rothschilds, whose names, hitherto, had been breathed with whispers of veneration, were now almost universally shunned; and in the most famous mansions of the Faubourg St. Germain it was considered a crime to be a Jew.

Meanwhile, Esterhazy had been tried by court martial and acquitted, while tension reached its height with the series of articles which Zola published in the *Figaro* in 1898, culminating in the famous indictment "J'accuse," which appeared a little later in *L'Aurore*, and each of whose separate points was found years later to be, if anything, an understatement of a campaign in which no crime, from forgery to murder, had been omitted.

"I have but one passion, and that is for light, and I plead in the name of that humanity which has suffered so greatly and which has a right to happiness," Zola concluded his protest; and immediately, a number of young men, henceforward to be known as the "intellectuals" drew up a petition demanding a retrial. Foremost among these was Proust, who hastened to the avénue Hoche in order to persuade Anatole France to head the list, and from there, to the old friend of his schooldays, the now renowned Professor Darlu, whose support he also obtained.

The political fervour which had already invaded the drawing-rooms of the Faubourg St. Germain, rapidly spread to the literary world, where gatherings became either predominantly Dreyfusard or anti-Semitic.

"I shall keep my Jews," said Mme Aubernon, who knew too well from which quarter came so much of the talent that made her theatrical performances successful; while Mme de Loynes, with her flair for utilizing all contingencies to increase the prestige of her drawing-room, became intensely anti-Dreyfusard, and sponsored the founding of La Patrie Française, the famous movement of the nationalists. Mme de Caillavet, on the other hand, herself a Jewess, and following France, became as fervently Dreyfusard, which made her house a continual bedlam, since her husband was a nationalist and never ceased to proclaim his views. Mme Strauss, also a Jewess, who had little interest in politics and many friends in both camps, refused to espouse either cause. If people could not come to her house without quarrelling, she announced firmly, then they must stay away.

Barrès, the gilded anti-Semite,[1] henceforward became one

[1] "The Semitic race," wrote Barrès, "may be recognized almost uniquely by its negative qualities: it has neither mythology nor epic, neither science nor fiction, neither philosophy nor plastic arts." Ironic, indeed, to compare such assertions with others with which, in recent years, we have become increasingly familiar.

of the most frequent visitors at Mme de Loynes'; while France, whose ears it had reached that his fellow academicians of La Patrie Française had been heard to say that, owing to the dissimilarity of his views they felt uncomfortable whenever they were in his presence, refused to set foot inside the Academy for the next fifteen years.

Proust found himself much in the same position as Mme Strauss, with friends of long standing as nationalist in their views as others were Dreyfusard. While continuing, therefore, to further the cause by every means in his power, he tried, at the same time, to avoid ruptures with acquaintances whose opinions differed violently from his own.[1] How little he considered his position in society, where it was a grave disadvantage to profess Dreyfusard tendencies, could now be seen. Indeed, he would not deign even to reply when he was included by some nationalist journal in a list of "shameful young Jews" who were alleged to compromise the position of Barrès by their discipleship; though he had been baptized in infancy and had never been anything but a professing Catholic. In the same way, when Montesquiou, with characteristic petty malice, continually tried to draw him out in public, and taunt him with his Jewish blood, he replied simply that, although he and his father and brother were all Catholics, his mother was a Jewess, and therefore he could never take part in any discussions on questions of race. Impartial in most of his views, he was completely unprejudiced about the whole matter. Although several of his most intimate friends were, like himself, half Jewish, he considered that race was little but an accident of birth which had comparatively slight significance. What aroused his deep resentment, however, was the fact that Parisian society, which was now exercising a fanatical fervour in excluding the Jews from its

---

[1] In spite of this, however, it is almost certain that their vitriolic anti-Semitism was the cause of his later estrangement both from Barrès and Forain.

midst, had for years been establishing the fortunes of its most noble families by wealthy "misalliances" with daughters of the race that it now affected to despise. Two of the most courted princesses in society had been born Heine, while Rothschild ladies had married into the princely houses of de Wagram and de Gramont. That such families should now protest the most bitter anti-Semitism seemed to him as false and despicable as did those writers who, married to converted Jewesses and using the dowries which had come to them from their Jewish parents to advance their social and professional positions, now employed themselves in writing to the nationalist Press the most slanderous and insane attacks upon the Jews.

At this period many of the more ardent Dreyfusards used to gather in the drawing-room of Charpentier, Zola's publisher and friend, which had now become almost the centre of the movement. For years indeed, this vast room, with its walls hung with canvases by Monet and Renoir, had been the scene of numerous and huge receptions. Now the somewhat vague character of its gatherings assumed a definite form. It was here that Proust, introduced by his friend, Louis de Robert, had first met Colonel Picquart and learned from his own lips of the known facts which proved conclusively the condemned man's innocence. It was hither that he would repair, in the distracted days before Zola's trial, to meet other Dreyfusards as fervent as himself, and to discuss the latest developments of the case. When these evenings broke up, there would be the same long walks to and fro through the deserted streets, while Proust and his friend would consider all the available facts again and again, express their indignation, assert their convictions and go through all the names of their acquaintances and friends to see whether any remained whose sympathies for the cause could be awakened, and whose prestige might add weight to the various petitions that were continually being directed to the President.

Louis de Robert was one of Proust's most recent friends. Proust had been first drawn towards him by the sincere and understanding appreciation that de Robert had accorded to his writing at a time when most of his acquaintances offered him little but ironic disparagement or equally superficial compliments; and this sympathy had deepened by reason of the great interest they both shared in the case. Every morning, throughout Zola's trial, de Robert was present in the Palais de Justice, hanging upon each word with absorbed attention; while in the evening he would meet his friend and narrate in detail the proceedings of the day.

When the great writer was condemned de Robert reported that terrible scene when a small group of men had been obliged to use force to save the victim from the enraged and hysterical mob which was shouting madly: "Kill him! Kill him!"

Once Zola had fled to England, feeling in France ran even higher than before. "It must stop," M. Méline said in his famous speech in the Chamber. "It must stop if only in the interests of those who have flung themselves into the campaign with such reckless audacity. If we are not careful, there is about to rise in this country a party which has never existed before. Enmities and hatreds are being sown which can fall only upon the innocent. If we do not take steps to stop it, we shall find ourselves, one hundred years after the revolution, marching towards a new era of intolerance."

With Zola in exile, Picquart cashiered from the army on half pay, and subsequently prosecuted for treason for denouncing as forgeries the new alleged "proofs" of Dreyfus's guilt, which the Army Council had just displayed triumphantly in the Chamber, the position of the Dreyfusards looked black indeed. Yet even among the most ardent nationalists, there was growing a certain uneasiness. It was said that in England Queen Victoria had interested herself in the case sufficiently to obtain from her nephew William II, a definite assurance that Dreyfus was innocent; that she had communicated this information to the exiled Empress Eugénie, who in turn had passed it on to the Princesse Mathilde.

And then, in the autumn of 1899 fell the great bombshell. Lieut.-Colonel Henry admitted that he had forged the famous papers in which Dreyfus was mentioned by name, and, after arrest and imprisonment, committed suicide. De Boisdeffre, the commander-in-chief of the army, was dismissed, the third war minister in three months resigned his position; and Mme Dreyfus again wrote to the President demanding a new trial. Public opinion had now reached the point of hysteria. There were irreparable feuds in almost every family. There was more rioting in the streets. Dreyfusards were dismissed from public positions, and duels were fought by deputies of the Chamber. Hundreds of new petitions were got up for a fresh trial. But the army remained adamant: Dreyfus was guilty. On the threshold of a new century, France stood on the brink of civil war.

CHAPTER VIII

MEANWHILE Proust had now contributed articles and sketches to several of the more literary journals, and the trend of his future life was beginning slowly to shape itself. Juvenilia from *Le Banquet*, as we have seen, were subsequently collected in *Les Plaisirs et les Jours*. Other pieces in the same volume had first appeared in *La Revue Blanche*, as did, in 1896, his essay, *Contre l'Obscurité*; while the year before, he had published two short articles in *Le Gaulois*. In 1897 there had appeared in *La Presse* an obituary he had composed in honour of Alphonse Daudet; while in 1900 he wrote, for the first time, an article for the *Figaro*, now edited by Calmette, to which he was to contribute, irregularly, until the end of his life.

This article, *Pèlerinages Ruskiniens*, marks the beginnings of Proust's rapidly growing enthusiasm for Ruskin, whose passionate admirer he remained for the next five years, during which time he devoted himself almost completely to translating two of his works. English literature altogether now made a deep appeal to him. Pater and Ruskin were his best loved essayists, while the novels of George Eliot, as he frequently averred, never ceased to move him to tears.

Although towards the end of the century, he had not yet given up hope that his asthma could be cured, and that one day he would be able to lead a normal life; his choking fits, usually at their most violent in the evening, made it necessary for him nearly always to remain in bed until about eleven o'clock at night, with the result that it gradually became his habit to sleep throughout the day.

On his return from Venice, the one long holiday abroad of

his whole life, the family moved to the rue des Courcelles. Almost immediately Proust's health took a turn for the worse, and there were periods of long months when it was impossible for him to leave his room.

It was now for the first time that he began to be deeply troubled by the sense of his wasted youth. Already, it seemed to him, many of his friends were beginning to distinguish themselves, while he himself had as yet done nothing. He had been among the first to congratulate Gaston de Caillavet and Robert de Flers upon their collaboration in those witty comedies whose success was steadily to increase: he knew that Louis de la Salle had published a volume of very creditable verse, that Robert Dreyfus was writing steadily and that Léon Brunschwicq had edited a new edition of Pascal's *Pensées*. As for the others, they all seemed to be equally well launched upon satisfactory careers, while he himself had nothing to show but one slim and precious-looking adolescent volume, and a few articles in literary or æsthetic journals. But although deeply dissatisfied with his own efforts, he still could find no subject for the novel which he was always intending to begin. He continued to fill notebooks, jotting down his most vivid observations and reflections; he continued to read with unabated persistence; but it seemed utterly futile to force himself to settle down to any prolonged and serious effort.

In the long hours afforded him for introspection, he was frequently overwhelmed with a terrible sensation of the futility and the emptiness of life. His evenings spent in society would seem to recede an immeasurable distance, and from the peak of his isolation he was compelled to look down upon them with a detachment which served merely to emphasize their long littleness in high relief. Yet there still persisted in him all the old urgent necessity for self-expression, even while the possibility of his gratifying it seemed continually to recede. Each time he tried with honesty and patience to consider a subject worthy of serving him for some important work, a thousand different ideas and figures would leap to his imagination, but so diverse and diffuse that there seemed no possible means of grouping them on the same canvas. So from week to week he continued to delay; while each day that he did so afforded him further time to assimilate the vast mass of material accumulated within him, and which already contained the seeds of his future work.

On the other hand, he still had many contacts with the outside world and was even making new friends. Now it was that he formed a particularly intimate friendship with the Princes Emmanuel and Antoine Bibesco and their almost inseparable companion, Comte Bertrand de Salignac-Fénelon. The Bibescos, who lived but a few doors away, were young men with tastes very similar to his own. Their mother, who was passionately devoted to music and literature, and had been on terms of friendship not only with Liszt and Wagner, but with many of the eminent writers of the day, had inculcated into her sons a deep respect for culture; added to which their interest in philosophy, their intense Dreyfusism, and the fact that they moved in the same circle, caused them to form a small band which congregated frequently in the invalid's room for hours of fervent and earnest argument and discussion, and expressed itself by means of a number of personal, significant, yet almost undergraduate terms and phrases. They turned their names into anagrams, and referred to each other respectively as Lecram, and the Ocsebibs. They invented a number of intimate and secret idioms which they alone could understand and which frequently interspersed their conversations and their correspondence. They expressed agreement by using the latin "sic," and emphasis by its superlative "sicissime," and referred to the state of their friendships with the vocabulary of the Stock Exchange. Their frequent, almost daily meetings, were composed of a series of animated transitions from serious conversation to secret confidences, and from secret confidences to gossip about their mutual acquaintances. During Proust's long periods of exile from the world, his three friends would often call to see him late in the evening, and share with him all their latest news: how the Dreyfus case was going, and who most recently had been won over to the cause; which of their acquaintances had fallen in or out of love, which of them had quarrelled, which of them had left the city. From Prince Antoine, Proust learned many of the obscure mannerisms of society people; and there was no detail too slight for his interest and curiosity. Questions of precedence, of family alliances, of when and when not to elide the particle before a proper name, were all entered upon and discussed with the same minute analysis as were problems of æsthetics or philosophy.

Prince Emmanuel, on the other hand, influenced him more deeply in his deepening love and appreciation of the Gothic cathedrals. He had an unusually fine collection of photographs which, when the invalid was sufficiently well, he would often go to look at: and when conditions were favourable, he would sometimes arrange with his friends expeditions to visit the cathedrals themselves.

Soon after Ruskin's death,[1] Proust had been reading, in the works of his master, of a little figure on the façade of Rouen that he longed to see for himself. Setting out with some friends, they spent a whole day scrutinizing the sculpture, only discovering the figure they sought at the end of the day, dwarfed among the noble ranks of prophets, saints and kings, by its own miniature proportions. Learning from the sacristan that he well remembered Ruskin, Proust's joy was unbounded. For a long time he remained talking to him, striving, through his innumerable questions, to recreate for himself a portrait of the Prophet of Brantwood. Nor could he tear himself away until it was time to catch their train. Even then, although he had already tipped the man with charac-

[1] On January 21st, 1900.

teristic generosity, urged on, no doubt, by his master's advice "Pay your sacristan well and make friends with him" he was impelled to turn back to give him more. "A man who knew Ruskin surely deserves that" he excused himself to his impatient companions.

Now, under the tutelage of Prince Emmanuel, he went to look at the cathedrals of Laon, Senlis, Lisieux, and many other towns. To be sure that he would be ready in good time to start, Proust would get up and dress late the night before, and read until it was time for his friends to call for him. During the journey he would be so happy to be out, that, even though he could take nothing but coffee for fear of bringing on an attack, he would leave tips for the waiters which were even more prodigious than usual. In the clear light of spring, everything, after his long confinement, would seem superlatively beautiful: and the countryside, with its fields and meadows, its apple-trees in flower, would bring back to him all the force and clarity of his impressions in the old days at Illiers.

As soon as they arrived, they would make a survey of the cathedral from the outside, walking slowly round, while Emmanuel Bibesco explained to his companions the features of special interest. Although already exhausted, Proust would insist on climbing up to the belfry, leaning on Bertrand de Fénelon's arm for support. The higher they went the more difficult it became for him to proceed. His friends would insist upon pausing awhile, so that he could regain his breath, and when they were ready to move on, de Fénelon would break into song in order to encourage his companion. Such moments as these Proust never forgot and when, years later, he began to write his book, it was this young aristocrat, with his fair hair and complexion, his brilliant blue eyes, his extraordinary courtesy and easy elegance of manners, that he used as the physical prototype for Saint-Loup.

In addition to this trio, there was a larger group of companions with whom they were intimate—George de Lauris, René Blum, Prince Radziwill, the Duc de Guiche and the Marquis d'Albuféra, who also came sometimes to spend their evenings with Proust, at the rue des Courcelles. Some of these young men, who knew little of his real talent and understanding, were drawn to him simply on account of his wit, his good spirits and his extraordinary friendliness, and would think nothing, while they were doing their military service, of using a short leave in coming to Paris specially to visit him. These gatherings where the only attractions were cider and conversation, caused no little interest in the outside world, where it seemed extraordinary that young men should be content to employ their infrequent leisure in so strange, though harmless a manner.

On those occasions when he was sufficiently well to get up, Proust would spend his evenings either writing or receiving his friends in the family dining-room. Here, where there was always a huge fire and where the large dining-table was covered with a red plush cloth, there would be many a night spent in talk until the dawn. Seated round the hearth in comfortable arm-chairs, Proust would do everything in his power to entertain his companions. One of his greatest pleasures was to be able to make them laugh, and to laugh with them. The most trivial details of their lives were of interest to him. He would listen to them, when they were alone, with the utmost sympathy and attention; and knowing his immense tolerance and the breadth of his understanding, they would pour out to him freely all their problems, and share with him their most intimate hopes. Of himself, however, he would say but little. When he spoke, it was usually of his opinions and ideas rather than of his personal life. These dissertations were received with great respect, for among such friends he had already achieved the reputation of being a man of great ability.

His circle at this time was increased, too, by the arrival of the latest star, the young, beautiful and talented Comtesse de Noailles, elder daughter of the Princesse Bassaraba de Brancovan, and related both to the Bibescos and to Montesquiou. Proust was impressed no less by the charm of her personality and the passion and courage of her convictions than by the quality of her poems; for she exhibited not only a rare intelligence but a sensibility and a spontaneous understanding that matched his own. While he was the only person for whose opinions Mme de Noailles ever had sufficient respect to alter, on his advice, the phrasing of a line; he, on his side, wrote her enthusiastic letters of appreciation, and never ceased to quote her verses to his friends. Even greater, was his affection for her younger sister, the Princesse Alexandre de Caraman-Chimay, who possessed a simplicity and a sincerity of character before which he felt so completely natural and at ease that, when he was sufficiently well, he would often call upon her unexpectedly for the sheer pleasure of talking with her throughout the night.

These nocturnal visits that he was inclined to pay his friends at a moment's notice, however, were not unattended with disadvantages. Not that they were ever unwelcome. Invariably he was received with a warm and spontaneous pleasure. But as the night passed, and still he showed no signs of leaving, his hosts would begin reluctantly to consider with dread having to go through the next day with only two or three hours' sleep. Finally, when the group broke up in the full light of day, they would anxiously consult their watches to consider whether it was even worth while going to bed at all.

Sometimes in the summer, completely forgetful of the season, Proust would accept an invitation to dine in the country, and would arrive, faultlessly arrayed in evening dress, with top hat and white gloves, just as the party were about to go out on some expedition in country clothes. It was on one such occasion, after a dazzling display of conversation, that the father of his friend requested, as he was about to sign the visitors' book: "Above all, sir, no epigrams, please."

Gone, now, were the evenings when he could spend hours with his friends in restaurants, while they regarded with affectionate amusement the generousness of his hospitality and the prodigality of his tips. When he wished to entertain, he must do so at home, arranging, with the same assiduous care, the same earnest intention of giving pleasure, dinner parties in which, after an immense amount of thought, friends from various different spheres were successfully brought together. There were parties when Mme de Guerne and Reynaldo Hahn sang duets, and evenings when Montesquiou gave readings of his latest poems; on which occasions, it must be added, the Count himself invariably decided to whom should be extended the great honour of being present; and it was only after a tactful and persistent pleading that the host was permitted to include Lucien Daudet, still out of favour with the poet, among his guests. If his parents were away, Proust would undertake the whole supervision of these parties himself; otherwise there would be long and earnest discussions with his mother beforehand about the dishes to be served; and, while he played the role of host, his mother and father would preside at each end of the long table, the former beautifully proud to see her son so elated and so popular; the latter, courteous and smiling, but a little puzzled as to what there could possibly be about his boy that made all these people think him so attractive.

To these dinner parties, often of an almost traditional magnificence, would come, besides Montesquiou and Yturri, such writers as Anatole France, Barrès, de Régnier and Ganderax, often with their wives and daughters; some of the most celebrated and most beautiful hostesses of the Faubourg St. Germain, whose hospitality he wished to return; old friends such as Jacques-Émile Blanche and Gabriel de la

Rochefoucauld, and new acquaintances such as Charles Ephrussi, to whom Proust was greatly drawn by reason both of his great knowledge of art and his fervent Dreyfusism. On these occasions Proust would spare himself no efforts to please and to amuse his guests. Once, when he had invited Mme de Noailles, he had the table specially decorated in her honour with all the flowers named in her latest volume of poems; while in accordance with his earlier habit, he would himself eat before the meal was served, in order that he could offer his whole attention to the entertainment of his friends. Sometimes, pretending to eat, he would move his plate from place to place, taking each new course beside a different guest, so that he could devote himself exclusively to each in turn. He took particular pleasure in inviting to meet each other friends who, he knew, would be mutually sympathetic, but who moved in such widely different circles that without his intervention there would have been little opportunity for them to become acquainted; and as a host he was considered generally to be a great success.

But if this narrow and circumscribed life that his illness forced upon him must have deprived Proust of many pleasures, it nevertheless offered him certain compensations, chief of which were the terms of unusual intimacy and friendliness on which he lived with his parents. His mother, whose only thought was to serve her family with devoted affection, watched over him still with a unique solicitude and tenderness. When he needed rest, she ensured that he should sleep uninterruptedly in a calm which not the slightest murmur should disturb; when his friends called, she would herself make sure that he was in a fit condition to receive them, and insist upon his changing his vests as though he were still a child. Or when a letter arrived that she knew would particularly please him, she would herself take it to his room at once, handing it to him with an elaborately affected casualness, lest she should spoil for him the surprised delight which she knew the writing upon the envelope would evoke.

Between Proust and his father, too, there was growing a deepening understanding. Professor Proust now devoted himself almost exclusively to scientific investigation: he saw few private patients and was consequently much at home. Every evening, therefore, he would spend some time in his son's room, discussing such matters of literature and politics as he hoped might interest him; while Proust, on his side, deliberately tried to suppress certain traits in his character that he knew well his father actively disliked. It was inevitable, sometimes, that between men of such different years and experience there should be occasional friction; that when his father expressed views and ideas with which Proust passionately disagreed, he would react with an emphasis and a violence that later he would regret. But these misunderstandings were shortlived and entirely without bitterness; and at an age when the relationship between father and son is usually little more than one of polite estrangement, Proust was on terms of intimate friendship with his own. Particularly would he seek opportunities when he could draw out the Professor on the subjects of pathology and medicine, or persuade him to explain in detail the symptoms and methods of treatment of various grim diseases. Just as, in other circles, he would ply his friends with questions upon anything from higher mathematics to precedence, so now he would elicit, with the same interest and attention, all that he could assimilate concerning the functioning of the human body and its disorders.

This environment of family affection, an environment which he scarcely noticed consciously, since he had naturally come to accept it as one of the normal conditions of his daily life, brought him a dim, underlying sense of well-being and happiness that he was to lose all too soon. For in 1903 two events occurred to disrupt his life. His brother, with whom also he had always been on the best of terms, married, and consequently set up house elsewhere: and a few months later, his father was taken ill. Brought home one morning from his hospital in a critical condition, despite all his efforts to alleviate the anxiety of his family, within three days he was dead.

CHAPTER IX

To Proust the death of his father was a twofold grief. He had to bear not only his own sorrow but the greater sorrow of seeing his mother suffer, and of understanding that never to the end of her days would she regain her former happiness. He had known for a long time that his parents were so utterly devoted to each other that his own ill health had been their one great sadness; and now he realized that however deep his own love for her, he could never make up to his mother for this irremediable loss.

A few months previously he had completed arrangements with the *Mercure de France* for the publication of his first Ruskin translation; but it seemed to him now that he could best show respect to his father's memory by renouncing an ambition the fulfilment of which had for so long been his chief desire. In this, however, Mme Proust soon sought to dissuade him, assuring him that such a sacrifice would be not only profitless, but directly contradictory to his father's wishes, since he had for long been looking forward to seeing his son's new work in print.

The translation of the *Bible of Amiens*, accordingly, was published the following year. Proust had been engaged on it with laborious conscientiousness for over two years. His knowledge of the English language was not great, and having established, by the aid of dictionaries, the meaning of each separate word, he would often be forced to apply to one or another of his friends for the idiomatic translation of a phrase. The volume was dedicated to the memory of his father and contained, in addition to the translation itself, a preface of nearly one hundred pages, divided into four parts.

INTRODUCTION TO PROUST

This preface is well worthy of attention, because it supplies an illuminating link in the development of his thought between *Les Plaisirs et les Jours* and *Swann*. In it, Proust asserts that by reading only one book of any writer you may discover his individual features but never his essential characteristics; for these can be appreciated and understood only after prolonged and repeated study in a series of different works. It was this principle which, applied in this instance to æsthetic criticism, was nevertheless revolving in his mind round the question of delineation of character, and which later caused him to show, with the most careful deliberation, each personage of his novel in a series of completely different circumstances and environments.

But the critic, he maintained, should go even further. His function is not only to demonstrate essential characteristics, but to penetrate so deeply into the mind and work of the writer that he can extract for himself not only the truths which have been recreated, but the experience of which they are but a material reflection. By this means alone can the depths of his talent be assessed and understood. For the true artist, moreover, there can be but one real source of inspiration. This is the sense of a deeper and fuller spiritual life lying hidden beneath the world we know. This sense, haunting him incessantly, must become more than instinct and should serve him as his morality; for his ultimate duty is not only to understand it as clearly and deeply as his growth permits, but to retranslate it into such terms as may be both permanent and clear. To this end the whole of the creative life, mind, heart and being, must be continually directed.

This theory, as we shall see later, when it is much amplified and elaborated in *Le Temps Retrouvé*, is not only an apology for the work of his master, but the apology of his own. Here, however, it is only with the work of Ruskin that Proust is concerned, whose great value lies, for him, in an extraordinary capacity of inner discrimination, which permits him to express all his ideas, his emotions, his values, in terms of the spiritual inspiration which he found on every page of that Bible which he read "as if it had been written by the hand of God." This, to Proust, is the whole centre of gravity of Ruskinian æsthetics—the fact that art is assessed therein less in terms of beauty than of moral significance. Nevertheless, in the same capacity wherein lies his master's greatest strength, therein, he considers, lies also his greatest weakness. For not only was Ruskin's appreciation of the scriptures so deep that their cadences often moulded the form of his own phrases, but it dominated his being to the extent that it forced him even to find moral reasons for valuing certain works when to the sensibilities none whatever seemed to exist.

Such, in short, was the gist of the thesis with which Proust sent forth the first translation of a work by his Bergotte: a thesis which, while bringing him a certain credit from his more discriminating friends, did little to introduce his writing to a wider public. The book, like the articles he had recently been contributing to the *Figaro* on some of the famous drawing-rooms he had known since his youth, was addressed rather to the poets and littérateurs of his own circle: such friends as Montesquiou and the Comtesse de Noailles whom, doubtless, he still retained a certain desire to impress.[1]

These *Figaro* sketches, signed by the pseudonyms of Dominique or Horatio, were supposed to be anonymous: but since, in his characteristic manner, Proust let each of his friends, singly, into the dark secret, extracting promises from them that the information must on no account be made public, the knowledge soon became common property. Only Montesquiou, apparently, remained in ignorance: for a des-

[1] It is interesting to begin here to note some of the curious similarities between Proust and the writer who probably most influenced his ideas and his work. Ruskin also for many years lived at home with his parents, who provided him with a generous allowance, deliberately sought out writers and painters, and, despite a considerable *succès d'estime*, for years was generally considered to be merely a wealthy dilettante.

cription of one of his gatherings that Proust had published under the title of *Fête chez Montesquiou à Neuilly*, was privately printed by that gentleman for distribution among his friends, without any acknowledgments to the author, since the Count professed a repeated ignorance of his identity. Although Montesquiou had by now ceased to exert so great an influence on Proust as in the first years of their friendship, the two men still continued to visit and to correspond. It is very likely that the great attraction, from the poet's side, was Proust's considerable friendship with France, since Proust was frequently commanded to bring him, a somewhat reluctant victim, to the Palais Rose, the mansion at Vesinet built in imitation of the Grand Trianon, which Montesquiou inhabited after he had given up the Pavillon des Muses.

But whenever Proust was obliged to reject, owing to illness, certain of Montesquiou's invitations, which were always offered in the style of royal commands, the Count ceased to be sympathetic, and, disbelieving his excuses, wrote him sarcastic diatribes in his most characteristic vein. To one of these, in which he had likened himself to Solomon and his young friend to an ant, Proust wrote an almost indulgently polite reply, in which he remarked that of course he realized that Montesquiou always liked to take the best part. "What do you mean, take it?" the Count replied. "I have no need to take it, since I already have it." With Montesquiou there was little opportunity for anyone else to have the last word!

Actually, Proust's excuses were perfectly sincere. Even if he gave a dinner at home, it meant that he had to prepare himself for the event for several days beforehand, by reducing his diet to milk alone, and strictly refraining from all conversation. Once again, all serious attempts at work became impossible. For not only was he too weak now to write with any persistence, but he had not even sufficient energy to receive any vivid impressions from the outer world.

Far from being able to go out, there were whole months when he lacked the strength to dress himself; and his asthma was so bad that if anyone came to see him, he had to forbid them to smoke or to wear perfume of any kind.

By the summer of 1905, however, he was sufficiently recovered to be able to accompany his mother on a holiday to Evian. Thence he would take excursions,[1] as always when he was in this neighbourhood, to the Brancovan's beautiful country house, Amphion, which was situated in High Savoy on the edge of the lake of Geneva, and whose gardens were now richly aglow with the double purple of many fuchsias. Arriving at his destination in a carriage about midnight, he would be hailed with delight by his friends assembled on the terrace, and wrapped in his fur cloak, would remain with them, deep in conversation until the dawn.

But it was not only Proust who was now in bad health. Soon after they had arrived at their hotel, the fits of dizziness from which his mother had been suffering for some months, suddenly got worse, and she was taken seriously ill with uræmia. But despite all her son's entreaties, she still refused to consult a doctor. Probably she knew too much of the limitations of medicine to expect to derive from it any lasting cure. Although unable to eat, in order not to alarm him, she persisted in rising at her usual hour every morning, and going downstairs, even when she could scarcely walk and it was necessary for her to lean on two people for support. For days Proust watched her with a deepening anxiety, concealing from her his fears, just as she was striving to conceal from him her own. When another week passed and she got no better, but continued to refuse both food and medicine, his alarm increased. Whenever, in the past, he had forced himself to face the fact that one of them must die first, and so leave the other, he had always hoped that the one who must

---

[1] It was these journeys in the local train that supplied material for the train journeys from Balbec to La Raspelière, in *Sodome et Gomorrhe*.

live on alone might be himself, so that his mother might never know the agony of losing him also, as she had lost his father. But now it seemed probable that, after all, it might be himself who would survive, he flinched from facing the possibility. Every day he would search her face with tender solicitude, hoping to discover the faintest signs of improvement. But there were none.

Finally Mme Proust consented to let him take her home. Doctors were summoned at last, and specialists consulted. But it was too late. With characteristic calm, she continued to preserve her attitude of courageous resignation, while her son watched her slowly slipping from him. She, who must have known that soon she was to leave him for ever, still forbore to speak lest she should cause him grief; until at last the power of speech was taken from her. Nor dared he let her know by the faintest sign that he realized that the end was near, lest her knowledge of his agony should but increase her own.

With outward composure, Proust watched her lose all consciousness of him; followed her coffin to the grave and heaped upon it the first clods that were to bury it in the earth. With outward composure, he thanked people for their flowers and condolences, and replied by letter to their many tokens of kindness and affection. Actually, he was stunned with shock. He knew that in losing his mother he had lost the greatest affection, the greatest devotion he would ever know: but the realization was only to reach its fullest depth after many weeks.

CHAPTER X

THE man who, as a boy of fifteen, had unhesitatingly admitted in a drawing-room confession that the greatest tragedy of his life was to be separated from his mother, was now separated from her for ever. He returned to his bed in the now melancholy and empty apartment in the rue des Courcelles. The place was much too big for him to keep on for himself alone, but for the moment he was too ill and griefstricken to be able to cope with practical arrangements. Its coldness and loneliness were unendurable. A dozen times a day he found himself waiting for the sound of his mother's footsteps, her knock upon his door. Her absence only served to emphasize to him more deeply the beauty and selflessness of her devotion. No more she would come to him with some unexpected letter, no more announce the arrival of some expected friend. No more, when he was going out, might he go to her to do up his shoes for him, lest his bending down should bring on a violent attack of coughing, and no more, when he returned, find her waiting for him in the hall to make sure that he had not suddenly been taken ill. Instead of the passing weeks helping to alleviate his sorrow, they only made it the more poignant. Now it was the habitual sweetness of her smile, now a peculiar warm intonation of her voice, that would suddenly return to revive his suffering with a terrible intensity.

By the new year, the sense of his loss was so acute that it was imperative for him to make some change in his existence. He had not yet utterly lost hope of one day leading a more normal life, even though he realized that years of illness had so undermined his constitution that he could never hope to be completely cured; and as, for a long time various friends had urged him to try a succession of remedies, none of which had proved successful, he felt that it was high time to resort now to the most drastic measures. He at last decided, therefore, to try to improve his condition by undergoing a rigid treatment in a sanatorium. Yet in spite of being excessively expensive, this did him but little good. Within a few months he was back again in the rue des Courcelles making plans for spending the summer at Trouville or Cabourg.

Since his mother's death it was to Mme Strauss that he had turned most naturally for practical advice, and now, since he was unable to do so himself, he asked her to try to find for him a suitable house that he could rent. Many letters were written explaining his exact requirements, the amount he could afford to pay and the desirability of taking a villa rather than a suite in a hotel. But like so many other projects in the past, when there had been endless correspondence with one or another of his friends about some intended holiday in Switzerland or Italy, he was forced at the last moment to abandon the plan altogether. This time, however, it was the serious illness of an uncle that made it necessary for him to choose some other place nearer Paris.

Meanwhile the Dreyfus case had drawn to its sensational and romantic close. Three years ago, the prisoner had been brought back from Devil's Island so ill that it was believed he could not live. At the famous court martial at Rennes, where a murderous attack had been made upon his counsel, Labori, and, despite the exposure of the whole campaign of lies upon which the victim's guilt had been maintained, the former verdict had been upheld, "extenuating circumstances" had been found, and his term of imprisonment reduced to ten years. Again the whole of enlightened European opinion was scandalized, and Zola made another bitter protest in *L'Aurore*. There were fresh agitations and fresh discoveries, and once more Dreyfus applied for a new trial. This, at last, was granted in the summer of 1906. It dragged on for several days, but his innocence was at last established beyond all further doubt. A special Bill was passed to invest him with military honours; Picquart was reinstated in the army as Brigadier-General, and the ashes of Zola, who had recently died, were conveyed in solemn pomp to the Panthéon.

These events gave Proust much cause for melancholy reflection. He remembered the days when he had lain awake sleepless at the thought of an innocent man being condemned to a life of degradation and imprisonment. Now justice was triumphant in the matter of a romantic drama and ten years of misery wiped away by a spectacular public reparation. In this respect, he thought, victims of judicial errors, of political injustice, were not wholly unfortunate. For them there was always hope. Whereas for the essential tragedy of life there was no hope. This ultimate tragedy lay, for Proust, in the fact that in no sense could the life he knew correspond with the ideal life of the imagination. He realized too well that the best of his days were over. He had lost all those to whom he had been most devoted, and never would there be anyone to take their place. The happiest period of his life, his childhood, was continually receding further into the distance, while the future could hold little for him save greater disillusion and more serious illness. Love such as he had always desired was impossible for him, and by now he had ceased to believe even in friendship. In all his relations he had longed to give to the utmost capacity of his nature, but in no single one, save that with his mother, had he found anyone willing to reciprocate completely.

The only thing he could do to prevent himself from succumbing to complete despair was to work. Now at last, no matter how great the task, he must set himself to transfer from that perishable and precarious receptacle that was his brain, to the more abiding form of letters, those imperishable truths that were the chastening legacy of the accumulated experience and suffering of his life.

While he was thus preparing himself for his stupendous task, his second Ruskin translation appeared—that of *Sesame and Lilies*.[1] This had been completed early the previous year, but once again, publication had been postponed, this time owing to his mother's death.

The volume was dedicated to three different friends: the preface to the Princesse Alexandre de Caraman-Chimay, the first part to Reynaldo Hahn, the second part to Mlle Suzette Lemaire.

Once again, the introduction is of particular interest, not merely because it indicates many of the writers who were influencing him at this time—among others Marcus Aurelius, Ribot and Schopenhauer—not even because it contains a long and beautiful description of the days of his childhood which were enchanted by his love of books, a description no less vivid and delightful than anything to be found in the Combray scenes of *Swann*, but because it marks a further step in the growth of his ideas on literature and self-expression. The function of the writer for him now is, by presenting his readers with the key to a different world, to help them to dissipate for themselves "the clouds of heaviness and insignificance which leave us unamazed before the universe." Thus the reading of books can produce an alternative result—good when it leads us, by our own thought and effort, to discover a world of truth that without its aid we should never have known, but bad when, instead of awakening a new life of the mind, it is indulged in without deliberate intention and intelligence, and merely superimposes upon our habitual sloth of mind a different series of pictures passively assimilated and

---

[1] *Sesame and Lilies*, which, unlike most of Ruskin's earlier writings, had become immediately popular, in England reached its sixty-fourth thousand by 1903.

consequently devoid of meaning. Yet the friendship of books, he maintains, can be immeasurably superior to human friendship, since it may be at once more sincere and more disinterested. Further, it can be devoid of all the petty, tedious trivialities of our habitual life. For all of us, with the various formalities of the friendships we have initiated, do no more than spin about our essential being the threads of a cocoon, which, daily becoming more dense, finally shut us off completely in an oblivion as dark as death. Every thought that has crossed our mind, every word we have spoken, every habit we have formed, must produce in us at last a reaction pattern, stale and sterile, from which we can never deviate. Whereas reading, being without such formalities and habits, confers upon us the blessing of receiving from another mind those ideas which, in conversation, we merely dissipate; and of penetrating them to that depth when, recreated in ourselves, they can become our own.

Such, then, set forth here in his characteristic style, were some of the ideas that were still developing in his mind, when, during his summer at Versailles, he contemplated the structure of his future work.

He had taken an apartment at the Hotel des Réservoirs, which, to his consternation, cost him far more than would have any villa by the sea. But no sooner was he comfortably installed than he fell ill; and, imprisoned in his vast and sombre bedroom, was forced to spend long weeks gazing helplessly at the innumerable and indifferent pictures which lined the walls, and the profusion of pretentious bronzes which created about him an atmosphere of princely gloom. Although he had gone to endless trouble to ensure that the chimney should not smoke, his cough was continually aggravated by fumes which drifted in from neighbouring rooms. Added to which, he again found it impossible to sleep, so that it seemed now that he must reconcile himself at last to a life of inconvenient habits and abnormal hours.

INTRODUCTION TO PROUST

Very soon his holiday became a nightmare. When it was not smoke that aggravated his cough, it was pollen from the trees outside his window, or dust from the street below. To complete his misery, some woman had taken the floor underneath him on a long lease and was now engaged upon making extensive structural alterations. The continual hammering drove him almost insane. He dared not go out, since he could never rely on the necessary sleep with which to replenish his exhausted energy, and he could not go to his new flat because it was in the hands of decorators. For weeks he was forced to remain at Versailles, where a steady succession of workmen never ceased to riot in the rooms below, creating such an uproar that he expected, when he got downstairs at last, to find that they had erected at least something in the nature of an Eighth Wonder of the World.

At the same time, however, the many different themes he had been considering for his book were gradually beginning to take shape. Of one thing, now, he was convinced: the state of his health would never very much improve, and since he might die comparatively soon, the whole of his material must be included in one single work. This meant that the book which very soon he must force himself to begin should not only recreate the whole of his past, should not only describe the process of his development through each phase of experience and subsequent disillusion, should not only portray the social life of his period and the transformations in its drawing-rooms, the tendencies of its morals, its politics and its arts; but must stand firmly rooted in those theories of memory, imagination, habit, love and time which alone helped him to understand the meaning and manifestation of the life about him. Moreover, for the right portrayal of character it would be necessary for him to employ an enormous canvas, in order that each figure could be shown, not only from one aspect in one point of time, but in many different attitudes throughout the whole period of its development. Such were the difficulties with which he was confronted, and the problems he was forced to solve for himself before he could begin. And thus the main structure of the book was planned and determined long before even the first paragraph was written.

CHAPTER XI

LATE in the autumn of 1906 Proust moved into his new flat in the boulevard Hausmann. It was a comfortable but ugly apartment set in the middle of dust and trees; and though he cared neither for its aspect nor position, he had chosen it because it was situated in a family property which possessed for him innumerable associations of his mother. In this house her old uncle had died, and several times, during his last illness, he himself had accompanied her to make inquiries as to his progress. To this house he had often come with her in his youth to lunch or dine, to offer congratulations upon a birthday or good wishes for the New Year; and since the flat in the rue des Courcelles was now both too large and too expensive, he felt that here at least he would not be shut away from the atmosphere of her presence.

In the two austere reception rooms stood the furniture he had brought from his old home; massive, familiar and unused. For henceforward Proust lived almost exclusively in his bedroom. Here, where, on the advice of the Comtesse de Noailles he had had the walls lined with cork, to preclude the torture of all violent sounds; where the windows were always shut, to keep out, not only the noise of the street below but all particles of dust or pollen that might aggravate his asthma; where the blinds were nearly always lowered to exclude the sunlight which he was convinced had become hurtful to him, he began to work at the prodigious task he had set himself.

For the next six years he devoted himself almost exclusively to his book. Day after day, week after week, month after month and year after year, he wrote in bed, propped up by his pillows, scene after scene of his tremendous novel. At his bedside there was a table piled to overflowing with newspapers, magazines, new books and letters. On his bed, the counterpane was scattered with notebooks and innumerable loose pages of manuscript. When he was too ill even to sit up, he would work lying flat on his back, his paper held over him with his left hand. In this awkward and painful position were written, too, many of his innumerable letters. For if he no longer believed in friendship, he still had many friends. This fact is not as paradoxical as it might at first appear. He no longer believed in friendship, because at last he realized that a human relationship of complete and mutual understanding and affection could seldom exist. But the knowledge of those psychological laws that made this ideal unrealizable, no less than the complete isolation in which, for long periods at a time, he was compelled to live, created in him an immeasurable tolerance which, in its understanding of human weakness and vulnerability, made him more quick to respond to the faintest signs of sincerity and goodness; and anxious most of all to express the essential sympathy of his nature by recreating for himself those moments in his life when he had experienced a vivid, if but short and transient, sense of unity with those he loved.

So long as he was able to work, life remained bearable; but in those periods, and they were not infrequent, when his spasms of choking had been so acute that they left him too exhausted even to hold his pen, he became a victim of moods of despair in which it seemed that, to the end of his days, he was doomed to lead a life not only deprived of the capacity to write, but in which there could enter never again such simple yet necessary joys of human existence as the sights and sounds of the country, orchards in flower, sunlight and the laughter of companions.

By now, the ravages of constant illness had left deep traces on his appearance. He had grown a beard, in contrast to which the pallor of his complexion was almost startling;

while his cheeks had fallen in, and his eyes shone brilliantly with the feverish light of the chronic invalid. From time to time, when one or another of his friends came to visit him, they would find him sitting up in bed, dressed in two or three of the woollen vests he habitually wore to keep him warm. The air would be thick with the vapour of his frequent inhalations, but if there was the faintest trace of perfume on their handkerchief or on the flower in their buttonhole, they would be politely but firmly requested to place the offending object in another room. His questions now would be directed chiefly to such subjects as those on which he required particular information for his book. Whilst he never ceased to probe into the details of the lives of all his acquaintances, he would still spend hours exploring the ramifications and alliances which linked together various houses of the nobility, almost childishly delighted when he discovered some important marriage that had connected two families in a manner such as he had never dreamed. There was no detail for his book to which he did not devote the same ardent and punctilious attention. Fashions in dress, modes of hairdressing, the seasons of various flowers, the type of pastry displayed in the bakers' shops in a certain country district, the exact pronunciation of special English or Italian phrases, all these had to be verified beyond the slightest doubt. Usually, when he went into society, it was for the same reason. Then, taking up his position in a convenient corner, his face pale and haggard beneath the electric light, he would stare about him like a man from another world, his brilliant, searching eyes never for a moment still, while he refreshed his memory over details of deportment, and elaborated his observation of the varied manner in which the most trivial social duties could be performed. Such excursions had to be limited, however, as they were most exhaustive of his strength, and afterwards it would often take him several weeks to regain his normal energy.

When he entertained, it was invariably, and with customary extravagance, at the Ritz. In order to express his gratitude to Calmette for publishing his contributions in the *Figaro*, which he knew had but little popular appeal, he arranged the first large dinner party he had given since his mother's death, appealing to Mme Strauss to help him over the somewhat exacting task of arranging the places of his guests, and inviting such women from the Faubourg St. Germain whose presence he felt would most please his guest of honour. This was characteristic of his habit of always repaying what he considered to be a particular service, with the most lavish gratitude. On this occasion it was Fauré who played during the evening; on another it was Risler. As Proust had fixed no special terms with the second of these musicians, throughout the whole evening he was in a fever of doubt as to how much he should offer him. Even when he had settled the question, he felt compelled to seek confirmation from Mme de Noailles and Mme de Clermont-Tonnerre that he had given enough. Nor was he fully reassured when his friends informed him, with indulgent laughter, that he had paid three times more than was expected. Without the faintest idea of the value of money, Proust was invariably prone to give too much for everything; and simple as was the routine of his life, his household expenses were enormous. As he used to tell his friends, with a half-complacent wistfulness, his mother had always said of him, as Mme de Sévigné about her son, that he found means of spending his money without getting anything to show for it, and of losing it without even gambling.[1]

Meanwhile he had told only the most intimate and trusted of his friends of the serious and colossal task he had set himself. Sometimes, indeed, such a one would persuade him to read a few pages aloud; but seldom would this be successfully

[1] This remark, not only quoted by his mother of the Marcel of the novel, is also to be found referring to himself in several of Proust's letters to his friends.

accomplished. For Proust was usually subject on these occasions to uncontrollable fits of nervous laughter, which forced him to give up at last in the middle of a passage. The majority of his acquaintances still believed that all his energy was being expended on the articles he was again contributing to the *Figaro*.

Early in 1907, the whole of Paris had been scandalized by the murder of a woman well known in society, who had been stabbed to death by her son, the young man immediately afterwards committing suicide. As Proust had been slightly acquainted with the murderer, and Calmette knew of this fact, he asked him to write an article on the subject. Proust complied with *Sentiments Filiaux d'un Parricide*, in which the episode, enriched with many classical allusions and references to Shakespearean tragedy, was treated in a manner intending to show how crime, far from being of necessity the manifestation of a debased and brutal mind, could perfectly well be committed by a sensitive and affectionate nature. When this was published, it caused a mild sensation. Several people expressed themselves deeply shocked, and the only appreciation Proust received was from Ludovic Halévy. This article was followed by several others, *Journées de Lecture*, a long extract from his introduction to *Sesame and Lilies*, *Les Éblouissements*, a tribute to the Comtesse de Noailles, *Une Grand'mère* and, in November, *Impressions de route en Automobile*, which described a journey he had taken by car from Cabourg, where he had spent the summer. The fact that most of his acquaintances ignored these efforts with elaborate care, presumably because they considered them stupid, and their own opinions of such great importance that they could not bring themselves to mention them with an even superficial politeness, was amply compensated for in the eyes of the author when he received from Agostinelli, the chauffeur who had driven him on this expedition, and to whom his valet had sent a copy of the article, a note of appreciation that amazed him on account of both its intelligence and its spontaneous evidence of literary taste. At a time when Proust was beginning to realize that the love of art, of music and of letters was far less widespread than he had imagined, it delighted him to find that it could be discovered, nevertheless, in the most unexpected places. Henceforward, whenever he was well enough to go out and required a car, he always insisted upon having this man to drive him, whose natural understanding he found so unusual that later, when the manuscript of his book was ready to be typed, he employed him as his secretary.

During the two following years Proust published, also in the *Figaro*, his sketches on *L'Affaire Lemoine*. Lemoine had falsely claimed to have discovered the secret of making diamonds, and had even received a million francs from Sir Jules Werner, the President of de Beers, on condition that he should divulge it to no one save certain experts in his company. It was soon discovered however, that his manufactured diamonds were actually real stones, with the result that the "inventor" was prosecuted, found guilty of fraud, and sentenced to prison for six years. With this as his theme, Proust produced a series of parodies on various well-known writers—Balzac, Flaubert, Sainte-Beuve, Henri de Régnier, the Goncourts, Michelet, Faguet the dramatic critic, Renan and Saint-Simon. While of no great importance, all these pieces, which are pungently skilful, show to what a pitch of perfection he had brought the art of mimicry, which is as vivid in these pages as ever it had been in his famous "imitations." Apart from one or two other short and trivial pieces, however, these were the last sketches he contributed to the *Figaro* until three years later there began to appear various short extracts from the long novel upon which he was still at work.

By now his excursions into society had become less and less frequent. Even during his summer holidays, which he took nearly every year in the Cabourg of his youth, he very seldom left his room during the day. Sometimes, when he was too ill to work, his friends would come and visit him, or while he played dominoes with Agostinelli or his valet, Reynaldo Hahn would sit by his bedside, and, apparently impervious to all distractions, continue to compose the music for *Le Dieu Bleu* which Diaghileff was shortly to produce in his next season of ballet.

Here at the Grand Hotel, where it was rumoured that he always took the four surrounding rooms besides his own to ensure complete silence, he would often entertain his friends at dusk on the terrace facing the sea. Such now, was his acute dislike of the sun, which he was still convinced aggravated his asthma, that he would appear with an umbrella in his hand, even at sundown, and wait on the doorstep until he was quite certain that the last rays had disappeared. Then, seated behind a large table, he would play the host, offering his companions, with customary generosity, the finest champagne and cigars, and delighting them with innumerable anecdotes of his youth. Sometimes he would give one of his celebrated imitations, sometimes he would discourse on his favourite writers. His memory was prodigious, and he could quote, if he wished, not only long poems, but several pages of prose, without a single hesitation.

At Cabourg, with characteristic benevolence, he had become interested in an old nobleman[1] who, though of the highest aristocracy, had been left derelict by his wife and family and, ill and half paralysed, was usually treated with insufferable insolence by the hotel staff. Proust did his utmost to improve the conditions of his tragic old age by surrounding him with innumerable unobtrusive acts of courtesy. Sometimes, too, if he heard that some friend was staying a short time in a neighbouring village, he would brave the sun-

---

[1] This character appears later in *Sodome et Gomorrhe*, as Pierre Verjus, Comte de Crécy, the first husband of Odette.

light and himself walk miles through dust and heat in order to be able in person, to invite him to dinner. Wearing a dark town suit, a deep stiff collar, and a straw hat set at an extraordinary angle, or else enveloped in a long black velvet-lined cloak, he would arrive at length exhausted and dishevelled, but touchingly pleased to have been able to find an opportunity for showing his friendship.

Later in the evening he would probably go to the Casino in order to watch the people. Just as, in town, whenever he went out at night he would invariably wear a heavy fur cloak, so here, no matter how hot the weather, he would put on, not only, beneath his dinner jacket a thick woollen cardigan, but on top of it a heavy overcoat, which, in the manner of his youth, he wore unbuttoned. With superb unconcern he would wander through the gaming rooms or the restaurant, where the crowd was attired faultlessly in evening dress, with his straw hat in his hand, his woollen waistcoat much in evidence, and his pockets bulging clumsily with magazines.

Sometimes he would discover here some solitary acquaintance, whom he would invite to join him: then, while his brilliant eyes with their deep rings beneath them never ceased to rake the room, he would discourse with whimsical irony upon the foibles, the pretentiousness and the stupidity of the people about them.

Throughout all these years, Proust never ceased to correspond with his most intimate friends, though several of them had begun slowly to drift away from him. In their bereavements, he sent them sympathy, not as a matter of form, but with a spontaneous warmth that made him plan to alter the whole routine of his life in order that he could be near them in their grief: or, if he fancied them in need of money, he would offer to place his resources at their disposal, only glad of some opportunity to serve them. But if he was thus eager to aid his friends, nor did he refrain from applying to them whenever he himself required advice or help. Sometimes, if he was in doubt of the genuineness of a man's good will, he would go to the length even of borrowing money he did not need, simply in order to measure his sincerity.

About the time that he was finishing his book, Proust almost ceased to leave his room. Very rarely could he go now, and then only in a completely closed car, to the country, to see the hawthorn-trees in blossom or the apple orchards that he loved. Once when he had ventured forth at night to visit the rose gardens of some friends, which had to be shown to him by the light of the headlamps of his car, the slight exertion of walking brought on a fit of suffocation from which he recovered only after he had drunk about twenty cups of coffee. Such was the state of his health, indeed, that it was impossible for him ever to accept an invitation. Instead, on rare occasions, just as his friends were preparing to retire, he would arrive unexpectedly, and so would begin one of the nocturnal reunions that had by now become widely associated with his name.

One of Proust's deepest regrets during these years of retirement was his almost complete isolation from the world of art and music. Wistfully he would read the announcements of those exhibitions and concerts that he would have liked so much, though was scarcely ever able, to attend. Only once, with a friend, he ventured to look at some pictures by his beloved Vermeer at the Dutch Exhibition at the Tuileries, and then he came back so dizzy and exhausted that for hours he had not sufficient energy even to undress and crawl into bed.[1] As for quartets and symphonies, he had to content himself with such as were available on the theatrephone that had been installed at his bedside. With the increasing violence of his attacks, visits from his friends became rarer and rarer: while several of them, like Mme Strauss or Mme de Noailles, whose health was also delicate, it was impossible to see at all.

[1] This episode appears in his novel, applied to Bergotte shortly before his death.

At the one hour, late at night, when he could visit them, it was imperative that they should sleep, so that the only way he could communicate with them was by letter. But just as friendships with his own sex had always been necessary to him, so too had the society of intelligent and sympathetic women; and during these years, when he was able to go out, it would often be with Mme Sheikevitch, a lady deeply interested in literature, who had been married to the painter Carolus-Duran, and who moved much in intellectual circles. Proust had known her very slightly for several years, but now her genuine interest in his work drew him to her more closely.

To any writer, and particularly to a writer of the earnestness and sensibility of Proust, a certain amount of appreciation and encouragement is absolutely necessary. But Proust was far too sincere an artist, and too sensitive a man, to be able to accept praise that was anything but spontaneous and honest. If anyone ever spoke to him of his work, indeed, he would subtly cross-question him to make sure how much of it he had read and understood, before he was prepared to continue the conversation; and although now it was the object of all his attention, of all his energy, of all his hopes, he would mention it to no one of whose sympathy and integrity he was not utterly convinced.

It was impossible that so skilled a critic as himself should not be deeply aware of his own book's unusual complexity and power; yet nevertheless he was very much concerned with the problem of finding a suitable publisher. He well realized that his novel was far too long and too serious to become immediately popular, and he feared lest the chapters on inversion, even though they were treated in an austere and almost scientific manner, should prejudice the reading public against him.

But as soon as it was finished, find a publisher he must; and that too, without delay. Too well he knew that death might overtake him at any moment; and the idea that it might do so before his life's work was accomplished to his satisfaction never ceased to urge him to further efforts.

To help him in this all-important undertaking, he did not hesitate to use his friends. To Jean-Louis Vaudoyer, the editor of *Les Essais*, to whom he had recently been re-introduced at a performance of the Russian Ballet, he wrote many letters asking for practical advice. With Louis de Robert, whose old friendship, on the appearance of his *Roman d'un Malade*, he had also renewed, and to whom, subsequently, he habitually referred as "the first friend of *Swann*," he exchanged a voluminous correspondence about his ambitions and his plans.

After years of work, his book was finished. Written, at the fullness of his powers, with the utmost sincerity of which he was capable, composed of his most intimate ideas and experiences, his very life, he longed for it to be read without delay by those unknown friends who would appreciate and understand the keen intelligence and the passionate desire for truth which had dominated its composition. In order to avoid delay, in spite of the fact that several of his friends attempted to dissuade him, he was perfectly prepared to pay for the publication of the book himself. For one thing, long though it was—and the typescript must have been a formidable pile of nearly 2,000 pages—he was most anxious that it should be published in one volume. Otherwise there was the grave danger of its meaning and intention being completely misunderstood, since despite its prolixity and colossal length, the structure was such that every episode was interrelated, and this fact would not for a long time become apparent. This, de Robert assured him, for anyone with a reputation less than Zola's, was quite unthinkable. Even if a work like *Jean Christophe*, whose separate parts thousands of readers awaited with perennial eagerness, had been published at first in its entirety, it would have received nothing but complete indifference. As Proust, even worse than having no reputation, had first to dispel the fatal impression which his *Figaro* articles had encouraged rather than dispelled, that he was no more than a talented society amateur, such a project was impossible. Proust decided, therefore, to try for publication in two volumes of about 700 pages each, which he hoped might be put on sale simultaneously.

Now every writer, in his secret heart, has a publisher in his mind under whose imprint, could he but choose, he would like to see his work appear. For Proust, this was *la Nouvelle Revue Française* which, directed in those days by a group of distinguished writers which included Jean Schlumberger, Jacques Copeau, Jacques Rivière and André Gide, had started a small publishing house whose productions aroused his greatest admiration and respect. With their austere white covers decorated only by a narrow red border, unheralded by publicity and even derided by popular reviewers, the volumes which came from their press, accepted only after the most keen discrimination, exerted upon the more intelligent public of the day an unusual influence. In such companionship, more than in any other, would he have liked to have seen his own. Fortunate in the fact that his friend Prince Antoine Bibesco knew André Gide, Proust was able to approach the firm armed with personal introductions. Towards the end of 1912, therefore, we find him addressing to them an urgent series of letters, many of which, it must be admitted, failed to elicit even the courtesy of a reply. In vain he telephoned, sometimes, naïvely, several times a day, requesting an interview with one of the directors; no answer came. At last he resigned himself to another letter, in order to discover finally whether they would consider publishing the book at his own expense, and if so, when it could be put on sale. With customary politeness, but firm tenacity, he sought also a direct reply to several other important questions. Could the work be issued, as he hoped, simultaneously in two volumes? If this for some reason proved impracticable, could it be published in three or four volumes of the usual size and price? since he was anxious that it should be bought and read generally, and not predominantly, as with his other books, by rich society people. In any case, in view of the state of his health and in order to leave him ample time to correct the proofs, how soon could it be put on sale and when could the second volume follow? For it must be understood that acceptance of one volume must imply acceptance of the whole work. Regarding the passages on inversion, he was anxious to explain that in no sense was this phenomenon justified, and that as, in the book, the metaphysical and moral points of view so predominated, he felt that little exception could be taken to them. This new attack, however, produced nothing but another long silence.

The bulky manuscript was deposited with the publishers, however, and the anxious author composed himself patiently to wait. For a long time Proust's formidable pile of typescript lay neglected on an office table. Readers occasionally came, eyed it gloomily, and went away. After further appeals from Prince Antoine Bibesco, Gide himself opened the bundle somewhere about the middle, only to be confronted by a long string of ducal and princely names. Dubiously he shook his head. He remembered a young Proust he had met long ago at Mme Lemaire's; and society novels were not much to his taste. After a further long wait, the manuscript was returned.

Proust was dumbfounded. He had offered even to pay all the printing expenses, and still they had rejected his book—the *Nouvelle Revue Francaise*, the one firm he had expected might understand and appreciate his ideas. But although bitterly disappointed, he perfectly understood the value of his own work, and refused to let this act in any way interfere with his practical efforts. He had toiled at his book indefatigably for many years, and now, no matter what it cost his pride, he was prepared to fight for it. The next publishing house he tried was the *Mercure de France*; but they, too, declined. Then, at the suggestion of Louis de Robert, he tried Fasquelle. Here again, he did not shrink from employing the good offices of his friends. He begged Mme Strauss not only to speak to Fasquelle herself but to persuade Calmette, who also knew him, to do the same. But despite these interventions, after another anxious period of waiting, the book, although this time read completely, was once more declined. Still in despair, but doubly persistent, Proust accepted de Robert's new suggestion to try, under his protection, his own publisher Ollendorf. After another interminable period, the book was again returned. "I cannot understand," Ollendorf wrote in confidence to de Robert, "how a man can take thirty pages to describe how he turns over in bed before he goes to sleep." To Proust he merely sent a short and formal letter of regret. Amazed at this further blow, but still undaunted, Proust continued to exert himself with indomitable vigour. He remembered now, that René Blum was a great friend of Bernard Grasset and did not hesitate to write him a long letter asking for his help. In spite of the repeated protests of his friends, he was determined now in order to avoid further delay, to pay all the expenses of his work.[1] He even insisted that only upon these conditions would he submit it at all: and upon these conditions alone, at last it was accepted. Proust was satisfied. He had given to his book, during his last years, the whole of his life: and his one concern was to ensure that this sacrifice should not have been in vain.

Meanwhile, he had been intent upon that other exacting problem, the choice of a suitable title. For the whole of the book he had hovered, for some time, between *Les Intermittences du Passé*, *Les Intermittences du Cœur* and *À la Recherche du Temps Perdu*, finally deciding upon the last. But now it was necessary to find two, and possibly even three,

---

[1] It is certain that Proust could have considered this in no way derogatory. Had not the great Ruskin done the same?

more for the separate parts. To Mme Strauss, who had suggested *Conquête sur le Passé* he wrote that he had decided to call the first volume *Le Temps Perdu* and the last *Le Temps Retrouvé*, considering privately, as a possible intermediate, *L'Adoration Perpetuelle*: while in his correspondence with Louis de Robert, he had suggested a series consisting of *L'Âge des Noms, L'Âge des Mots* and *L'Âge des Choses*. Alternatively, for his first volume, he had considered *Jardins dans une Tasse de Thé, Le Printemps, Les Colombes Poignardés, Le Septième Ciel*, and *Avant que le Jour soit Levé*. Finally, deciding that he would prefer something more colourless, he thought of *Charles Swann* and then, in order to include the first chapters, *Premiers Crayons de Charles Swann*. But since neither of these seemed to the author to combine adequately the country scenes of Combray and the history of Swann's love affair with Odette, of which the first volume was composed, he finally struck on the successful *Du Côté de chez Swann*, under which name the work was finally published.

His book accepted, Proust felt that, without embarrassing them, he might now show his appreciation to those friends who had exerted themselves on its behalf: and, in several cases under protest, insisted on making them beautiful and expensive presents. His next task was to correct his proofs. This in itself was an exhausting occupation, since, in his "entangled and illegible hand,"[1] he corrected, recorrected and made such huge insertions that every available inch of margin was overscored, new sheets had to be pinned on, and only about one line in twenty of the original version remained. While the printer was complaining that they evidently expected him to set up a completely new book, Proust was writing to Vaudoyer to inquire whether, after giving so much extra work, he should write at once to Grasset to offer to contribute towards any fresh expenses that might be involved.

Only when the proofs had been returned to his publishers

[1] As it was called by Montesquiou.

could Proust at last permit himself a little relaxation. Then, having sold some carpets and furniture to Jansen through the kind offices of Mme Strauss, he bought himself a pianola; and was somewhat aggrieved to discover that the pieces he most wished to hear had not been recorded. Not a single one of their 15,000 subscribers, the attendant at the library coldly informed the servant who had been sent to get the roll, had asked during the last ten years for the 14th quartet of Beethoven that Proust so much wished to hear again.

When he was well enough to go out, he would sometimes accompany Mme Sheikevitch and Jean Cocteau to the Diaghileff ballet, which on its first appearance had been partly financed by the Comtesse Greffulhe, and had since won the allegiance of the whole of the fashionable world. Here, various acquaintances in the audience would greet his reappearance with exclamations of pleasure. Sometimes meeting a friend unexpectedly in the foyer or the bar, with all his old inimitable high spirits, he would start to "take off" Montesquiou, who, earlier, had bowed to him with benevolent condescension from a box, thus reducing both his companion and himself to fits of spluttering laughter. Though he still corresponded with that gentleman from time to time, their former friendship had almost petered out. Montesquiou, at present forestalling d'Annunzio in his public worship of Ida Rubinstein, had recently embarked on one of his characteristic campaigns of slander against Proust, and caused him great distress by the efforts he had been making to estrange some of his friends. Nevertheless, from time to time he would suddenly arrive at Proust's flat and stay talking hour after hour while his victim lay positively longing for him to go away.

As always, Proust's greatest happiness was to feel himself both understood and loved. At such times, he would still become as disarmingly frank and high spirited as in his youth: and once when he had arranged to join a party of Mme Strauss's at the play, he rushed out in such excitement that, instead of wearing his evening dress, he put on, with his white waistcoat and white tie, a dinner jacket; and never even noticed the fact until, when he arrived home, his valet asked him in great concern whether during the evening he had taken off his cloak.

At last the great day arrived for the appearance of *Swann*. It came out in the middle of November 1913, and was dedicated, as Proust had always intended, to the man who had "first given him the joy of seeing himself in print" —Calmette. The author had awaited it with mingled excitement, trepidation and concern. *De luxe* editions of the book were eagerly dispatched to his innumerable friends, dozens of letters written, and, since Grasset seemed to have completely ignored all forms of advertisement, Proust was even forced to resort to measures of oblique publicity on his own account.

With the same disregard of pride that he had evinced in his negotiations with publishers, he now sought to get extracts from reviews which had been written by his friends, inserted in various other journals at his own expense, naïvely hoping thereby to stimulate the interest and appreciation that his book unquestionably merited, but had not received. Indeed, apart from these tributes—one from Jacques-Émile Blanche in *l'Echo de Paris*, another from Lucien Daudet, who had helped him in the correction of several errors in his proofs, in the *Figaro*; and a third from Maurice Rostand in *Comœdia*, who said in his article that *Swann* was the most interesting novel that had appeared in the last ten years, Proust got but few reviews. The only critic who devoted to his novel the attention worthy of its importance, was Paul Souday in *le Temps*, and this was indirectly through the efforts of Mme Sheikevitch who, a friend of Hébrard the editor, had done her utmost to arouse his interest. And even this review was not particularly eulogious. It lamented the obscurity of the style, pointed out grammatical errors and railed bitterly at the mistakes that swarmed in the text. If authors did not know how to correct their proofs it was up to their publishers to engage someone to do it for them, remarked M. Souday, assiduously chasing one of his favourite hares.

Proust, who felt not only affronted by these columns, but was amazed at the critic's lack of comprehension, replied to him with a lampoon upon his own article: and was fortunately able to justify his work in a long interview which *le Temps* accorded him a few days later.

Nor was his book's reception amongst his own acquaintances much more successful. Certainly there were a few who appreciated its worth more now than ever had been possible on those occasions, when, long before its publication, he had shown them isolated extracts. But many of them were either indifferent or frankly hostile. It could have been scarcely encouraging for the anxious author, when he elicited an opinion, to be greeted in the manner of his old friend Albuféra, with whom the following remarks had been exchanged: "My dear Louis, have you read my book?" "Read your book? Have you written a book?" "But, Louis, I even sent you a copy"—"Oh, my dear Marcel, if you sent me a copy, then I have certainly read it. Only I wasn't quite sure whether I had received it." A conversation far more bitterly ironic than anything made up by Jacques Bizet or Robert Dreyfus! Many other people averred that they simply hadn't the courage to begin, while some even went about exclaiming: "What childish nonsense! When will all these amateurs learn to shut up?"

As yet the work had not penetrated even to the more discriminating section of the general public. Most of the novels of the day which achieved success were short, machine-made products, dramatic in form and competent enough in execution, but so superficial that they could be read in a few hours without requiring the slightest effort of attention. Small wonder, therefore, that Proust wrote soon afterwards to one of his sympathizers: "My book has had no success, and I can feel little pleasure in its publication."

The atmosphere of the following months was scarcely helpful to the general assimilation of so powerful and strange a talent. Coming events were casting their shadows before them, and the whole of Paris was excited and uneasy. In opposition to the Russian Ballet, jazz had just arrived from America, and to its novel negroid rhythms women in evening dress began to dance at noon. Slowly but inevitably, however, admiration of *Swann* began to be noised abroad in certain small intelligent cliques. Here a young clerk, poor and obscure but with a passion for literature, would lie reading the book, entranced, until the small hours of the morning, ungrudging of the exhausted weariness with which he would have to pay for his enthusiasm on the morrow. There a schoolmistress, lured by some chance remark of appreciation, would borrow it from a friend, and attain through it that new and astonished delight which can only be procured through the fresh and vivid revelation of a sensitive and exceptional mind. Of such admiration, the only deep and sincere understanding of his book, as yet Proust knew nothing.

Determined to finish the task he had set himself, however, he proceeded with his plans for the publication of the forthcoming volume. About two hundred pages of proofs, which had been intended primarily for the first volume, and subsequently laid aside for inclusion in the second, were now overscored and augmented with his usual punctilious care. It had been determined at last to issue the work in three parts; and announcements were already published of the two which were to follow, entitled respectively *Le Côté de Guermantes* and *Le Temps Retrouvé*. But just as a further section was to be put into type, all operations had to be suspended. A small cloud which had shortly before appeared upon the political horizon, had now assumed immense proportions, to break, finally, in the cataclysmic storm of war.

CHAPTER XII

RETURNING to his flat after a few weeks at Cabourg Proust relapsed into a state of illness more grave than any before. Oppressed by the horror of the war, by the absence of his brother whom he had accompanied to the train that was to bear him to his future duties at the front, by the separation from his friends, so many of whom were in the army, and by the final extinction of a love affair which, as usual, had ultimately proved abortive, he suffered willingly, tortured by the fact that he could not more actively share in the travail of his country. As with so many others, it seemed at first that his whole life was to be completely disrupted, and for the time being all thoughts of his book were put aside.

A few months before, he had been saddened by the death of his secretary, Agostinelli. Having earned a considerable sum by the typing of the prodigious manuscript, and been persuaded by his wife that the way to make his fortune was to take up flying, he had proceeded to do so, and had crashed fatally soon afterwards, on the Mediterranean coast. With characteristic kindness Proust had tried to obtain work, with one of his friends, for the woman who was discovered then, although they had been one of the most devoted couples he had ever known, to have been the man's mistress and not his wife. Now his valet, too, had been called up, and for a short time Proust was completely alone.

Fortunately, however, he was soon to obtain the services of that admirable housekeeper—the "charming and perfect" Céleste—who, eventually marrying Odilon Albaret, the taxi-driver whom Proust had employed ever since Agostinelli had become his secretary, was to watch over him with the utmost care until the end of his life. Moving about the flat so silently that the occasional rustling of her black taffeta dress was the only sound to be heard; assiduously turning out his rooms whenever he was well enough, for a few hours, to leave his bed; helping him to dress, when he was too weak to do so alone, with an almost maternal care; cooking, for such friends who could come to see him, sumptuous dinners which were at once her triumph and her pride, she was treated invariably by her master with the habitual consideration which soon won her complete fidelity and devotion. Sometimes, when he had been alone for weeks and badly needed companionship Proust would keep her in his room talking throughout the night, and would even entertain her with his imitations, overjoyed when he discovered that she possessed a similar talent and could "take off" to perfection such visitors as came to the flat with any frequency.

A strict routine now governed his existence. He usually woke late in the afternoon, though he was never called, and it was forbidden in any circumstances to disturb him until he rang. There would then follow lengthy inhalations, until the atmosphere of his room became dense with steam. He ate but little, and breakfasted on croissants and coffee: but this had to be as thick as essence and invariably boiling hot. Too weak, now, to shave himself, he let his beard grow and, when necessary, employed a barber to come in and shave him. He was a man of but few whims, but such as he had were punctiliously observed. Subject now to acute bronchitis, he was afraid of catching cold and his linen always had to be warmed in the oven before it was put to use. He insisted also that it should be of the finest quality; and once when Céleste had bought him some handkerchiefs which he considered too coarse, and then tried to rectify her mistake by carefully washing them, Proust, on their reappearance, solemnly tore them into strips, lest he should ever be afflicted with them again.

Every day he read the war news with feverish attention,

following the movements of the armies with flags stuck into a staff map, and was bitterly wretched that he could not serve with those of his old friends who were at the front.

During 1915 he received a note requesting him to go up for examination for military service. Despite the fact that by now he could scarcely walk upstairs, he presented himself (having misread the instructions) at the appointed place at three o'clock in the morning. The office was closed and empty: and his enthusiasm in complying somewhat excessive, since he could hardly get himself home without collapsing in the street.

As weeks, months and years passed, and one by one he learned of the deaths of those whom he had known in youth, the vast tragedy about him oppressed him ever more heavily, and his own isolation became like the isolation of a tomb. Bertrand de Fénelon had been the first of his friends to be killed; and Proust mourned him with Emmanuel Bibesco who was already dead. Then Louis de la Salle fell on the Champagne front in 1915, while, in the following year, Gaston de Caillavet died. And when Rumania was overrun, Proust's memories of the Bibescos made him feel the invasion as deeply as he felt the mutilation of those miles of his own loved country which already had been transformed from the smiling fields and orchards that he knew, to an unspeakable morass of mud and rotting corpses. Others of his friends were lost, too, in these years: and in his almost sepulchral imprisonment he learned of each new disaster with a grief that compelled him to recreate their presence as they had existed for him in the past. Nor had his anxiety for his brother ever lessened, since, in the early days of the war, Robert's hospital had been heavily bombarded, and, with shells exploding about him, he had insisted upon continuing to operate on his most urgent cases.

But if Proust experienced keenly within himself all the overwhelming suffering of the war, no one could have resented more bitterly the vulgar fanaticism that made it fashionable to decry all things German. When he read in some article a serious statement that it was only snobbery that had attributed genius to Wagner, he wondered ironically what diatribes might have been written had France been at war with Russia, against Tolstoy and Dostoievsky.

For the moods of despair that the devastation and carnage of these years induced, there was but one cure, as for all his griefs—to work: and how desperately and continuously he must have done so can only be understood when it is realized that by the time of the armistice his book had been amplified to almost three times its original length. The actual structure of the work had long been complete: but, to the skeleton which supported it, he continued to add the muscle and flesh of numberless elaborations that enriched immeasurably each aspect of its complex form, and enabled many of its characters to be displayed against the additional background of contemporary conditions.

The manuscript had by now become an amazing object. Writing covered every margin, every space, and, as with his proofs, overflowed on to the backs of pages and thence onto the further sheets that had had to be inserted with clips. Many chapters had been so much fingered that they were almost in tatters, and sheets had to be held together and patched up with long strips of adhesive paper.

Apart from this work upon his novel, and his correspondence with his friends, throughout the whole of the war Proust wrote but little. Disliking the idea that his name should appear while so many of his countrymen were at the front, the one thing that he published was a very short preface to a portfolio of drawings by the Comtesse de Maugny, and then only because she was the wife of an old friend and he wished to be of service to her. He composed also, however, a long and delightful preface upon the Auteuil of his youth for the volume *De David à Dégas*, upon which, at this time, his friend Jacques-Émile Blanche was engaged, but which was not published until 1919. For various reasons, this effort was the cause of a considerable amount of bitterness and misunderstanding: and in reply to a particular paragraph in one of his friend's letters on the subject, which had wounded him deeply, Proust wrote with characteristic sincerity that he would cut out the offending lines and burn them, in order never to be tempted to read them again.

Towards the latter years of his life, indeed, his acute sensitiveness, his vulnerability, increased rather than diminished. If he felt the slightest cooling off in any of his relations, he never failed to remark upon the fact reproachfully. A friend might treat him with the utmost kindness and consideration; but if his greeting lacked the warm and spontaneous smile of welcome whose memory Proust had cherished from other days, the fact would cause him infinite sadness and regret. Even a slightly more conventional ending to a letter than that to which he was accustomed would elicit an expostulation: and for him to read "Dear Marcel" when he anticipated "My dear old boy" was a minor tragedy.

All this time, despite the war, not only in France but in England and in Belgium, the first volume of *Swann* had been slowly gaining for itself a small but gradually increasing band of ardent admirers. At the beginning of 1914 the book had been read by several of the directors of *la Nouvelle Revue Française*. Jacques Rivière, the first to be struck by it, had now persuaded André Gide to read it attentively. Having done so, the latter had been unusually impressed. Bitter irony. Here was one of the most subtle, the most penetrating, the most extraordinary novels he had ever read, and his had been the carelessness responsible for its rejection. Now, he would have felt proud indeed had he been the man to sponsor it. At once he sat down and wrote to the author, expressing with complete sincerity his own share in the event and his very deep regret; to which, in spite of a somewhat natural irritation, Proust replied, heaping coals of fire on his correspondent's head by assuring him, with reciprocal politeness, that without the repeated rejections of the *N.R.F.*, he could never have had the delight of receiving so welcome a letter.

This overture was followed by an offer from the board of directors to take over the succeeding volumes of the work, paying all the expenses of production and allowing the author generous royalties.

Meanwhile, completely unaware of this offer, not only Grasset, but Fasquelle also had suggested publishing the forthcoming volumes at his own expense. Proust was in a quandary. He still wished to be published by the *N.R.F.*, but he very much disliked the idea of offending Grasset, who had, after all, published the book when so many other houses had refused it. There followed a long and complicated correspondence between Proust and his publisher with René Blum employed as an intermediary, who, while acting as an army interpreter in the neighbourhood of Amiens, did his utmost, at the same time, to obtain for Proust the release he desired. Hitherto Proust had always treated his publisher with an extraordinary generosity. He had refused to take the whole of the royalties due to him; and, although it was quite unnecessary from the terms of his contract, had insisted upon Grasset sharing with him any profits that should be earned by translations. In consequence he felt now that Grasset should free him without reproach.

Unfortunately, at the mere suggestion, Grasset, who was undergoing a cure in a sanatorium in Switzerland, suddenly discovered that Proust was the one author on his list whom he most admired. Other letters followed, not without several scarcely veiled grievances from both sides; but in the end Proust got his way. By the end of 1916, still fearful that he might die at any moment without warning, he could at least rest content that if he did so, his book would be assured of posthumous publication.

Later, when the end of the war seemed in sight, his new

publishers wished Proust to send them the next volume of
Swann, in order that it could appear immediately peace was
declared. This volume, *À l'Ombre des Jeunes Filles en Fleur,*
was composed of material that had occupied but a long
chapter in the original version, and had since been amplified
and rewritten to form a separate part. In order to make the
author some reparation for the way they had first treated
him, the *N.R.F.* decided also to publish at the same time as
his new novel, another volume containing a collection of his
more recent contributions to the *Figaro*; so for some time
Proust was occupied in getting his manuscripts prepared.

Meanwhile the war dragged on. Repeated air raids over
Paris were followed by the Russian revolution and the second
battle of the Marne. In his flat in the boulevard Hausmann,
Proust continued to lead a life of almost unrelieved monotony. For weeks at a time he saw no one save Céleste. Sometimes one of his friends, on leave from the front, would pay
him a long and unexpected visit, so that Céleste must be sent
out for beer and lobster, and roast one of her famous chickens.
Sometimes, when he was sufficiently well to receive visitors,
he would dispatch his housekeeper in her husband's taxi to
try to find someone whom he hoped might be free, at so late
an hour, to come to see him. Occasionally there were
tragedies when some friend who had promised to visit him
failed at the last moment to appear; and Proust, having
forced himself out of bed and, with the utmost difficulty,
dressed himself, was left to wander forlornly about his own
formal and unfamiliar rooms, opening drawers that had been
for long years closed, to inspect a little collection of souvenirs
that never failed to recall to him, with the bitterness of
despair, the bleakness of the present in contrast to the richness of the past.

When he felt he could bear this loneliness no longer he
would even drag himself out to some large reception in the
hope of encountering a few familiar faces; and it was this that

gave rise to a persistent legend that his health had improved and he was going much into society. Sometimes, too, he would get up to dine out with Mme Sheikevitch, or the new friend, Walter Berry, to whom she had introduced him. As always, he still felt the necessity in his life for active friendship; and when, at the suggestion of Mme Sheikevitch, Walter Berry, then a stranger, had sent Proust as a gift, in honour of *Swann*, a book from his library stamped with the arms of Paulin Prondre de Guermantes, it resulted in a meeting of the three of them, which proved so successful that it lasted from the early afternoon until well past midnight.

Whenever he entertained outside his home, it was, as usual, at the Ritz: though now he seldom invited more than one or two people at a time. Arriving, very often, over an hour late, with the air of a man who had not yet been able to tear himself away from his inner life, he would order nothing but a glass of water for himself, while for his guest he selected carefully all those things that he himself would most have liked to eat. Still his old susceptibilities persisted. Once, when he was dining with Mme Sheikevitch, imagining that a man at the next table was regarding her with an obtrusive familiarity, he sent him his card by a waiter, and was quite prepared to fight a duel until he discovered that the offender was one of her old friends.

Often, while he was awaiting his guests, and sometimes, very late, after they had departed, he would sit at his table deep in conversation with the waiters, questioning them with all his old eager pertinacity, not only about their own views and their own lives, but about each of the people who were still having supper; their professions, their manners, their habits, whether they came here frequently, and who were their friends. No mere idle curiosity, but a means—one of the few left to him—of verifying certain details or developing certain threads that were necessary for the completion of his book.

Then, if the weather was fine, smothering in his heavy fur

cloak, he would walk home to his flat, remembering sadly the long nocturnal walks of his youth, with their absorbing arguments, their moments of unexpected harmony. Suppers at Weber's with Gaston de Caillavet and Robert de Flers; afternoons at the tennis club at Neuilly, the first days of *Le Banquet*, Cabourg in his youth and his visits to the cathedrals, all would return to him, evoking a deep nostalgia for friendships which were no more, and so many eager projects which had come to nothing. And since the countries he had longed to visit he now would never see; since there was no way back to those moments of the past which were complete in a circle of their own, all he could do, in the isolation of his room, was to continue to strive after the essence of the days in which he had been happy, and to recreate them in a medium which would ensure them a perpetuity outside himself, continually altering and reshaping certain chapters of his book, that this might the better be achieved.

On the rare and exceptional occasions when he could go out during the day, his impressions would be as vivid as a child's, and he would absorb them with a child's delight: the more so as such excursions nearly always had to be paid for by weeks of complete seclusion.

For in addition to asthma and bronchitis, he now suffered appalling periods of insomnia; and to cure them he resorted to various forms of narcotics. None of the doctors he called in were able materially to improve his condition; and often he lamented that, without bettering his health, they merely depleted both his resources and his energy. He decided now, therefore, to live henceforward, as far as possible, without consulting them, and took to counteracting the lassitude induced by various drugs with strong and frequent doses of caffeine. Too much veronal, also, had the disquieting effect of impeding his enunciation; which, since he had never contracted any venereal disease, he was alarmed to think might be the first signs of some unsuspected malady of the brain.

In his more gloomy moments, he even feared that he was shortly to be seized, as had been his mother just before her death, with aphasia; in which case the most that he could hope for was to live in full possession of his intelligence until his book was finished to his satisfaction.

Nor was he without financial difficulties. The young man who could lose his money without gambling had, in his maturity, even resorted to this final means of further dissipating his fortune. Despite this fact, however, he remained always eager to help his friends, not only in their domestic and literary problems but, whenever he fancied it necessary, with offers of pecuniary assistance. Throughout the war he sent a large number of regular weekly parcels to various old servants on active service; and when, after the Russian revolution, he feared that Mme Sheikevitch's income must be seriously affected, he proposed the touching scheme that she should persuade her friend Hébrard to commission from her a regular column for *le Temps* on any subject, which he would willingly write for her but for which she alone should receive payment.

By now the war was drawing to its close. Shortly before the end, all Proust's old fears for his brother revived. In charge, now, of the medical supervision of several army corps, he had been involved in a car accident and had had his head badly cut open, in spite of which he insisted upon going back almost immediately to his job at the front.

At last the armistice was declared. But despite his great joy, Proust still could not forget the thousands slain. Nor, later, did the Treaty of Versailles arouse anything but his deepest forebodings. No one more than himself could have desired a lasting peace, satisfactory alike to the victors and to the defeated. But since he realized that this was but an unattainable ideal, and that one day Germany would inevitably desire revenge, it seemed to him tragic for his country that there should still be left to her the possibility of attaining it.

CHAPTER XIII

AFTER the first sense of deep release, the weeks following the armistice were filled, for Proust, with an intense activity of proof correcting. It was not only the novel now which demanded his usual concentrated attention, but his sketches also: particularly the *Lemoine* sketch after Saint-Simon which he had much amplified and in which he had incorporated, in accordance with one of his habits, the names of, and references to, several of his friends. Here there is mention of the Duc de Guiche, of the Comtesse de Chevigné, of the Duc de la Rochefoucauld and of the Marquis d'Albuféra. Here there is a pungent comment on the Bibesco-Asquith marriage and the fact that certain badly informed English people believed that Miss Asquith had not made a sufficiently good match, ignorant of the fact that these Bibescos, "along with the de Noailles, the Montesquious, the Chimays and the Bauffrements, by reason of their illustrious lineage, might well have worn the crown of France." Here there is a thumbnail sketch of Comte Robert de Montesquiou-Fézensac and his friend Yturri; and mention of Mme de Clermont-Tonnerre the sister of the Duc de Guiche; of Mme Greffulhe, born Chimay, of the famous princely house of the counts of Bossut; of Mme de Noailles, of whose verses Montesquiou had been the first to speak; and of Mme Strauss, whose face alone, without her wit, "would have sufficed to attract all those who crowded about her." There is even a line devoted to Olivier, head waiter of the Ritz, with whom the author had had from time to time so many protracted conversations. These passages are doubly interesting, not only as a final demonstration of that famous "niceness" which made him desire still, at all costs, to lose no opportunity of reciprocating any kindness that had been shown him, but because it supplies, beyond all doubt, the key to the prototypes of several of the Guermantes.

To Mme Strauss alone he sent proofs of this sketch, lest he should publish anything that might hurt her feelings; and in accordance with her wishes toned down, to suit her taste, a portrait which she considered made her appear too much like a "haughty Vashti." This volume of sketches Proust dedicated to Walter Berry, "advocate and scholar, who, from the first days of the war, before an America still undecided, pleaded with incomparable energy and talent, and finally won, the cause of France." When Walter Berry expressed a very natural embarrassment at being the recipient of so momentous a eulogy, the author replied, a little crestfallen but with characteristic naïveté, that, in despair lest his friend should leave Paris after the war, he had hoped that the phrase might help to get him elected ambassador!

The two volumes were placed on sale almost simultaneously: *À l'Ombre des Jeunes Filles en Fleur* at the end of December, and *Pastiches et Mélanges* early the following year. It had originally been intended to publish much of his new novel in serial form in the *Figaro*: but owing to the scarcity of paper, at the last moment the project had to be given up. Publication in volume form proved but another disappointment, however, and neither of Proust's books was accorded much attention.

By now *Swann* had won a considerable circle of admirers who received its sequel with pleasure, it is true; but amongst the general public and the majority of reviewers *À l'Ombre des Jeunes Filles en Fleur* slipped by almost unnoticed. Léon Daudet, however, from the first one of Proust's most fervent admirers, having prominently published a eulogy in *l'Action Française*, immediately proposed the work for the *Prix Goncourt*; but this was awarded instead to *Le Feu*, by Henri

INTRODUCTION TO PROUST

Barbusse, curiously enough one of Proust's old companions of *Le Banquet*. The greatest attention the book received, indeed, was from the *Figaro*, which, now directed by another of the same band, Robert de Flers, printed an important article entitled *Une Rentrée Littéraire* by Robert Dreyfus. It is interesting to discover that in writing to thank his old friend for his "too flattering" praise, Proust did not omit to mention the fact that he considered it was a pity that more attention had not been paid to the size of the type. How could he know that already he had caused chaos among the printers, since the review concerned, intended by his friends for the front page, had been relegated, in assembling the paper, to the second; from which insignificant position it had had to be rescued at the last moment with all the concomitant disturbance of completely resetting several columns?

Far more disturbing to Proust during these days, however, than this second cool reception of his work, was the fact that he was obliged to move from the flat in the boulevard Haussmann, where he had lived ever since his mother's death. Having heard indirectly that the house was being taken over by a bank, he had written to his aunt for confirmation, receiving in reply a "superb" letter in which she averred that she "preferred the sweet name of aunt to that of landlord, and that if he ever got well enough to see her again, her decision would have the advantage that in future they would be able to talk together of literature rather than of the house." Apart from the supreme inconvenience of having to move when his recent exertions made it necessary that he should do little but sleep, there were further financial complications. Owing to some money due to him from abroad, which he had been unable to collect on account of the war, he had had a verbal arrangement with his aunt that he should pay no further rent from the end of 1916 until peace should be declared. Now that the ownership of the property had been transferred, he was faced with the difficulty of finding a comparatively large sum at a moment's notice. It therefore became necessary for him to sell some more of his possessions. In the past, when he had wished to unburden himself of some carpets, Mme Strauss had displayed them to Jansen for him at her house. Knowing her to be too ill now to be troubled with a matter of comparatively small concern, he applied instead to Walter Berry who, as President of the United States Chamber of Commerce seemed a likely person to be able to help him. As it was impossible for Proust to have people to inspect the things at his flat for fear of disturbing his sleep, he asked to be allowed to house them at the storerooms of the Chamber of Commerce, so that he could direct there such acquaintances or dealers as might consider buying them. Tapestries, sofas and crystal chandeliers were consequently sent away; and eventually Proust was much dismayed to find modern and worth very little pieces which connoisseurs like Montesquiou had claimed to be both old and valuable.

Despite the fact that the Marquis d'Albuféra assured him that he could not legally be turned out of his flat for several months, the prospect of remaining there while workmen were engaged in heavy structural alterations was intolerable. One day Proust would consider turning this misfortune to advantage by making it an opportunity to visit certain Italian towns that he had always longed but never managed to see: another, he contemplated retiring to some quiet villa somewhere between Nice and Monte Carlo. But such projects were little more than idle dreams, and after weeks of letters, of searching, the Duc de Guiche helped him move to a furnished apartment in the rue Laurent Pichat, owned by Mme Réjane. Paris was now packed with visitors, and it was the one possible place he could find. But no sooner had he recovered from the first exhaustion of moving than his life became a repetition of the terrible days after his mother's death in the hotel at Versailles. The flat above was being decorated, so that once again he was continually kept awake by an orgy of hammering that lasted from morning till night. Besides this the walls were so thin that even when the knocking ceased, he was disturbed by the sound of his neighbours, whose every word was as distinct as though they had been just outside his door. To increase his distress, pollen from the trees in the Bois aggravated his asthma, and it soon became imperative that he should move again without delay.

What he required was a small flat, quiet and high up, well away from dust and trees, and as far from the damp of the river as he could get. When he heard that there was such a place to let next door to Robert Dreyfus he was delighted: but, alas, it was taken before he had time even to go and see it. At last, since he could find nothing more suitable, he was forced to accept another furnished flat, this time at 44 rue Hamelin. While the rent was exorbitant, it was as poorly equipped and uncomfortable as any servant's bedroom, but, once he was installed, though he had intended to stay but a few weeks, he continued to remain there until the end of his days.

While the author for some months had been a wretched wanderer, his book had fared considerably better. Léon Daudet, still indefatigable in his admiration, had once more nominated his friend as a candidate for the *Prix Goncourt*, and a few days later Proust received a letter to inquire whether, should he be offered this prize, he would accept it. Meanwhile this news had aroused furious opposition from certain factions in the Press, in which Proust's chances were treated with a mixture of enraged hostility and derision. He was far too old for this distinction, they said; or if he was not too old then he was too rich; or if he was not too rich, then he had not fought in the war. Fortunately the judges were less prejudiced and a few days later Proust was awarded the prize.

The opposition received the news with an insensate rage. If

they had broadcast his age formerly as being an insuperable obstacle, now they claimed that it was shameful for such a distinction to have been conferred upon a man who was nearly sixty. "This time the prize has been awarded to an author who is really unknown: and unknown he will remain," wrote one anonymous critic, with a malice exceeded only by his incompetence. Others protested that Daudet had proposed Proust only because he wished to recognize his former anti-Dreyfusism: a somewhat galling rumour to a man who had for years prided himself upon being the "first Dreyfusard."

Added to which, *La Croix de Bois* by Dorgelès was advertised so hugely in the Press, with *Prix Goncourt* preceding it in vast letters, and below only a very minute little "4 votes out of 10," that for some days there was doubt in the minds of many people as to whether Proust had actually won the prize or not. Soon, however, there were tributes from other sections of the Press, and in his barren little flat in the rue Hamelin the author was inundated by hundreds of telegrams and letters of congratulation. They came from his family, from old childhood friends, from the people in his immediate circle, from dozens of society acquaintances, from enthusiastic critics, from publishers who had rejected his book and from delighted admirers in every part of Europe and America. Success had been long in coming, but now it burgeoned with an almost excessive luxuriance. Like Byron, Proust woke up one morning to find that he had become famous in a night.

First of all the flood of letters had to be answered. Excitement had not improved his health, and only those from his most intimate friends could be acknowledged in his own hand. The others, with punctilious care, were dictated to his secretary, an almost destitute young Swiss upon whom he had recently taken pity but who was, unfortunately, remarkable neither for his intelligence nor his zeal. Next, there followed a series of magnificent dinners. Almost deliriously anxious to show his gratitude to everyone who had helped him: to the few friends who had always believed in him, to the critics who had praised him, to the acquaintances who appeared overjoyed at his success, he arranged at the Ritz a series of parties in order that his old and his new friends might meet each other. These functions, however, were not without an element of tragedy. His health more precarious than ever, frequently he could send out invitations only a few hours before the projected gathering; and, at the last moment he might be discovered—a Proust who, having shaved off his beard, wore now only a small moustache, and seemed thus to have put on a new appearance with his success—a forlorn and almost solitary figure, standing, with the two or three friends who had been able to come at such short notice, before the magnificently prepared table, waiting in vain for further guests to arrive.

Sometimes there would be small and joyful reunions at the rue Hamelin. Céleste, her larder empty, would be dispatched post haste to the Ritz for a chicken, to Rumpelmayers for cakes, and in sundry other directions for beer and fruit. Proust still had as little idea of the value of money as a child. On the one hand he spent recklessly; on the other he steadily sold shares which formed part of his capital, squandered the money, gave Céleste paradise feathers for her hat, and looked hopefully to his royalties to make up the deficit caused by his unbounded extravagance.[1] Sometimes one of his friends would remonstrate with him over his ridiculous excesses. "You see, I go out so seldom," Proust would seek to excuse himself. Then, if they still protested, he would add: "Anyhow, I'm too old to change my habits now."

Indeed, life about him had much changed, but owing to his prolonged isolation, his own habits and opinions had become fixed. His invariable punctilious politeness could not adapt

[1] Another curious similarity to Ruskin, who gradually frittered away a vast fortune, and was forced, at the end of his life to rely upon the large royalties which by now, fortunately, his books had begun to earn for him.

itself to post-war manners. He would never dream of calling a princess by her Christian name, though he had known her for over a quarter of a century, and the latest newcomers to society would do so without demur upon a second meeting. In the same way, he felt almost affronted when some critic referred in print to Anna de Noailles. "She never signs herself thus," he protested, "and I, who have known her since she was a girl, would not dream of speaking of her otherwise than as the Comtesse de Noailles."

But success did little to alter his persistent industry. No sooner was *À l'Ombre des Jeunes Filles en Fleur* off his hands, than he was deep in the final version of *Le Côté de Guermantes*, which, like its predecessor, received an equal due of amplification and revision. To the end, the best of his thoughts and the best of his energy were for his work. Everything to do with its progress and its future absorbed him. He never ceased to write to his publishers about its welfare. Now he did not consider sufficient attention was being paid to distribution; everyone was reading and talking about his book, but nowhere could he see a sign of new editions. Now it was the question of an English translation that was of paramount importance. Since his work had received much praise from English critics,[1] and since English literature had always aroused his passionate appreciation, he was particularly anxious that his novels should be available to the general public in England as soon as possible. Then there was eternal quibbling about his proofs. He considered that his publishers had no right to reproach him for his method of continually rewriting, since they knew well, when they asked him to join their list, exactly what were his methods of composition. In addition, he could never get his galleys from the printers without waiting interminable weeks,

---

[1] Among Proust's early admirers in England were such distinguished writers as T. S. Eliot, Virginia Woolf, Aldous Huxley and Compton Mackenzie.

and when finally he did so they still swarmed with faults: no small matter for a man whose energy was limited and who could work only when the state of his health permitted.

Thus, in the next two years, he saw the publication of the various parts of Le Côté de Guermantes which he dedicated, out of gratitude and friendship to Léon Daudet, and of Sodome et Gomorrhe. From the isolation of his room, he kept up a long correspondence with the new friends that his book had made him. Immediately responsive to the faintest signs of appreciation and intelligence, he wrote letter after letter to such critics and admirers as Jacques Boulenger, Paul Souday and Mr. and Mrs. Sidney Schiff. His greetings, beginning as "Dear Sir," following as "Dear Sir and friend"; continuing eventually as the preferred "Dear Friend," show clearly his continual reaching out for sympathy and comprehension, not so much for himself as for his ideas. With the utmost candour he would write pages to refute unjustified criticism, and seek to make clear those of his theories that he felt had not been sufficiently understood.

During his recent peregrinations, he had developed an increasing fear that he might not receive all his letters. In consequence, the heading of his own took up, in some cases, a long paragraph of careful instructions. "8 bis rue Laurent-Pichat" he would begin, following, in brackets, with "(But 37 rue Madame, please forward, would be safer, as I shall not remain here. If you forget 37 rue Madame, you could, at the worst, write to me at the Ritz, where they would forward the letter without a doubt.)" During his increasingly long periods of isolation these letters were his one link with the outside world, and he would risk no chance of having it accidentally broken.

Occasionally, with these new friends, there would be meetings. Eminent critics came to dine at his bedside. The Schiffs came over from England specially to see him; and there was a tragic evening when he waited for them for hours at the

Ritz, while they waited as vainly, owing to some misunderstanding, at Foyot's. He saw them, however, on other occasions but all such excursions into life now had to be paid for very dearly. When he went to the Ritz, now about the one place where he would venture, he had to have a private room specially heated for him. If this was impossible, and he was forced to use the dining-room, then all the windows of the restaurant had to be closed, for fear lest he should catch cold. This was invariably done, with alacrity, upon his arrival: the waiters had all benefited by his lavish tips and were ready at a nod to obey his slightest whims.

So rarely could he now go out, indeed, that there was even friction among his friends as to whom he should see. Old friends reproached him for preferring to spend his time with acquaintances who had never even heard of him until he was successful, and new friends protested that none of his old friends had ever sufficiently appreciated his talent. Added to which, even though he was often too weak even to reply to an invitation, no one would believe it when he assured them he was a dying man. People who caught sight of him at some huge crush to which, after several months of isolation, he had dragged himself for some specific reason, continually made mischief with hostesses whose cards had received no acknowledgment, by disseminating fresh rumours that he was again going much into society.

But if, during his last years, he was still making new friends, he was also losing some of his old ones. He had long known, however, that this would be inevitable. "Don't you think that your book will make you many enemies?" a companion once asked him. "Now that my work is finished it doesn't matter," Proust had replied. Mme Laure Hayman, whom, in his youth, he had so much admired, wrote to him reproachfully that people were saying that she was the model for Mme Swann. He replied to her that Odette was one of the most invented of his characters, and if she recognized some object in Mme Swann's drawing-room that he had remembered from her own, he had also placed there flowers which he had taken deliberately from a Guermantes lady, who indeed had written to thank him, never dreaming for a moment she could be taken for Odette. His old friend Albuféra, too, after so many years, suddenly began to ignore his existence, and Proust could only imagine that it was because, for some reason or other, he fancied he saw himself in the character of Saint-Loup. And with the further appearance of de Charlus in *Sodome et Gomorrhe*, Montesquiou had grown livid at what certain people were hinting was a portrait of himself. Old and disappointed, the great triumph of his later years having been an invitation from Isadora Duncan to give her a child, he was now furiously jealous of Proust's success.

"I see I shall have to call myself Montesproust. I too would like a little fame," he had remarked indulgently during the first days of *Swann*. Since then his feelings had become steadily less amicable. Referring acidly, after the *Prix Goncourt*, to Proust's "fat dividends," the poet wrote accusing him of no longer bothering, now that he had become fashionable, even to answer his old friends' letters. After this, the Count had grown increasingly bitter as the success of his former disciple increased; which did not prevent Proust from exerting himself to obtain, by roundabout methods, for his old master, some journalistic work worthy of a talent he recognized too well had never been sufficiently appreciated. Montesquiou had set out to become a dictator of Arts, much as earlier, in England, Ruskin had aspired before him. But whereas Ruskin's writings, unsuccessful at first, had gradually achieved accumulated weight, Montesquiou's were steadily becoming more and more neglected. But Montesquiou was not appeased, and rumour was abroad that he was writing his memoirs in which he intended to say many unpleasant things about his former friend. Much distressed, Proust received assurance from the publishers that nothing derogatory to him would be passed for publication,[1] and to the end of his life, despite the increasing coolness of their relations, preserved for Montesquiou a curious affection. One of his last regrets, indeed, when he knew that Montesquiou, too, was seriously ill, was that he had omitted to write and congratulate him upon the appearance of his last volume of verse.

In these last years his health was steadily deteriorating.[2] He suffered terribly from cold, and in the winter, despite a huge fire, would have his bed filled with hot-water bottles and piled high with blankets and a fur rug. In addition to his various other ills, he was now afflicted with heart attacks and, towards the end, uræmia; all of which were aggravated by his careless or excessive use of drugs. To increase his physical tortures, he would sometimes make mistakes in the

---

[1] This promise, however, owing to a subsequent change of publishers, was not fulfilled. Although, in the main text of *Les Pas Effacés*, Montesquiou dismisses Proust, with a patronizing and indulgent condescension, as a man capable of sporadic moments of penetration, who might have written a masterpiece had he not always been too ill, the tone of a long note subsequently devoted to him, is very different. Here he asserts that Proust's sudden success was the result of a specious theatrical trick: that, having reached his fiftieth year without having attained such a position of pre-eminence as alone could satisfy a man who was a "cross between a Christian and a Jew," his friends, Hahn, Flers and Daudet, had therefore conspired to raise to the highest rank a man whose work was obviously second rate. Then, ignorant of, or deliberately distorting the facts of the *Figaro* article, he claims that "an article of Robert Dreyfus which appeared in some newspaper in an inconspicuous position, was actually reprinted the following day, owing to Proust's furious rage, upon the next page." He continues, while admitting that the book is not without some little merit, by asserting that it was deliberately constructed in a salacious manner to whet the appetite of the mob, just as the title *Sodome et Gomorrhe* was chosen to attract a huge crowd of prurient readers. This, after all Proust's fears that after its publication not only many of his readers, but his friends, would turn their backs on him! However, while such observations help to show us nothing about Proust, they certainly show us a great deal about Montesquiou.

[2] Undoubtedly Proust was an ill man: but even so, it is a little difficult not to consider that many of his lamentations were either greatly exaggerated, or else employed deliberately as an excuse to prevent people from coming to disturb him.

Perhaps even in unconscious imitation of Ruskin, whom, in this respect also he so greatly resembles, his letters for years were full of incessant complaints of debility and exhaustion; a d interminable explanations of how he could neither sleep, nor digest, nor walk.

doses of his medicines, and once severely burnt his intestinal tract by taking undiluted a medicine that should have been mixed in a large quantity of water. He had sudden and distressing lapses, too, not only of speech, but of memory, which, although caused by his persistent overdoses of caffeine or adrenalin, terrified him by the thought that they might be further signs of approaching insanity.[1] And, worse even than all this, he was slowly losing his sight. Having been troubled with his eyes for years, he had continually put off visiting an oculist, until at last, when he could scarcely see to correct his proofs, it was impossible for him to leave his bed. The periods of complete exhaustion during which he was unable to correct his proofs, or read, or even sit up in bed to eat, became more frequent and more prolonged. By now he had completely lost all faith in doctors, and though there were times when he would willingly have consulted his brother, the fact that he himself could only go out at night, and Robert had to be at his hospital early in the morning, restrained Proust from disturbing him.

At last, the formidable task of seeing his work finished and published in its entirety began to oppress him: after *Sodome et Gomorrhe*, there were still two further parts to be revised, whose proofs later would need interminable correction; and the fact that he might not have strength to complete them weighed upon him heavily.

Now that it became almost impossible to receive from the outside world any of the impressions of nature with which he had sought to nourish his inner life, he had to substitute for them such fortuitous effects as the play of light on a half-filled beer mug, or the fantastic shadow of a pile of books upon the floor. At such unexpected glimpses of beauty he would gaze long and intently, with just the same passion of intensity as that with which, as a child at Illiers, he would pause to

---

[1] This, again, was quite possibly due to his earlier preoccupation with the tragic declining years of Ruskin.

gaze at some wild flower or a strange cloud formation in the sky. And since, too, he could no longer go out to see pictures or to hear music, he arranged, in a final burst of extravagance, for a quartet to come to his apartment to play a work by Poulet that he had long desired to hear. So generous was his appreciation of their performance, that he was surprised to receive from them the next day, an enthusiastic letter of gratitude for the friendliness and consideration with which they had been treated.

When it was possible for him to see his friends, however, which was extremely seldom, he would become as eager and as spritely as they had known him years before. He would frivolously discuss mutual acquaintances, and loved to entertain them with amusing anecdotes either about himself or about his work. The fact that Lord Derby had once remarked that Proust had impressed him more than anyone else in France, because he was the only man he had ever seen dining in a fur cloak, tickled the author no less than the American woman who had recently written him a gushing letter and, prefacing her request with the information that she was both young and beautiful, begged him, since she had been reading his books night and day for the past three years and still had not the faintest idea what they were about, to tell her in two lines exactly all he meant to convey.

The same vein ran through many of his letters. It became necessary for him to change his secretary, but before doing so, he wished to find him a position in a bank. "He is rather idle, and doesn't much like figures ..." he whimsically informed such friends as he hoped might be able to employ him; despite which glowing reference, he was eventually able to dispatch him to a new job in America and to employ a niece of Céleste in his place.

Even in his last months, there persisted his desire to do a dozen small services for people, some of whom he did not even know. Now it was on behalf of some comparative stranger, to augment whose chances of winning a literary prize, that he exerted himself, not so much because Proust admired the man's talent as because he was a widower who had been wounded in the war, and, with but slender financial resources, had two small children to provide for; now it was some acquaintance of his own who badly needed work. Erroneously imagining that one of his new friends was in need of money, he wrote with his usual impetuous generosity to offer him a loan.

But his greatest pre-occupation was always his book. Apart from a single preface, which he wrote for his friend Morand's novel, *Tendres Stocks*, an essay on style largely adapted from that which he had written years ago for *La Revue Blanche*, all his energy was concentrated upon its completion. A dozen practical details of its welfare occupied his attention. He was worried about finding a suitable title for *La Prisonnière*, the third part of *Sodome et Gomorrhe*, which he was completely rewriting for the third time: he was anxious because he heard that some of the parts had been allowed to go temporarily out of print, and that *Sodome et Gomorrhe* was not being nearly so well displayed or advertised as he expected. "Without expecting that, as for Morand, you should put 5,000 copies sold in ten minutes," he wrote to his publishers, "I wish that you could give my books a little publicity." He could not understand, with the extraordinary reputation he had won, why his sales were not larger. *Nène*, he remarked reproachfully, although the subsequent Goncourt Prize winner, and consequently published over a year later, had already sold thousands of copies more than *À l'Ombre des Jeunes Filles en Fleur*. As for the proofs that he was daily receiving from the printers, they still were so full of faults he had already corrected, that his work was almost as arduous as writing a completely new book. These continual obstructions and delays finally caused him to insist that they should be sent to an entirely different printer.

Most of all, he was concerned because he learned that the general title of his work had been announced in England as *Remembrance of Things Past*,[1] a title which corresponded not at all to the meaning contained within his own, and which he lamented destroyed the whole significance of his thought.

To his great satisfaction, however, his books were steadily winning him an increasing admiration and respect. *À l'Ombre des Jeunes Filles en Fleur* had been published in a limited *de luxe* edition, with a heliograph of his portrait by Blanche and pages of his corrected proofs inset in each number; and no sooner had he been awarded the *Prix Goncourt* than a group of Academicians wrote to inform him that they had wished to offer him the *Grand Prix*. Bibliophiles desired to buy his manuscripts, and numbers of literary reviews clamoured to publish extracts from his forthcoming volumes. Far from the author not being accorded sufficient attention, he was now even accorded too much, since the popular Press never ceased to print the most extravagant rumours as to his life and habits. It was considered a privilege to review his novels, and contributors to important papers vied with each other to be granted the distinction. His portrait was exhibited at the Exposition du Cercle Interallié, he was decorated with the Legion of Honour, at the same time as Mme de Noailles whose poetry he had always so much admired; his name was coupled not only with the greatest of all novelists and poets, but even with such contemporary scientists and philosophers as Einstein and Bergson; and to crown it all, his work was being translated into almost every European language.

In October 1922, on one of his rare excursions into the outside world, he caught a chill. In spite of the consequent increase in temperature, however, he refused to give up working. He was now correcting *Albertine Disparue*. He knew that his death was imminent, and, despite the advice of his

[1] Although, of course, it is quite obvious why Proust's talented English translator chose this rendering of his title, *In Search of Lost Time* would more adequately have expressed the author's inner meaning.

doctor, who begged him not only to pay far more attention to his diet but to rest completely, he was passionately determined to get it finished. A week or so later, Proust had reason to go out again. No sooner had he left his flat, however, than he was forced immediately to return home. He was shivering violently, and could not stop himself from sneezing. But having dragged himself to bed, despite his doctor's orders, he insisted upon continuing with his work, easing his conscience by sending his medical adviser huge bouquets of flowers. He was quite willing to die, if only he could finish his book. He worked feverishly, without giving himself time to eat; took innumerable cups of strong coffee, and drank iced beer which was sent in to him from the Ritz. He knew that he was dying, that no doctor alive could save him, and begged Céleste not to let anyone try ineffectually to prolong his life. Preparing for his end, he sent for Jacques Rivière, and gave him details of his uncorrected manuscripts and instructions for their publication.

A few days later he felt a little better. Having broken his prolonged fast, he then determined to deny himself for another week the rest for which his body clamoured and to complete *Albertine Disparue* while he still had strength. It was November 17th. About three o'clock the following morning he realized that he was about to die. He was now too weak to write himself, but, sending for Céleste, he dictated to her some passages on Bergotte's death, and showed her exactly where, in the preceding volume, he wished them to be inserted. When this was done he consented to lie down. Until ten o'clock he dozed intermittently, while Céleste sat anxiously at his bedside. Then, rousing himself, he asked her to go quickly to the Ritz to get him some more beer. As she hesitated at the door, he implored her to hurry, remarking, with bitter pathos, that otherwise, like everything else in his life, it would probably arrive too late.

While she was away he fell asleep again; but by the time

she returned he had become delirious and was crying out about some fearful hallucination. Immediately Céleste ran downstairs to telephone both for his brother and for the doctor. When Robert arrived, he tried to raise Proust up to enable him to breathe more freely. But an abscess on one of his lungs had broken, and the effort to move was unbearable. It was evident that little could be done. A few hours later, Proust was vanquished at last in one of those grim struggles for breath that had haunted him throughout the whole of his life.

He was a man of fifty, but when, on the morrow, some of his friends came to look upon him in his last sleep, his face had reassumed all the expressive beauty of his youth.

PART TWO

CHAPTER I

THE third part of *Sodome et Gomorrhe*—*La Prisonnière*—was published in 1923; *Albertine Disparue* in 1925 and *Le Temps Retrouvé* in 1927. Not until five years after his death was it possible to assess Proust's work in its entirety. Nevertheless, no sooner was he dead than he became an almost legendary figure, and the real man was completely obscured by exaggerated tales of the fur cloak, the cork-lined room and the magnificent dinners at the Ritz. All sorts of wild rumours that had been rife immediately after he had won the *Prix Goncourt* were revived and repeated; and, while there were a number of eminent critics, both French and English, to do him honour, his novel enjoyed a temporary and spurious popularity which was soon succeeded by an inevitable reaction. Many people bought his books; women got their portraits painted with them displayed prominently in their hands, or placed them with conspicuous negligence upon the tables of their drawing-rooms; yet though even the popular novelists of the day took care to see that their heroines were following the fashion, comparatively few people actually read them, and even among those who did, the essential meaning and significance of his work was but little understood.[1]

It is impossible to arrive at a fair estimation of Proust, either as a man or as a writer, unless all his novels are considered together as one work. "I ignore the purely worldly opinion," wrote Proust in one of his most interesting letters to Sidney Schiff, "that you prefer the man to his book.... Between what a man says in company, and the truths he

[1] It is possible to find, even in books published as late as 1935, caustic references to Proust's "veronal, his padded cell, and his black philosophy."

extracts from his inmost being when he is alone, there is a world of difference." And indeed, the real man is to be found less in those many vivid and expressive portraits which his friends have left us, less in the most spontaneous and extravagant passages of his correspondence, than in the book the writing of which was his vocation, and which will stand as his abiding monument.

After all, those unexpected and excessive protestations of affection in his letters, did they really mean so very much? Surely, in most cases, they were little more than the effervescence of a few transient moments of intoxication? Who, better than himself, realized the impermanence, the unreliability of all human feelings? Very few of his friends really understood him, and no one realized this more poignantly than Proust himself. His greatest tragedy was not so much his illness as his essential loneliness; and his loneliness was the result rather of an unusual intellectual stature than of any external conditions of his life. It was the loneliness of the man who, head and shoulders above the people about him, was forced eternally to try to communicate with the generations to come, in the hope that among them he would find those who could share the revelation which forced him persistently towards creation.

À la Recherche du Temps Perdu is one long complex novel. It is not a sequence of novels, each complete in itself, which together form a cycle that need not necessarily be considered as an inseparable whole. It was published in six parts,[1] with separate titles and sub-titles, simply because, for purely practical reasons, it was not possible to publish the whole work together. In its entirety, it totals approximately a million and a half words; its scope covers the half-century preceding the Treaty of Versailles, and it has a cast of over two hundred

[1] i.e., including *La Prisonnière* as part of *Sodome et Gomorrhe*, as did the author.

INTRODUCTION TO PROUST

characters. Therefore in order fully to appreciate the book, it is helpful, before a first reading, to be aware of the outline[1] which supplies a basis for the various interwoven themes. Written in the first person, with the writer[2] as the centre of his own world, and the chief characters grouped about him in accordance with the roles they play in his life, the book at the same time is developed in a manner that gives them an existence completely independent of his own. Although all the principal ideas of the Marcel of the book are undoubtedly Proust's own, the novel must be considered less as autobiography than as a deliberate effort to present various aspects of the life he had known, in a reconstructed form that would the better express the truths he had been able to extract from it. To this end the form is arranged so that the growth and development of Marcel's inner life is coincident with vast objective pictures of the social life of his period.

SWANN'S WAY

Excavated from the long and drowsy midnight hours, during which past memories from different phases of his life ceaselessly return, so that on waking fully he is not at first aware even in which room he lies, there come back to Marcel with peculiar vividness those days in the country at Combray, when as a sensitive and delicate child, he would lie in bed every evening, while the rest of the family sat sipping their drinks and gossiping on the terrace below, longing for the moment when his mother would come up to say good night to him. So much did he look forward to this last kiss, that often he reached the stage of hoping that it would come as late

---

[1] The *précis* which follows is inserted for the benefit of those not already well acquainted with the work, and should be omitted by those who do not require it to make all that follows fully comprehensible.

[2] It is not until the middle of *La Prisonnière* that we learn that the narrator of the novel, who does not necessarily represent Proust himself, is called by the same Christian name. For convenience in the following outline this has been adopted throughout.

as possible, simply to prolong the sweet yet melancholy pleasure of anticipation. Yet in vain when she appeared would he entreat her to stay with him; for this persistence only aroused on her face a look of sorrowful displeasure for his weakness.

But wretched as he used to be at the shortness of her visits, such evenings were blessed indeed when compared to those others upon which their neighbour Swann was invited to dinner, and she did not come up to him at all.

After Swann's unfortunate marriage, which it was understood he had made only on account of his daughter, to whom he was devoted, these visits became less frequent, because Marcel's family did not care to receive his wife. At this time they were completely unaware of their visitor's brilliant position in society, partly on account of his natural reserve and discretion, and partly on account of the rigid caste system to which they strictly adhered; so that, knowing that their friend had been born into a wealthy family of stockbrokers, they could never have conceived that now he was one of the most sought after men in the aristocratic world.

On such evenings, when Marcel used to dine earlier than the others, and come into the dining-room afterwards for dessert, he would sit at table until eight o'clock, wretchedly conscious that his mother, for fear of annoying his father, would never give him in public the series of kisses she might have allowed him had they been alone, and that all too soon he would be obliged to content himself with one alone, which must be preciously guarded all the way upstairs and cherished tenderly long after he was in bed.

One evening, even worse. Because he looks tired, and his mother is already dressing, Marcel is sent up to bed early without even being able to kiss her at all. Desolate and miserable, he forces himself upstairs; but long after he has undressed, he lies awake in a state of misery too intense and poignant to be borne. So acute is his suffering, that no matter what penalties may be inflicted upon him he must see his mother before she goes to sleep. With the audacity of despair, he writes her a note, which he entrusts to their servant, Francoise, to deliver. And while he waits, with passionate impatience, for his mother to reply, he imagines how much her visitor would despise him were he to see the note being delivered and be able to guess its contents; whereas in reality Swann would probably have been the one person who could have understood the anguish which had prompted it, since he himself had known so well the pain of being separated from the being he most loved.

But his mother does not appear, and Marcel receives at length the reply that there is no answer to his message. Sorrowfully he shuts his eyes and with them tries to exclude from his consciousness the voices of the party, which drift up to him from below. Eventually, realizing that, in his present state, sleep will be impossible, he decides to brave the most dire humiliation and even to hazard the terrible punishment of being sent away to school, and to waylay her later when she comes upstairs to her room.

At last the moment arrives. From his position on the landing Marcel sees the light of her candle. She climbs the stairs. As soon as she is within reach, he throws himself upon her. With surprise and anger on her face, she tells him to run away before his father catches him, and, only because he refuses to move, promises that she will come later and see him in his room. But already his father is upon them. All is lost. Even the worst may happen and he be sent away.

But, miraculously, acting from expediency rather than principle, Marcel's father not only makes no mention of punishment, but even suggests to his wife that, since she is not tired, she may just as well sit up with the boy—even have the spare bed in his room made up, and spend the night there.

Marcel is filled with inexpressible gratitude; but he dare not speak, for fear lest his father should consider his transports sentimental.

So all night long his mother stays with him. At first he weeps uncontrollably, until she too is moved to tears. Then, getting for him the books which his grandmother has already bought him for his birthday, she begins to read to him from *François le Champi*.

His agony soothed, Marcel allows himself to be borne unheeding upon the current of his perfect happiness. He knows that he can never hope for such an experience to be repeated. To-morrow, at bedtime, he will again suffer all his insupportable anguish, and his mother will no longer be at his side. But to-morrow, as yet, is deeply buried in the mysterious obscurity of the future.

Such is the sole recollection of Combray that he can wrest from oblivion for many years, until one afternoon, in a different epoch of his life, the savour of a madeleine dipped in tea brings back a host of vivid associations that no deliberate effort of memory could revive. In that moment, like those Japanese flowers which, when soaked in water take on colour and distinctive shape, become flowers and houses and people, so all the flowers, the people and the countryside of Combray quiver with life before him, sprung from his cup of tea.[1]

For there, at Combray, where the family used to go for their holidays year after year, his "great aunt" Leonie would give him a sop of her madeleine dipped in tea when he went into her room to say good morning. This redoubtable old lady, his grandfather's cousin, had, since her husband's death, wilfully submitted herself to a process of gradual incarceration; until at last she refused to leave her bed, and conducted her existence, like a princess immured in her tower, under the most rigid conditions dictated to her by her sorrowing widowhood, and the neurotic obsessions to which she had willingly succumbed. Here, day by day, week by week, and year by year, she held her court; and her family, the local curate, her

[1] This explains the discarded title of *Jardins dans une Tasse de Thé*.

old friend Mme Sazerat, and the "retired" servant Eulalie all have to come regularly to pay their dutiful respects; and here, she diverts herself for hours at a time by gazing from her window into the village street below, where every trivial occurrence, whether the appearance of an unfamiliar dog or the passing of a neighbour, serves as an unfailing source of interest to be chewed over voraciously with Françoise, the only servant who has gained the right of entrance to her room.

At Combray, too, is a little room, usually unused, which evokes for Marcel many memories of his late Uncle Adolphe, visiting whom one day, he met a charming lady dressed in pink with a beautiful rope of pearls; a fortuitous accident, alas, which distressed his parents and through a series of accidents, finally estranged him from his uncle.

He recalls in the most vivid detail his attendances at Mass in the noble Combray church, with its beautiful belfry and its famous stained-glass windows, whence, on their way home they would so often meet their neighbour, Legrandin, a man who, though tempering his airs and graces with great simplicity of dress, is nevertheless an unconscionable snob; and, while he has added to his profession of engineer the secondary labours of a man of letters, and launches continual tirades against the aristocracy and the world of fashion, always ignores his old friends whenever he happens to be in the company of some lady of rank; and although he learns that Marcel is shortly to go to Balbec, firmly refuses to offer him an introduction to his sister, Mme Cambremer-Legrandin, who has a country house near by.

Then, after lunch, one of those bountiful country luncheons of Françoise, where every dish is selected for some special feature, and each course a work of art, Marcel would retire upstairs to read in his little room, into which drift all the sounds and scents, the lights and shadows of the summer afternoon.

Absorbed in his book, he believes implicitly in its philosophic truth and beauty, and desires above all to appropriate these qualities to himself. Only later, sitting in the garden, his imagination kindled by descriptions of far places, he would long passionately for the cool of rivers and mountains and the woman inevitably associated with these remote and attractive scenes; seeking thus to replace every commonplace of his ordinary life by wonderful adventures.

On such an afternoon, while he is poring over his favourite author, Bergotte, whose books have been recommended to him, in his usual inflated, affected style, by his Jewish schoolfriend, Bloch, Swann, who has been calling on his parents, tells him that this novelist is his daughter's greatest friend. Since Marcel is by now probably Bergotte's most fervent admirer, attributing to his work every subtlety and beauty, he bombards the guest with an excited list of questions about his idol; and, learning that his favourite actress is Berma and that he has written about her a pamphlet which Gilberte Swann has in her possession his incipient desire to meet this girl blazes into a wild longing.

From the local curate on one of his visits to his "aunt" Leonie, Marcel first hears of the Guermantes, whose mansion is not far distant, and of their illustrious ancestors, the Abbots of Combray, the Lords of Guermantes and Counts of Brabant; and so deeply are these names imbued for him with enchantment, that when his grandmother mentions that there are some Guermantes connected with her old school friend, the Marquise de Villeparisis, he joins the rest of the family in ridiculing any such idea.

Here it is at Combray after their weekly presence at church, that Marcel usually sees M. Vinteuil, his aunts' old music master, now retired on a small estate of his own, where, in his intervals between strenuous composition, he devotes himself with loving tenderness to the welfare of his motherless and stolid-looking daughter. And here, too, upon one of his long country rambles on one of the two "ways"—the one which leads towards Tansonville, Swann's country house—during a walk rich with impressions of racing clouds and streams, of innumerable wild flowers, of hawthorn, cornflowers, poppies and apple-trees, he first sets eyes on Gilberte Swann, through the hedge of her garden: a little girl with fair and reddish hair, a face powdered with freckles, and black eyes that for years he is to see in his imagination as blue. He falls in love with her now more madly than ever, so that henceforward the most insignificant details connected with her life or with her father are of inexhaustible interest to him. But before he is able to make any contact with her, she is called away by her mother and departs in an enigmatic manner that leaves him with a thousand questions, and to be gazed after by a man in white ducks with staring eyes, whom his father at once puts down as M. de Charlus, Swann's great friend and, as is generally believed in the neighbourhood, the lover of his wife.

It is on another of these walks, whereon he is haunted by his first desire for a woman, and while he is near M. Vinteuil's house at Montjouvin, that he sees through a window an amorous and perverse scene between Mlle Vinteuil and her Sapphist friend, whose liaison has long since been the scandal of the countryside and is said to have driven the girl's father to his grave; and on his walks on the Guermantes way that he dreams so often of the Guermantes themselves, who, although he dimly realizes that they are real people, are still bathed for him in all the fabulous beauty of the figures in a stained-glass window. Often he would fancy that Mme de Guermantes, taking a sudden capricious fancy for himself, would invite him to her home, where, all day long, she might remain at his side, fishing for trout. And when evening came, she would take his hand in her own, and, leading him tenderly through her private flower garden, would make him tell her about the poems he meant to compose and the books that he intended to write.

But when, one day, Mme de Guermantes appears in Church,

a lady with fair hair, a large nose, piercing blue eyes and a billowy scarf, his disappointment is immense. In all his dreams of her, he has always pictured her as living in another century, as being of different substance from the rest of mankind, and has little imagined that she might have a red face and a mauve scarf. By chance, however, her glance, straying vaguely about the pillars of the old church, falls for a moment upon his face. He is entranced anew, and finding now only beauty in her own, assures himself that true nobility and perfection reside within her countenance.

So these two "ways" remain linked for ever with the incidents and impressions which, buried in the deepest layers of his mental soil, and forgotten for many years, are to cast reflections upon the whole of Marcel's later life.

In the old days before his marriage, Swann often used to meet Odette de Crécy at Mme Verdurin's, where her "faithful" were ruled by means of a rod as stern and inexorable as that of any Spanish inquisitor. Here, if you were genuinely of her "little clan," you had your place laid every evening she was at home; but only on condition that you religiously agreed that the young painter and the musician whom she had taken up that season were geniuses, and that all entertainment offered by society was so excruciatingly boring that even the smartest hostesses had to offer fabulous inducements to get anybody to visit them.

Indulged with lavish hospitality and persistent adulation, the "faithful" had to comply with but one other condition—to pursue all their most cherished activities in her company, even to the conducting of their love affairs. Any allegiance less passionate was anathema, and suppressed with the ruthlessness of a medieval Pope. And since Odette was one of the most zealous adherents of the group, Mme Verdurin was only too eager that her new romance should mature under the propitious influence of her benevolent eye.

Swann, alike the glass of fashion, paragon of taste and idol of society, who hitherto had always been an incorrigible philanderer, was so enamoured of his new mistress, that he would eagerly suffer a society that formerly he would have despised, in order to be able to pass his evenings at her side; even although, when first he had been introduced to her, her style of beauty had not only left him unmoved, but even evoked in him a sort of physical repulsion.

She it was, indeed, who had made the first overtures of friendship, writing, with charming diffidence, to ask him whether she might not come to look at his collections. First she would sometimes visit him in the afternoons; next she persuaded him to share at her house in the solemn rite of afternoon tea, an invitation which, for long, he struggled to avoid. At last, when their relationship became intimate, he willingly endured at the Verdurins, night after night, the exasperating and fatuous remarks of Dr. Cottard, the complacent, affected tirades of the young painter, the cruel humiliations wilfully inflicted upon the guileless Saniette, the vulgar commonplaces of the pianist's aunt and the exaggerated praises of the young musician himself, whose performances at least afforded him a subtle pleasure. For it was he who often used to play the *andante* from the Vinteuil sonata for piano and violin, a piece which Swann already knew but had never been able to identify; and which had made so profound an impression upon him that it brought him not only curious happiness, but a renewal of his old belief in life itself. So much did he love it, that a certain phrase even became for him a symbol of his love, as listening to it so often by his mistress's side, it served as a prelude to the intimate and charming drives back to her house, to which, at the end of each evening, he used to escort her.

Thus his feelings for her, nurtured at first with the most tender care, since he doubts his own capacity to feel again the full emotion of love, proceed inevitably through all the phases of indifference, curiosity, gratified interest, tenderness and passion. As his love for her becomes crystallized, so his interest in other women wanes, and no longer does he pester his friends, with customary persistence, for introductions to the ubiquitous women who usually attract his wandering glances. For now, though at first it scarcely attracted him, Odette's face, like that of a Botticelli[1] nymph, dominates his imagination with such insistence that he dreads to think there may come a day when she will grow weary of him.

Yet apart from the evenings they spend together at the Verdurins, and the precious hours they share alone, he knows little of her life. Whenever he wishes to introduce her to his friends, she dissuades him, always offering vague excuses, for fear lest someone, knowing her reputation, may speak evil of her to him. So Swann, anxious to draw closer to her, to share all her pleasures and her thoughts, willingly sacrifices the gratification of his own cultivated tastes for those mediocre pursuits that form her life, and leaves the exclusive drawing-room of his old friend the Princesse des Laumes for Mme Verdurin's, where, for the sake of being invited with his mistress, he tries to find in every vulgarity signs of intelligence and good nature.

But this state of felicity does not last. Mme Verdurin, feeling that he does not enter into the worship of the faithful with sufficient singleness of mind, and sensing that he finds Cottard a buffoon and Professor Brichot a pedantic idiot, or because he cannot be got openly to confess that he finds all society people the most colossal bores, very soon begins to compare him, greatly to his disadvantage, with their newest recruit, the Comte de Forcheville, who, while infinitely more stupid, is at the same time very much more appreciative of the wit and talent of her clan. Lamentably informing the

---

[1] Proust himself had no doubt acquired the Botticelli cult from Ruskin; and several descriptions of paintings in his work are obviously derived from "Modern Painters." In the novel, the Ruskin influence is shown exerted on Marcel partly through Swann, and partly through Bergotte.

"mistress" one day, in answer to a direct inquiry, that he considers those arch bores, the la Trémouïlles, charming, Swann at length brings down upon his head her despotic vengeance. Indeed, the naïve and excessive enthusiasm of the newcomer so magnifies Swann's defection that Mme Verdurin decides to excommunicate him.

Meanwhile, although Swann generously indulges Odette both with jewels and money, he never imagines for a moment that she has ever taken a penny from anyone before. But it might have cost him but little suffering to discover that her affection for him was based on a sound commercial instinct; for although he has often reflected that in no way is she very remarkable, he is immensely gratified whenever she causes it to be known that he occupies a unique position in her life.

From this pride in her possession is born his jealousy. She lies to him over some trivial incident, and this jealousy increases. He becomes importunate: pries into her movements, questions her about her friends, her habits, every minor episode in her life. One evening, when the Verdurins dismiss him without inviting him to some expedition they have been planning in his hearing, the "mistress" insists upon driving Odette home in her carriage with de Forcheville, leaving Swann to go home alone. He suffers the paroxysms of complete despair, and, with a wild revulsion of feeling, inveighs to himself bitterly against his hostess.

So the drawing-room which had once helped to keep them together now keeps them apart; and whenever he learns of some expedition to the country which Odette is making with her friends, he must plan all manner of ways in which, as though by chance, he may meet them at their destination.

For many months his moods oscillate through every shade of feeling: from desire, adoration and gratitude, to suspense, jealousy and even hatred. So much anguish does this infatuation for Odette cause him, that there are times when he looks forward hopefully to the day when he will love her no longer. The more hopelessly enamoured he grows, the more cold she becomes, accusing him now, whenever he desires to be seen at her side in public, of having no more consideration for her than if she were a woman of the streets.

After this, Swann begins to hear hints dropped about her past life. He begs his friends to tell him about the men she has known; seeks, with tortured persistence, to find out how she spends every hour when she is not with him. He even persuades his old friend, the Baron de Charlus, to escort her as frequently as possible to plays or concerts, in order that he may find out later exactly where she has been and to whom she has spoken; while he accedes to Odette's lightest wish with an almost fervent gratitude, trying to find in her most casual phrase some hint of interest or affection.

One day he goes to a party at Mme de Saint-Euverte's. Owing to his long absence from society, and the melancholy in his face, his old friend the Princesse des Laumes imagines he has been ill. A concert is in progress, and once again he hears the piece by Vinteuil that, ever since he met her, has always been associated in his mind with his feelings for Odette. His whole relationship with her passes before his eyes, with all its tenderness, its suffering and its disillusion; and for the first time he realizes that all he has hoped from it can never be realized.

He decides therefore to wait for a suitable opportunity to break with her. But always an expedition she has planned with someone else arouses his jealousy, and he cannot bring himself to do so. One day he receives an anonymous letter, telling him not only that she has been the mistress of several other men, giving their names, and among them that of de Forcheville, but insinuating, also, that frequently she has had perverse relationships with women. At first Swann believes these accusations groundless. Gradually, however, his suspicions grow, and curiosity and anguish with regard to her affairs become a perpetual torture. He persecutes her with questions, wrings from her partial confessions that tear his heart. At all costs, he feels, he must prevent her from gratifying such inclinations again. He tries to increase his vigilance. He continues his interrogations. Odette lies, retracts, contradicts herself, grows evasive, and lies again. He becomes obsessed with the idea of her vices, and every new incident, every answer to his questions, inflicts upon him further wounds.

At last there is a respite. Odette goes away with the Verdurins for a long cruise.[1] During her absence his sufferings become dim. His jealousy is frantic and incessant no longer. Aroused, for the last time, by a strange dream, it disappears with the light of morning, leaving him desolate with astonishment that he has wasted years of his life, that he has even longed for death, on account of a woman who did not really ever please him and who was not his type.

Like the poet whose heart was stolen away by the resonant names of the mountains of Ecuador, for a long time Marcel is entranced by the names of Florence and Venice, and even more by that of the little seaside town of Balbec, which represents to his imagination a splendid setting for magnificent storms and tempests, and is notable for its remarkable Norman Gothic church, almost Persian in appearance, of which he has once heard Swann speak with admiration. But the state of his health forbids his journey to all such places, just as it prevents him from hearing the sublime Berma, whose genius Bergotte has proclaimed; and he must content himself instead with daily visits to the Champs Élysées in the charge of Françoise, who, since his "aunt's" death, has been

[1] It is interesting to note that Mme Verdurin frequently refers to Odette as her "little piece of perfection," and to compare this with the fact that Mme de Caillavet also had a friend, Mlle Laprévotte, whom she nicknamed Mlle Perfection and often used to take cruising in her yacht.

in his family's service. It is here, one afternoon, that he sees again Gilberte Swann as she is saying good-bye to a friend with whom she has been playing. All Marcel's old love for her is rekindled and henceforward he haunts the Gardens in the hope of seeing her again. Eventually his persistence is rewarded, and one day, when she has not enough companions to make up a game of prisoner's base, she sends one of her friends to ask him if he would like to join them.

After this, there is only one question of any importance to him. Will he find Gilberte in the Champs Élysées to-day or not? Every morning he observes the weather, weighed down with apprehension if it seems too cold or rainy for her to be allowed out. And one afternoon, joy of joys, he sees her running at full speed towards him, obviously prepared to accept him among the number of her friends.

But often he is less fortunate. Gilberte remains at home, or is occupied on some mysterious mission with her family, and he can only wait for her, hour after hour, in abject misery. He is certain, now, that he loves her deeply. The overwhelming question is whether his emotion is reciprocated. Alas, there is little cause for him to think so; even though their friendship progresses, and one day Gilberte buys for him, and begs him to keep in memory of her, a marble which he adores because it is the colour of her eyes. She even brings him, tied up with ribbon and sealed with wax, the essay on Berma by Bergotte, which for long he has wished to read. More gracious still, she suggests that they should call each other by their Christian names. But if, at times, she shows him such marks of affection, there are other occasions when she wounds him deeply by her lack of pleasure in their meetings, and very often on those special days on which he has most counted for the realization of her affection.

Whenever she is absent, he is in despair. At such times he imagines her writing to tell him that she loves him; kisses the marble she has given him, adores Bergotte with increased ardour, since he is still her friend; begs her passionately, on their next meeting, since their friendship seems to remain static, to join him in laying the foundations of a new one.

He even keeps by his side a plan of Paris, marked with the street in which her family live: introduces their name into the conversation at home whenever possible, writes their initials over and over in the spare pages of his exercise books, and even attempts to copy Swann's mannerisms, coveting above all his impressive baldness.

When his mother informs him one day that she has met M. Swann buying an umbrella at the Trois Quartiers, he is filled with a melancholy satisfaction that increases to amazed delight when he learns that Gilberte's father has even inquired after him. The fact that M. Swann is perfectly well acquainted with his identity, from the occasions when he has sometimes come to fetch his daughter or watch her at her games, seems to connect them in a further intimacy.

On afternoons when he knows Gilberte will not be going to the Champs Élysées, he forces Françoise to take him past her house, so that, by feasting his eyes upon it, he can imagine himself in contact with her: or else, learning that Mme Swann walks almost every day in the Allée des Acacias, he demands to be accompanied there in order that he may pay her homage, as, attired with her characteristic elegance, the cynosure of all eyes, walking quickly on her way home or driving with an enigmatic smile in her carriage, from which she receives with a fleeting bow the attentions of the gentlemen who continually salute her, he may indulge in the exquisite pleasure of pulling off his hat to her with so lavish and prolonged a gesture that the passers by cannot repress a smile.

So vivid are these impressions of the Bois in spring, and Mme Swann, gracious and elegant, performing the ritual of her morning stroll, that never in later years can Marcel return there without seeing her again vividly in his memory, and being saddened by the irreparable changes wrought by time.

WITHIN A BUDDING GROVE

Yet despite the illustrious position the Swanns have attained in Marcel's eyes, when his parents give a special dinner, the menu for which is conceived and executed by Françoise in a frenzy of inspiration, and their guest is the distinguished diplomat the Marquis de Norpois, it is Cottard, now one of the most eminent physicians of the day, and not Swann, that they would have preferred to meet their guest. For Swann, ever since his marriage with Odette, has been trying to create for her a place in society, and since none of his own aristocratic friends will consent to receive her, is to be heard ceaselessly bragging about the mediocre invitations they have received from undistinguished ministers and their dowdy wives.

When M. de Norpois arrives, the question of Marcel's career is broached, and his desire to become a writer is given a slight encouragement. More important still, on the diplomat's advice, he is at last permitted to go to the theatre with his grandmother to see Berma act in *Phèdre*.

The proposed performance, bathed by his imagination in a sea of wonder, is a bitter disappointment; and his admiration is aroused rather by the frenzied applause of the audience and the subsequent praises of the critics in the intellectual reviews, than by any beauty he himself can find in the actress's interpretation.

Since M. de Norpois mentions in conversation the Swanns, whom he happens to know, Marcel questions him ardently about their habits, and even begs him to mention his name to them when next he is at their house. But his plea remains unanswered. The new year comes, and still Gilberte does not appear in the Champs Élysées. At last she returns, only to tell him in reply to one of his ardent speeches in admiration of her parents, that they, for their part, cannot abide him. So great is his infatuation, however, that soon afterwards, when he is suddenly taken ill, refusing to forgo the pleasure of seeing her, he arrives at the Champs Élysées with a high temperature and has a terrible attack immediately he returns home. Cottard is sent for, who treats him with his characteristic curtness, a series of his old, inane puns, and unquestionable skill. But no more, alas, is Marcel permitted to go to play in the Champs Élysées. The sorrow of this great misfortune is only mitigated at length by a note from Gilberte herself, inviting him to tea. A kind word whispered into the ear of Mme Swann by Professor Cottard has aroused her interest in him. The golden gates are open at last, and henceforward Marcel is a continual visitor to the house. Here, at Gilberte's tea parties, Mme Swann, fresh from one of her "at homes," would sweep in for a moment to say, "How de do," and offer some further invitation for the morrow; for now that at last he has become their daughter's accepted friend, the Swann's continually appeal to him to exert his influence upon her, and to escort her everywhere.

Meanwhile Mme Swann, a worthy pupil of her late "mistress," is busy forming a drawing-room of her own. But as yet she has had but little success, and the two lions of her modest menagerie are Mme Cottard and Mme Bontemps, the latter, wife of the Permanent Secretary to the Minister of Posts, as Swann is continually at pains to explain, and aunt of the already much discussed Albertine, a little girl who used to go to Gilberte's dancing lessons and who is said by her to be sure to grow up dreadfully "fast."

And so at last, admitted freely to the house, invited for luncheon, to the theatre, to accompany Gilberte to her dancing lessons, to stand behind Mme Swann and turn the pages as she plays Vinteuil's sonata, to long afternoons walking with the family to the Jardin d'Acclimatation, and, greater honour still, even to meet Bergotte, Marcel is formally invested with the official dignity of being Gilberte's greatest friend.

Shortly afterwards, he is taken by his friend Bloch for the first time to a brothel, where he is offered a young Jewess, Rachel, whom he nicknames "When from the Lord" and who, despite her obvious intelligence, does not attract him. Still ardently in love with Gilberte, he sells many of the beautiful things his "great aunt" Leonie has left him, to lavish flowers upon her mother, and even renounces his diplomatic career lest it might estrange him from her.

But his relations with Gilberte have already reached their peak; and now that all opposition to their meeting is removed his grief is renewed by the increasing indifference and irritation she begins to display at his frequent attentions.

Realizing at last that he merely bores her, Marcel is so grief-stricken that he decides to put an end to their friendship; for his love and admiration for her so far exceed her interest in himself that their continual meetings have begun to bring him little but unhappiness. By refusing her invitations with the same polite indifference that he would show to anyone he did not wish to see, he hopes that his apparent lack of interest will revive her desire for his company. This, he realizes, could only be aroused by his protracted absence, which he intends to prolong until in the end he will no longer love her. So while he continues to visit Mme Swann, he does so now only upon occasions when he knows that Gilberte will be away from home; and thus reassuring himself that, should their estrangement prove too painful, he can put an end to it at any time, he declines with vague regrets all the invitations which Gilberte indirectly sends him. Yet still he hopes, with passionate persistence, that one day she will write to him herself. Eventually his longing for her overcomes all resolutions, and, having sold a valuable bowl in order to be able to give her some handsome present, he decides to call upon her without delay. But when he reaches her house, it is to learn not only that she is out, but, from the butler's manner, that the whole household tacitly considers that he is persecuting Gilberte with unwelcome attentions. In renewed despair, he flings himself from the house, his wretchedness only increased by the fact that, on his way back through the Bois, he fancies he sees her with some other young man.

He arrives home utterly wretched. Again there follows the old sick round of imagination that one day she will discover her need for him, while at the same time he is torn with jealousy to think that even now she may be bestowing her favours upon some happy rival. At all costs, to soothe this pain, he must refrain from seeing her again. Inventing some fictitious misunderstanding that he pretends is responsible for keeping them apart, for a long time he maintains a sterile correspondence with her, until at last, in the middle of one of these letters, it suddenly comes to him that his great affection for her has already become a thing of the past.

Two years later, when he has arrived at a state of almost complete indifference to Gilberte, Marcel is taken by his grandmother to Balbec, in the hope that the sea air will improve his health. His first impressions both of the town and its "Persian" church, are very disappointing. The Grand Hotel, where they are staying, however, is full of interest; and once he has accustomed himself to this new environment, to the Manager, to Aimé the head waiter, to the numerous staff; the different visitors with their innumerable idiosyncrasies and petty snobberies, all provide him with continual amusement. Besides Mlle de Stermaria, the stiff, reserved young daughter of an obscure but very ancient Breton family, by whom he is much attracted, there is also staying in the hotel that Marquise de Villeparisis whom Marcel's grandmother always maintained was somehow allied to the Guermantes. Eventually the two old ladies resume their former intimacy, and Mme de Villeparisis, who smothers both Marcel and his grandmother with graceful attentions, surprises them equally by appearing to be intimately acquainted with the movements of his father, who is on holiday in Spain with his friend M. de Norpois. Through Mme de Villeparisis, Marcel soon becomes acquainted with her nephew, Robert de Saint-Loup, a young man to whom he immediately becomes deeply attached, and who, on leave from his military service at Doncières, is remarkable not only for his aristocratic birth, his wealth, his good looks and the smartness of his clothes, but also, by reason of his exquisite courtesy and his intense veneration for the things of the mind.

Marcel then reintroduces this new friend to Bloch, who is also staying in the neighbourhood with his somewhat unpleasant Jewish family, whose ostentation and vulgarity are a continual source of embarrassment, but with whom the two young men eventually go to dine.

A few days later when calling on Mme de Villeparisis, Marcel meets her nephew the Baron de Charlus, his new friend's uncle and brother-in-law of that famous Duchesse de Guermantes who, even in the old days at Combray, had captured his imagination—a man so haughty and so courted that even his nearest relations dare not assume the privilege of presenting their friends to him, and whose remarkable eccentricities and strange manifestations of interest immediately succeeded by insolence or icy indifference, together with his exaggerated scorn of effeminacy and his extreme sensibility, for a long time leave Marcel deeply puzzled as to his character.

While his friend Saint-Loup is deeply miserable on account of the mistress on whom he is squandering both his passion and his fortune, and is brooding tragically over the fact that she will not let him go to her in Paris, Marcel sees for the first time that frieze of girls against the sea, who seem to him the very embodiment of blossoming girlhood that his whole nature ardently desires. As he lingers to watch them, first one and then another seems most to appeal to him, until gradually his attention becomes focused upon the dark, carefree and engaging Albertine, who slowly detaches herself from the little band to fill the now empty horizon of his romantic imagination.

Dining one evening with Saint-Loup at the neighbouring watering-place of Rivebelle, where they often pass together the long glamorous summer evenings, they see the famous impressionist painter Elstir, who, in response to a note they address him in the full flush of their youthful admiration, invites Marcel to visit him at his studio.

During the following days, however, encountering her several times by chance in a dozen different attitudes, the fascination Albertine exerts upon him begins to crystallize, and Marcel postpones going to see Elstir in order to lounge about the front every day in a different suit and tie, in the hope of attracting her attention. At last he pays his visit, and having looked at Elstir's paintings with the greatest interest, is deep in conversation about the beauties of the Balbec church, which hitherto he has failed to appreciate, when he discovers with delighted surprise that Albertine also is a friend of his host. Immediately the painter loses all interest in his eyes, save as a possible medium between them. He begs to be introduced to her, and eventually Elstir invites them to meet each other. But the girl Marcel then sees corresponds but little with the image he has already formed of her. And one day later, when he is accosted on the beach by a girl in a toque and carrying a muff, he can scarcely recognize Albertine at all. He joins her in a walk, however, hoping she will at last introduce him to her band of friends, but she does not do so. They agree to meet later, instead; and so, almost imperceptibly, their acquaintanceship deepens, until at last Marcel becomes caught up in all the activities of the little band that comprises Andrée, Albertine's special friend, Octave, a young man known as "in-the-soup", Gisèle and Rosamonde.

Attracted by Gisèle, Marcel plans an abortive affair with her, only to be reclaimed more strongly by his fascination for Albertine, which increases steadily despite his continual waverings. Blissfully absorbed by this new companionship, he avoids equally Mme de Villeparisis, Elstir, Bloch and even Robert de Saint-Loup, irked by every obligation that might cause him to lose a moment of her company. One day, during one of their games, in a mood of childish gaiety, Albertine passes him a piece of paper on which she has scribbled, "I love you." Marcel is determined that, henceforward, his romance shall be with her. With tireless persistence he sets himself to win her and to get himself introduced to her aunt, Mme Bontemps, with whom she often stays. For hours he discusses her in minute detail with her friend Andrée.

The evening before her departure, Albertine comes to the hotel to spend the night before catching an early train, and gives Marcel permission to come up to her room to say good-bye. When he enters she is already in bed. Intoxicated with joy he bends to kiss her. She threatens to pull the bell, and as still his face continues to approach her own, he hears a shrill blast rend the silence. Nonplussed by her behaviour, he tries in vain to fathom whether it springs from ignorance, prudishness or even coquetry, until she assures him that in all her previous relations with young men, they have always been satisfied to be good friends. It is, therefore, on a note almost of brotherly affection, that Marcel finishes the season at Balbec and afterwards returns to Paris.

THE GUERMANTES WAY

Here, his family has moved to a new apartment almost above that of the Duchesse de Guermantes; and all the enchantment which the historic associations of her name, together with her proud and inaccessible beauty used to arouse in him, recaptures him anew. Meanwhile every domestic detail of her establishment is a source of inexhaustible curiosity to Françoise; as is the tailor in the court below, one Jupien, who, together with his charming niece, a little dressmaker who has already a smart private connection of her own, has aroused her highest feelings of admiration and respect.

More than ever now, since his father has made the acquaintance of the Duke, and Mme de Villeparisis, her aunt, has already invited him several times to visit her, does Marcel dream of one day meeting the Duchess herself. One evening at the theatre, as he is watching her in the box of her beautiful cousin, the Princesse de Guermantes, never moving his eyes from her throughout each interval, she recognizes him in the stalls below, and raises a gloved hand in friendly greeting. Dazed with bewilderment and delight, henceforward every day he posts himself in the street upon the route she usually follows in her morning walk, simply for the delight of bowing to her as she draws near. At last, by Françoise's cold and disapproving manner as she helps him to get ready for these excursions, he learns indirectly that the Duchess is only irritated by these constant meetings. But so deeply is he in love with her that he cannot give them up. And when soon afterwards he goes to stay with Saint-Loup at Doncières, where he is still on military service, he begs him to introduce him to his aunt and to speak of him to her beforehand, not only with his usual friendly enthusiasm, but even with premeditated exaggeration. This his friend promises to do, but since his mistress has recently quarrelled violently with Mme de Guermantes, owing to the humiliation to which she was exposed when she gave a recitation at her house, he has no immediate opportunity of doing so.

Back in Paris, Marcel continues to meet Mme de Guermantes on her morning walks, and tries to dissimulate his pleasure each time he sees her, by overacting a surprise and indifference that at last make him appear insolent and even ill-bred.

When Robert comes to town, he invites Marcel to meet his mistress, who turns out to be none other than Rachel "When from the Lord" who now, an actress of the most advanced school, and very intellectual, is living in a little country house in Versailles which her lover has given her, and is driving him distracted by her indifference alike to his infatuation and his wild generosity.

In the restaurant where they lunch, in which Aimé is now employed as head waiter, Robert is furiously jealous every time Rachel looks at another man, and the afternoon becomes filled with a series of embarrassing quarrels and reconciliations. Moreover, seeing a messenger from M. de Charlus arrive with a note for the head waiter, Saint-Loup is furiously angry because he believes his uncle is spying on him and joining his other relatives in their plot to separate him from his mistress.

Late the same afternoon Marcel calls on Mme Villeparisis, whose drawing-room, owing to her past indiscretions, although famous in certain circles as a "school of wit," apart from the presence of her own irreproachable relations and a few royalties who are old family friends, is largely composed of very mediocre people from the middle class. Here, at last, where he catches Legrandin in one of his most sycophantic roles, meets Bloch again, now a rising dramatist, discovers that M. de Norpois has been the Marquise's lover for over twenty years, and watches M. de Charlus sitting so close to Mme Swann that his feet are completely buried in her skirts, he at last encounters the Duchess herself. After an hour of listening to interminable talk about the Dreyfus case, and a display of her famous wit, and having been introduced to Saint-Loup's mother, Mme de Marsantes, who is blessed with a reputation almost of saintliness, Robert finally arrives, and speaking for a moment with his aunt in private, is obviously responsible for the Duchess subsequently addressing a few words of greeting to him. At last his goal is almost reached. Mme de Guermantes has formally acknowledged his acquaintance.

Later, M. de Charlus, who, shortly before, has given him the most frigid greeting, invites Marcel to walk home with him, and makes him the most mysterious offers of friendship and patronage.

Arriving at the flat, it is to find his grandmother seriously ill. Cottard having been unsuccessful in restoring her to health, they call in Dr. du Boulbon, who maintains that if only she will get up and lead a normal life, she will be well. Forcing herself to go out for a walk, she is accompanied one afternoon by Marcel to the Champs Élysées, where she has a stroke.

On their way home, they meet by chance a famous doctor, a friend of his father, whom Marcel persuades to examine his grandmother at once. His opinion is that there is not the slightest hope.

During his grandmother's subsequent illness there are many calls of inquiry. Bergotte comes every day to spend a few hours with Marcel, a benefit, like most others, which comes too late, since he no longer admires him with the same ardour as in his boyhood. Meanwhile the patient grows worse. Temporary blindness is followed by temporary deafness, and this last by an impediment of speech. At length her pain becomes so great that she attempts suicide. After this she changes completely and becomes a sullen haggard and doddering old woman. Every remedy is tried without success, and in a few weeks she is dead.

One evening some time later, Robert de Saint-Loup, whose family have at last succeeded in separating him from Rachel by getting him posted in Morocco, having met Mme de

Stermaria, the girl whom Marcel first admired at Balbec and who has since divorced her husband after only three months' marriage, arranges for his friend to invite her to dinner. On this very day, Marcel receives an unexpected call from Albertine, of whom he has thought but little since his return from Balbec. But it is a very different Albertine from that of the seaside who now confronts him; an Albertine older, more intelligent, with a sophisticated vocabulary, and no longer averse to kisses: an Albertine, indeed, who evinces for him now an affection that far outsoars his own. As soon as she leaves him, Marcel dresses himself to go to an evening party at Mme de Villeparisis', and here, at last, now that he has given up his habit of following her about and regarding her, whenever they meet, with passionate and hungry eyes, Mme de Guermantes sits and talks to him for some time and, since he is completely indifferent to her, even invites him to her house to dine.

But nothing can excite him now save his imminent meeting with Mme de Stermaria, which he dreams about in every solitary moment. While he is preparing to visit the restaurant to order the dinner in advance, Albertine calls to see him again, and he begs her to accompany him, half imagining Mme de Stermaria disappointing him, in order that he might invite her in her place. But next day, when he is ready and waiting for the carriage, and receives a note to say that his guest cannot join him after all, Marcel is deeply dejected and scarcely consoled when Saint-Loup, on leave from Morocco, calls unexpectedly instead to take him out to dinner.

A few days later he fulfils his engagement to dine with the Duchesse de Guermantes, and, having kept the whole party waiting while he examines her Elstirs in another room, finds it difficult to believe that this, the most brilliant society in Paris, can really be composed of the people he meets, who, although excessively agreeable, indulge in conversation even more malicious, pretentious and trivial than any that is customary in the middle classes they would never deign to meet.

Later in the evening he calls, in accordance with a previous invitation, upon the Baron de Charlus. After being kept waiting over half an hour, he is at last ushered into the presence, where his host treats him anew to that same strange mixture of affectionate insolence and theatrical pride that before he has been unable to understand. This time his conduct becomes so insulting that at length, when Marcel is about to leave the house in a towering rage, he is besought by his host with an extraordinary tenderness to remain, and, soon afterwards, is driven home in the Baron's carriage.

Now that he has once dined with Mme de Guermantes, he receives invitations from many of her friends, and finally, one from the Princesse de Guermantes herself, which astonishes him so much, since he has never met her, that for a long time he cannot believe that he is not the victim of a hoax.

CITIES OF THE PLAIN

Soon afterwards, when Marcel witnesses a curious scene between M. de Charlus, who has just been calling on his aunt, and Jupien, about to set off for his office, the meaning of the Baron's unusual contradictions of mood, his strange offers and even stranger retractions, become suddenly clear. The Baron, meanwhile, once having established relations with Jupien, makes him his private secretary, and recommends his niece to all the fashionable women of his acquaintance, who are only too glad to pander to their beloved Palamède by patronizing her.

The same evening Marcel goes to a vast reception at the Princesse de Guermantes', where most of the fashionable world is assembled. Here he has further opportunity for studying the Baron's social manœuvres, now suddenly illuminated by the scene he has watched that afternoon. Here also he meets Swann again, who, ill with some mortal malady, explains to him how he has just had a long conversation with the Prince, who has suddenly been converted to the cause of Dreyfus: a conversation which has been perceived by many of the guests and has already given rise to a host of curious whispers among them, that the Prince, aware of his friend's notorious Dreyfusism, has just asked him to leave his house. He also asks Marcel to write to Gilberte, who often speaks of him. Nothing could be further from Marcel's desires. In refraining from seeing her, his purpose has been more than gained, for now Gilberte means less than nothing to him, and the prospect of sending her a few lines, an insufferable bore, the more so as he is expecting, on his return home, a visit from Albertine.

When Marcel arrives, she has not yet come. At once he fancies that she has found some more pleasant distraction, and begins to suffer. He waits impatiently for her to telephone. But as soon as she does so, he professes indifference. Only when he perceives that she intends to put him off, he insists upon her keeping her engagement. When she arrives she is so affectionate and charming that he gives her as a keepsake, the book-cover for Bergotte's essay, that he has long since ceased to treasure, although Gilberte had given it to him many years before.

A few weeks later, partly on account of the Baroness Putbus's maid, for whom his desires have been aroused by a description given him by Saint-Loup, and partly for the sake of his health, Marcel returns to Balbec. And now, for the first time since his grandmother's death, he feels an irremediable sense of loss. All that she must have suffered, all the unnecessary grief he himself must have caused her during her lifetime, floods his being. He is informed that Albertine has called. He no longer wishes to see her. He can now think only of his grandmother, and of the terrible fact that he will never see her again.

Some days later, Marcel receives a visit from the old Marquise de Cambremer and her daughter-in-law, who, while formerly ignoring his existence, now realize that he is friendly with the Guermantes and invite him, in consequence, to dine with them.

His desire for Albertine reviving, Marcel sends Françoise to fetch her. She is away so long that he begins to despair of her success. At last she returns with the girl, who, when she perceives his melancholy, offers with affectionate meekness to come and see him whenever he feels in need of her. But he is not now in love with her, and desires her only at intervals when he is not dreaming of enjoying the favours of other women. Only when she ceases always to come at his bidding, and a chance remark of Cottard first implants in his mind the idea that she may be attracted towards her own sex, does he begin to suffer deeply on her account. Then, at their subsequent meeting, he treats her with harshness; pretends that it is with Andrée that he is in love, and tries to wring from her a confession of Sapphic tastes. In vain Albertine protests that such ideas revolt her. Remembering all the stories he has heard of Odette and Swann, Marcel refuses to be convinced. Feeling, now, that she can never reciprocate the love which he begins to feel for her, he decides that he should leave the place at once and never set eyes on her again. But an affectionate reconciliation temporarily soothes his doubts. Henceforward they spend together, sometimes alone and sometimes with the rest of the little band, many long sun-drenched afternoons. But the more their intimacy delights him, the more his jealousy revives, and he regards with despair any woman in the vicinity who gives the impression of being attracted to her.

At La Raspelière, the villa near Balbec that she has rented from the Marquise de Cambremer, Mme Verdurin is giving a series of her famous "Wednesdays". Through her partisanship of Dreyfus, her drawing-room has increased in importance, and, although it has not yet blossomed into its final period of splendour, is nevertheless rapidly becoming known as the "Temple of Music". One day, on his way to visit her with Albertine, whom, under the pretence of her being his cousin, Marcel now takes about with him everywhere, he meets, at a wayside station, M. de Charlus, who asks him to cross the line and summon on his behalf a young relation who is on the opposite platform. This proves to be a youthful and extremely handsome cadet named Morel, whom Marcel recognizes at once as being the son of an old servant of his uncle Adolphe. This young man, a brilliant violinist, is the most recent *protégé* of the "mistress" to whom, at her next "Wednesday," he introduces the Baron. The little clan, of whom Brichot, Saniette and Cottard are all still faithful members, has been increased, since the old days of Swann, by the Polish sculptor Ski and the Princesse Sherbatoff, an outcast from society, who is nevertheless considered the brightest star in the "mistress's" constellation. After so many years Brichot has grown more pedantic, more sententious, even, than of old; Cottard more futilely complacent, and Saniette more ridiculous and inept; while the "mistress" herself, slowly but steadily advancing to higher social spheres, is still a martyr to music and neuralgia.

Every day Marcel goes out with Albertine, driving with her in the motor-car he has hired for her pleasure, watching her while she sketches, visiting ancient churches or rustic inns, or taking her to see his friends. De Charlus, meanwhile, becomes inseparable from Morel. He takes him about with him whenever the lad is not on duty, and listens equally complacently to recitals of his depraved desires or to his ambitions as a musician, carefully educating his taste and lavishing upon him attentions of every kind.

Meanwhile Albertine shows such affectionate docility in their relationship, that Marcel's anxieties are by now completely calmed; though whenever he hears her make an engagement with someone else, no matter how bored he is becoming with her continual proximity, they immediately revive: nor will he leave her alone for a few moments even with Saint-Loup. Added to which, his mother's disapproval, by threatening the security of his attachment, makes it impossible for him to see his mistress less often.

By this time M. de Charlus also visits the Verdurins whenever possible, willingly sacrificing his insensate pride for the sake of sharing the company of his new *protégé* and complacently in ignorance that their relationship is obvious to the whole of the party. So enamoured has he grown, that he submits, from his favourite, to such insolence and humiliation that everyone is amazed by it. And when Morel, growing bored, refuses one day to go to him, the Baron, since by this device he hopes to assure himself of his company, goes even to the length of inventing the incredible fiction of fighting a duel to protect his *protégé's* good name.

Now that his jealousy is assuaged, Marcel decides that to marry Albertine would be madness; and soon after, when his mother proposes to spend a few days at Combray, he is glad to be able to assure her that he has decided to give the girl up.

But that same evening, on their return from the Verdurins, when he intends to break with her, Marcel begins by telling Albertine how tired he has become of these continual parties. He will go to the Verdurins once more, however, he says, since he wishes to elicit from Mme Verdurin some special details of a musician whose work interests him deeply. Albertine inquires the musician's name. "My dear child, when I tell you his name is Vinteuil, will you be any the wiser?" Marcel inquires with patronizing condescension. "How you amuse me," Albertine replies, and explains that she can herself get him all the information on that subject he requires, since one of her own friends has for years been the close friend of Vinteuil's daughter. Immediately Marcel remembers the scene when, as a small boy, he looked through the windows of the house at Montjouvain. At once he is convinced that Albertine must possess the tastes of which he has always suspected her. An agony of jealousy possesses him. Begging her to spend the night at the hotel, he assures his mother in the morning, before she leaves, that it is absolutely necessary to his happiness after all that he should marry Albertine with as little delay as possible.

THE CAPTIVE

His parents being away, Marcel now takes his mistress back with him to Paris, where her constant presence with him, and her separation from her friends, afford him some relief from his jealousy: but where, beginning once more to grow bored in her company, the thought of marriage becomes intolerable. Since he has to remain much in bed, he hires a car to take her for drives, and arranges for Andrée to escort her, so that he can find out exactly whom she meets and what she does during his absence, just as, in the old days, Swann used to get de Charlus to go out with Odette. Very soon Marcel's suspicions are aroused anew; so, for fear of losing Albertine, who had developed exquisite taste, he consults Mme de Guermantes as to the best furriers and dressmakers from whom to obtain the beautiful clothes he showers on her.

One day, on his way home, he encounters M. de Charlus with Morel on their way to tea with Jupien and his niece, the girl who is now received by certain rich and smart women of the middle class, being deeply in love with the violinist, to whom, indeed, under the Baron's patronage, she is betrothed.

Meanwhile Marcel continues to watch Albertine closely, always on the alert for signs that will disclose her weakness; while imperceptibly their intimacy deepens, until his feelings for her become almost conjugal. For just as, in childhood, he could never close his eyes before his mother had kissed him good night, so now it is necessary to his peace of mind to receive Albertine's last embrace before he can sleep. One day Albertine announces her intention of calling to-morrow on the Verdurins. Because her manner suggests a particular reason for desiring to do so, Marcel immediately fears some assignation, a possible meeting with Mlle Vinteuil, and makes her promise instead to go to a performance at the Trocadero. In the morning, lying in bed with her in his room, listening to the street criers below, now that she has given up her project it seems scarcely to matter to him what she does. But this indifference lasts only until a few hours later, when glancing through the papers, he sees that Léa, a woman notorious for her Sapphic tastes, is going to play at the theatre to which he has sent his mistress. At once he is in a turmoil, and his one anxiety is to get her to return to him without delay. He sends Françoise to fetch her immediately, who telephones from the theatre to say that she has found Albertine and that they will be back shortly. Immediately his fears are allayed. Albertine returns and Marcel takes her for a drive; but as usual, in spite of the charm of her companionship, he only feels now the limits which her presence sets to his freedom.

The same evening he decides to go to the Verdurins himself to see if he can discover whom Albertine intended to meet. On the way, he falls in with Brichot and M. de Charlus; and the latter never ceases to discuss, in a manner intended to be impersonal, his own peculiar desires and tastes. As soon as they arrive, Marcel realizes that it is a very special occasion; and later Morel plays the Vinteuil septet to an audience recruited specially by M. de Charlus from the highest society, from whom most of the "mistress's" own friends have been excluded, in order that nothing should dim the brilliance of his *protégé's* success. During the performance, as he listens to a phrase similar to that which has often enchanted Swann, it seems to Marcel that such a work of art must indeed correspond to some spiritual reality; though as soon as the music ceases, all his old doubts revive.

And now the great ladies who have condescended to visit Mme Verdurin only on account of their beloved Palamède, unwittingly bring about the Baron's downfall. Enraged by the haughty manner in which he has refused to allow her to invite even the most illustrious of her "clan" to meet the Faubourg St. Germain, and fearing that his ascendancy over Morel is becoming so strong as to imperil his presence, which is one of her greatest assets, in her drawing-room, she determines to effect a breach between them. This is precipitated by the insolence by which she is treated by her guests, who, invited by M. de Charlus, greet and take their leave of him, not only ignoring Mme Verdurin completely, but even making insulting remarks about her in her hearing. As a crowning humiliation, the Baron, while congratulating himself to her on the success of the party, informs her that the Duchesse de Duras has already engaged Morel to play at one of her forthcoming receptions, and, ignoring all reference to herself, that he will try even to obtain an invitation for M. Verdurin to be present.

This is the hour for the "mistress's" revenge. Determined that Morel shall play nowhere without her consent, she decides to make him choose between herself and M. de Charlus. M. Verdurin is instructed to take the violinist aside and explain to him the terrible scandal caused by his liaison with the Baron, while she herself aids in his enlightenment with venomous relish, informing him not only that he is the talk of the Conservatoire—the one thing calculated to wound him most deeply—but that the Baron has the vilest reputation, is received by nobody decent, and is even notorious with the police; while Morel himself is pointed out with derision by everyone in society, and his career as a musician is being ruined. She even invents the lie that the Baron always speaks of him insultingly among his friends, and has spread a rumour that he is no more than his servant.

Morel is so wild with rage and indignation that when M. de

Charlus enters with infatuated delight to congratulate him upon his wonderful success, the violinist insults him publicly; whereat the Baron, instead of pulverizing his *protégé* with one of his customary diatribes, is so stunned that he can scarcely speak.

In vain he seeks a reconciliation, and later when he is taken seriously ill, his prayers that this youth, on whom he has lavished so much affection, should be brought to visit him, are all unanswered. For Morel, having also broken off his engagement with Jupien's niece, is afraid to speak to him and even believes that, were he to do so, the Baron would murder him: a project, indeed, that at the height of his rage and despair, M. de Charlus had actually contemplated.

On his arrival home after this performance, Marcel becomes embroiled in one of his usual scenes with Albertine, in which lies on her side, and jealous subterfuges on his, reduce him to a state of nervous exhaustion. In his frenzied desire to wring from her the truth about her relations with Mlle Vinteuil, he learns only the pathetic fact that she has never even met her, but that since they had a distant acquaintance in common, and he appeared so absorbed in Vinteuil's music, Albertine had thought that, by inventing the friendship, she would consequently make herself more interesting in his eyes. Their quarrel continues. At last, in despair, Marcel pretends to his mistress that his feelings for her have changed and begs, in order that they may part as friends, that she will leave the house quietly the next morning before he wakes.

This request is a deliberate lie, uttered simply in order that Albertine may be abashed and that later he can effect a reconciliation without loss of dignity. Still he continues to wring from her confessions on matters about which, hitherto, she has always lied; and not until she seems overwhelmed at the prospect of leaving him does he make it up with her.

Henceforward Albertine never ceases to try to dispel his suspicions; yet in spite of a greater docility, he detects in her a restlessness, a latent dissatisfaction, that appals him with the thought of how unhappy she must really be, shut up in his flat with an invalid. In future he indulges her more than ever, buys her innumerable hats and dresses, starts her with a collection of antique silver, and talks even of giving her a motor-car.

So winter passes and spring comes. One evening while they are out driving, when Albertine seems more irritable and distracted than usual, Marcel is assailed anew by the desire to travel, to go to Venice, for all the freedom of action and contemplation of which Albertine's constant presence robs him. Presently she becomes morose, even abrupt in her answers, and at length he reproaches her bitterly for her lack of gratitude. Feeling that his words were cruel and unnecessary, he begs her to forgive him and explains that his violence was caused by the deep concern he feels at the stories people are continually telling him about her relations with Andrée. Albertine is both angry and indignant. For the first time Marcel cannot induce her to return with tenderness his goodnight kiss; and she remains aloof and cold with him the following day. Gradually, however, as her coolness disappears, his desire for Venice returns; and he awakes one morning determined to break with his mistress at last and to set off on his travels alone. But when, a little later, Françoise comes into his room, it is to tell him that she has already left.

THE SWEET CHEAT GONE

Albertine has gone. A moment ago he had imagined that he desired this separation. In anguish he realizes now that she is the one person in his whole life he cannot live without. At all costs he must get her back: even if it means giving her, in future, absolute freedom. If she wishes, he will even marry her. Immediately he must arrange matters so that she returns to him at once, but without her return seeming solicited by himself. He therefore persuades Saint-Loup to follow her to Touraine to her aunt's, to try to influence her secretly to come back. But Albertine sees through this deceit and writes to her lover to inquire why, if he wants her, he does not write to her himself, in which case she will be delighted to return. In reply he protests that he does not now wish her to do so. He had just reached a decision to marry her, and had even ordered her a yacht; but since she finds she cannot live happily with him, it is better for them to remain apart. Confident that this letter will bring her back, he awaits her answer through all the vicissitudes of hope and despair. When at last it arrives, it is charming, but resigned to his decision.

Marcel has failed again. His next move is to inform her that, since he cannot live alone, and does not wish her to be pained by hearing of it first from someone else, he has invited Andrée to come and stay with him. To this message he receives no reply. Anxiety and jealousy reach such a pitch that he contemplates taking his own life. At last, when he can bear his suffering no longer, forsaking all deceit, all pride, he telegraphs to Albertine begging her to return to him at once on any terms that will make her happy. But no sooner has this message been dispatched than he receives another from her aunt, to acquaint him of the tragic fact that Albertine has just been thrown from her horse and killed.

And now Marcel's whole life seems to be wrenched from his heart. A few minutes later he receives two letters in Albertine's own hand, that must have been written just before her fatal ride. One is a meek reply to his own: the second, a fervent request that she may be allowed to return to him without delay. His suffering, now, can only cease when each memory he holds of her in his heart shall be erased.

Henceforward the world is full of images, each of which, by association, brings him back inevitably to his appalling loss. He has now only one hope, that a day may dawn when he will forget her. All his terrible jealousy of her past, of all the incidents of her life that he could not share, revives again. If only he could see her but once to ascertain the truth. In desperation, he employs Aimé to go to Balbec, to Touraine, to make inquiries about her tastes; while himself he questions all her friends. But because of a thousand lies, a thousand doubts, a thousand fears, he never learns the truth. The essential questions: in her heart of hearts what was she? what were her thoughts? what her loves? remain for ever unanswered.

Time passes. Marcel's grief for Albertine, like his former grief for his grandmother, becomes intermittent. Attracted one day by a girl in the street who, with two companions, is calling on the Duchesse de Guermantes, he decided to visit his old friends in the hope of meeting her. In the Duchess's drawing-room, a few days later, he finds that the girl is none other than his first love, Gilberte, now Mlle de Forcheville, since Mme Swann has married again after her husband's death, and the daughter has taken her stepfather's name. Now at last, though she cruelly and persistently denied her old friend the pleasure of presenting his daughter to her before he died, the Duchess willingly receives her. For having been left a considerable fortune by an uncle, Gilberte is now generally considered to be an eligible heiress.

Months go by, and at last Marcel realizes his dream of going to Venice. Here, in a restaurant where his mother has invited Mme Sazerat, whom they have met unexpectedly, to dine, he is surprised to see the Marquise de Villeparisis and M. de Norpois on holiday together. When he informs his mother of the fact, Mme Sazerat becomes visibly agitated, and begs him to point them out to her. She explains that it was this woman who years ago, as the Duchesse d'Havré, first ruined her father and then deserted him; and since she herself in consequence has been forced all her life to live in a humble position at Combray, she must at least see the woman, wonderfully beautiful as she was said to be, who has been the evil genius of her life. But when Marcel points out Mme de Villeparisis to her, all Mme Sazerat beholds is a hump-backed, red-faced, hideous old woman; so that she can scarcely believe there is not some mistake.

A few days later, when Marcel returns to his hotel, he is handed the following telegram. "My dear, you think me dead, forgive me, I am quite alive, should like to see you, talk about marriage, when do you return? Love, Albertine." Amazed by the missive in his hand, he feels not the faintest spark of joy. Having become, with time, another person, a person to whom Albertine is now no more than a bundle of thoughts, she means to him at last less than nothing. As with his passionate love for Gilberte, time has done its work. So utterly dead, indeed, is all his past love, that in order to avoid having to take any action, he even pretends to the hall porter that the telegram has been delivered to the wrong person.

Only on his way back to Paris, while he is reading a letter from Gilberte, announcing her proposed marriage to his friend Saint-Loup, Marcel realizes that, owing to the mistakes caused by her extravagant calligraphy, the telegram he has recently received must have come from her. At the same time he learns of a second engagement. Mlle d'Oleron, Jupien's niece, upon whom this noble name has been bestowed by her adopted father, the Baron de Charlus, and who has long since been abandoned by Morel, is to marry the young Marquis de Cambremer. This beautiful and charming young girl, however, dying shortly after her marriage, leaves her young husband as a consolation to the Baron, whose tastes he shares.

Meanwhile, Gilberte has become Mme de Saint-Loup, and, in the same way as with Mme de Guermantes, now that Marcel no longer embarrasses her with excessive attentions, is delighted to renew their friendship. But her marriage, alas, has not proved happy. For Robert, following in the footsteps of his uncle, publicly compromises himself with a series of fashionable mistresses in order the better to cloak his secret passion for Morel, to whom he is now deeply attached; while Gilberte pathetically copies Rachel's style in every possible way, in order to win back the affections of her husband.

TIME REGAINED

By the middle of the War, Mme Verdurin and Mme Bontemps have become the Queens of Paris. Despite her husband's death, the "mistress" still entertains regularly, now at the Ritz, inviting people in to "talk about the war," a delight which is daily augmented by Morel's playing—over whom the "mistress" has still retained her ascendancy (and who, though no one knows it, is a deserter from the army)—and by superior jeers at Brichot's articles in the newspapers, which have at last become highly popular in society, though laughed at with merciless persistence among the "faithful." The other star of her drawing-room is now "in-the-soup," the young golfer of Marcel's first days at Balbec, now an author of distinction, who has married Andrée. It was with this young man, Marcel has since learnt, that the Verdurins were planning a marriage for Albertine, which was not improbably one of the chief causes of her leaving him.

Meanwhile Saint-Loup is at the front, where he is eventually killed in action; while his wife, leaving Paris with her small daughter to escape the Taube raids, arrives at Tansonville, her country house near Combray, where she remains for two years, convinced at last that she has only left the city in order to save her property from the invading enemy.

M. de Charlus, at the same time, continues to go about his pleasures. Having now reached, in regard to his vices, the lowest depths, he has established Jupien in possession of a brothel for people of tastes similar to his own, where he himself can now obtain satisfaction only by being chained and beaten.

While the war moves to its close, Marcel is confined in a sanatorium, and it is only later, when he returns to Paris and attends a party given by the Princesse de Guermantes—the late Mme Verdurin, who, after becoming, for two years, the Duchesse de Duras, has now, after the death of the Duke, married the Prince de Guermantes and so resigned herself to a life among terrible bores, that he notices the transformations which have taken place among the people who have been his friends.

He has just met outside M. de Charlus, who, convalescing from a stroke of apoplexy, and no longer in full possession of his wits, is watched over like a child by the attentive Jupien. Now he sees the Duchesse de Guermantes, fast withering despite her black lace dress and her famous jewels, bored with her own fame, and no longer even firmly ensconced upon the rock of social eminence to which she has clung for many years. Her former exclusiveness almost a legend, she now consorts with actresses and dancers, her greatest friend being Rachel, now celebrated, but become a horrible old woman. Here, too, is Gilberte, whom at first Marcel fails to recognize, a stout middle-aged woman growing daily more like her mother, who introduces to him her daughter, a young girl who unites for him in her person all the many threads woven into the two "ways" of his boyhood. Odette herself, whose cheeks seem to have been injected with paraffin to prevent them from sagging, presents the appearance of a courtesan of an earlier day who has been carefully embalmed; and, no less beautiful than of old, she is now the mistress of the Duc de Guermantes, who, ruined in health but still magnificent in appearance, spends all his time at her house. Legrandin, who has acquired a title, and Bloch, who has changed his name and his appearance, have now both attained position in the society they stormed for years in vain; while Morel is a most highly respected member of society, and scarcely anyone can remember a time when the position of all these men was not established. With such emphatic reminders before him of the passing of time, Marcel realizes that he has no more time to lose. Such of his life as remains to him must be devoted to the effort of creating a work in which all these people will appear, as they appear to him now, when he remembers the many different points of their lives at which he has known them, like so many monsters embalmed in Time.

CHAPTER II

SUCH, in its bare bones, and stripped of the "moral and metaphysical" aspects which we shall examine later, is the superficial outline of the plot of *À la Recherche du Temps Perdu*—superficial because the deep, persistent underlying meaning and intention of the book is to express the author's continual search for and temporary achievement of the reality which lies for him in the experience which he describes as the recapture of "lost time." Without being aware of these two main streams which, arising from the same source, are closely inter-related throughout the whole work until, finally, they once more coalesce, it is difficult for a long time, owing to its enormous length, its general diffuseness and its long digressions, to realize that the novel has any form at all.

But form it has: the inevitable and symmetrical form of an organic growth that can only attain its complete stature in the fullness of maturity. The passage of time, indeed, and the ceaseless changes that it works, is the most predominant and the most persistent of all Proust's themes. His chief problem was, not only by its means to illuminate, as with a searchlight, a whole series of phenomena of which, in the ordinary course of life, we remain completely unaware; but to emphasize these in such a way as to produce the emotional shock without which they cannot fully be realized.

Intellectually, of course, we are perfectly aware that men are born, grow old and die, and that everything in the universe is in a continual state of flux. But if we can repeat, with a parrot-like, impervious complacence, that it is the crassest folly to put our trust in princes, we nevertheless continue fatuously to believe that princehood is as abiding as the seven seas. We may accept with our mind the fact that time changes all things, but it seldom prevents us from considering every moment of the present immobile, and of accepting each phenomenon we encounter, each person we meet, as a completed figure rather than a cross-section of an extended body that must change its appearance as often as we perceive it from different points. We believe, irrationally but implicitly, in the immediate aspect of everything that strikes us at an impressionable moment, and so regard as for ever young the young faces we have known in youth, and for ever successful those noted figures who, at the very moment we have met them, may have suddenly plunged from obscurity into fame, or as well just reached the point where they are about to fade into oblivion.

Time is the necessary, and indeed the only, medium, in which we can examine and measure the changes which are taking place continually in the conditions which surround us. Through its agency alone we can observe the continual transformation which is as the flow of blood to those organisms we call the worlds of society, of politics or of art; just as it is through its agency that we must measure our own development, or the development of those who form part of our environment. But this we can only do by a simultaneous perception of two different points, when the interval between them can be felt by the emotions as clearly as it can be measured by the intelligence. It was this realization that caused Proust to extend the development of his novel over so huge a scale and to substitute his peculiar form of inner drama in place of the usual emotional tension created by external action.

But if we fail to perceive the ceaseless changes which time effects in the external world, we fail equally to realize that we ourselves are creatures of time, since we continually regard the future as an unbroken whole, and seldom admit that, being no more than the inevitable extension of the past, it can differ from the past but little. For the past is as much part of the future as the fingers are of the hand; and may be likened to a long and narrow tunnel, up and down which, by the aid of memory, man is for ever moving, only very rarely coming to rest for more than a few seconds at one point.

Having reached such conclusions, it became necessary for Proust to construct his novel in such a manner as would manifest the form of man in the dimension which traces the path of his life from birth to death, and so to illustrate that a character considered from one point bears only the partial and superficial relation to the whole man, as does one surface of a cube to the cube itself. His intention was to portray a psychology in time which would contain the same depth when compared with the conventional psychology of fiction, as does geometry in space to a theoretical plane geometry whose significance is purely formal.

Thus, in *À la Recherche du Temps Perdu*, the time dimension may be likened to the backbone of a skeleton whose ribs encompass the vast and intricate pictures of those characters who continually reappear in different relationships at the various receptions throughout the book, and who can be realized only through the whole series of evolutions which they perform, none of which, if studied separately, can illustrate more than one aspect of their being.

Each of these receptions, no matter how widely separated from the last, forms an integral part of Proust's manifestation of society in a state of disintegration, and affords him at the same time the means necessary to record the transformations which continually affect the individuals which compose its amorphous mass.

They appear, in the novel, arranged in the following order:

Mme Verdurin's "little clan" in the days when it was frequented by Swann.

The evening party at Mme de Saint-Euverte's when Swann first realizes the hopelessness of his passion for Odette.

INTRODUCTION TO PROUST

The drawing-room of Mme Swann in the days when Marcel frequents it and has decided no longer to see Gilberte.

The afternoon reception at Mme de Villeparisis', when Marcel is introduced by Robert de Saint-Loup to Mme de Guermantes; and the evening party in the same house when Mme de Guermantes first invites him to dinner with her.

The dinner party at Mme de Guermantes', where Marcel is first able to observe the smartest society of the Faubourg St. Germain.

The evening party at the Princesse de Guermantes', where Marcel observes M. de Charlus in the light of his newly acquired knowledge, and has a long conversation with Swann for the last time before his death.

The "Wednesdays" of Mme Verdurin at La Raspelière.

The concert at Mme Verdurin's, when she effects the rupture between M. de Charlus and Morel.

The final afternoon party at the Princesse de Guermantes' (late Mme Verdurin) during which Marcel becomes aware of the changes that time has wrought upon all his friends, receives new inspiration, and decides to set to work without delay upon his book.

By means of this series of groups, in which the individuals are continually changing their positions, like those of Hogarth in *The Rake's Progress* or *Mariage à la Mode*, Proust is able to show, and with an equal power, the unceasing and apparently minute alterations in the features and expressions of his various characters, which accompany the inner crystallization of the degeneration that is the reciprocal aspect of their outward evolution.

Having seen something of the drawing-rooms which Proust himself frequented, it is not difficult to guess from which sources he derived the material for the drawing-rooms in his book. Mme Verdurin's, for example, in its various transformations, has in it something of Mme Aubernon's and something of Mme Lemaire's, just as Mme de Guermantes' displays features both of Mme Strauss's and of Mme Greffulhe's; and the rise of Mme Swann as a social figure, caused indirectly through her always being at home in the late afternoon, and much helped by her staunch nationalism in the Dreyfus case, is strongly reminiscent of certain features in the career of Mme de Loynes. But in the same way that nearly all his major characters are synthetic, so also is the formation of his social groups. For if the "mistress" leading her conversation, and her "little clan," which when we first meet it, is for years composed, apart from Odette and a few "sacred monsters," almost entirely of men, suggests very clearly Mme Aubernon; so too do the "school of wit" and the theatrical performances which are the reputed stock in trade of that somewhat fallen queen, Mme de Villeparisis. And if Mme Verdurin's passion for music recalls Madeleine Lemaire, no less so do those flower paintings at which Mme de Villeparisis is usually at work when she receives her visitors.

Similarly, Bergotte's place in the house of Mme Swann is identical with that occupied in the home of Mme de Caillavet by Anatole France; though when, later, Mme Swann's drawing-room undergoes an unexpected transformation, and from being filled with the most prosy women such as Mmes Cottard, Bontemps and Trombert, it becomes, shortly prior to its invasion by a bevy of social queens, frequented by some of the smartest men in Paris, it is quite possible that, as earlier with Odette's chrysanthemums and her Dresden china, despite Proust's very natural denials, he really had in mind the environment of Mme Laure Hayman. Much of the stately etiquette at the receptions of the Princesse de Guermantes, together with the long gallery around which the newcomers are guided by the older habitués, is copied from those of the Princesse Mathilde, just as the latter's stupid maid of honour is to be found, at Mme de Guermantes' dinner party, attendant upon the Princesse de Parme.

Such similarities, however, while interesting from the point of view of discovering how a writer first collects and then transforms his material, are of no great importance in themselves. The significance of these pictures of social life lies in their implicit satire, which is doubly mordant by reason of its subtlety and serene detachment. The Marcel of the novel but seldom obtrudes himself into his observations. He merely watches and records, and frequently omits to give the reader even the quiver of an eyelid lest he should miss the point.

But the study of these drawing-rooms offered the author far more than any comedy of manners. It was the supreme means by which ultimately he was to understand the most deeply implanted frailties and follies that govern human nature. The Proustian world of society is like a form of scum at the surface of the social structure, and composed of innumerable small particles in an incessant motion of rise and fall. Its artificial, alluring face, its famous and historic names wrapped in all the mysterious splendour of a distant past, the magnificent brilliance of its receptions and its balls—all these may well seduce the imagination of aspiring youth: but let him penetrate but a little closer below the surface, and how soon will he find himself confronted with all the features of another Sodom and Gomorrah. Yet its nullity, its vanity, its callousness and its amorality are as profitable to the moralist as are any of the prophetic books of Israel.

From his earliest youth, people who could not "feel what was good" were Proust's greatest aversion; and his book shows very clearly how, throughout the whole of his life, this attitude could have undergone no change.

The figures in Proust's society nearly all typify and illustrate such great fundamental psychological laws as are formulated by Pascal and La Rochefoucauld. They are driven by vanity, lust, self-love and the incessant necessity for diversion. Their whole scale of values—as, in many cases, is their sexuality—is inverted; and they spend the whole of their lives spinning on a fixed point in a process of inner decomposition, while under the flattering illusion that they are steadily climbing upward. The form of their universe is purely chimerical, and their snobbery just as futile as that of the fatuous barrister and his cronies who patronize the Grand Hotel at Balbec. None of them ever realizes—just as Marcel does not realize until he sees the two "ways" of his childhood united in Gilberte's daughter—that the segments into which we slice up life are purely arbitrary, and correspond not to any aspect of life itself, but only to the deficient vision through which we perceive it. The separate worlds of Mme Verdurin, Mme Swann and Mme de Guermantes are essentially the same world, and it is only a vain eclecticism that has ever separated them. They are the same world, not because Mme Verdurin finally marries the Prince de Guermantes, Swann's daughter eventually marries Mme de Guermantes' nephew, and Odette herself crowns her career by becoming M. de Guermantes' mistress, but because each of them moves in an orbit formed by a similar superficiality of being.

With all their apparent differences, and the wide separation in their origins (Mme Swann came almost from the gutter, Mme Verdurin from a wealthy family of the middle class and Mme de Guermantes from one of the most princely houses of France) essentially the three women are the same, and it is therefore inevitable that, in time, their apparently quite separate paths should converge. Human beings, with the same capacity as water, are destined to find their natural level: and what difference can there be between a Mme Verdurin who for years professes all society people to be bores, while steadily aspiring to join their ranks on the first possible occasion, and a Mme de Guermantes who for a like period, prides herself on her smartness in not permitting Swann's wife and daughter to bow to her, but who receives Gilberte immediately after the girl becomes an eligible heiress?

Indeed, the ambitions and desires of nearly all Proust's

characters would be ludicrous were they not, by reason of their very triviality, so essentially tragic.

Thus, for example, the young Mme de Cambremer. Legrandin's sister, and infected with the same snobbery, she manages, through her large fortune, to marry into a provincial but aristocratic family that for some time she imagines fondly to be one of the most eminent in France. Very soon after she has achieved her title, however, she ceases to be convinced that her new connections are sufficiently illustrious. She is furious with her mother-in-law for condescending to be friendly with any one whose rank she considers inferior to their own, and longs passionately to be received into the more exalted milieu of the Guermantes. When, at the theatre, she sees the Duchess and her cousin in their box, she is unable to tear her eyes from their faces, fascinated the more that for the last ten years she has been assiduously cultivating their acquaintance without success. Attacked by some inexorable disease, her one great fear is that she may die before her ambition can be realized. At last, when she has reached the stage when she can seldom leave her house, the Duchess begins to leave cards on her. Such people as the Verdurins now become far too inferior to be accepted with anything but the most obvious condescension. When she deigns to visit Mme Verdurin at the seaside—but only because she is her tenant—she arrives with the air "haughty and morose, of a great lady whose castle, owing to a state of war, is occupied by the enemy, but who nevertheless feels at home and makes a great point of showing the enemy that they are intruding." The literary and musical pretensions for which she is noted are based on much the same species of snobbery as is her social climbing, and when Morel, out of mischief, plays for her Meyerbeer instead of Debussy, like everyone else she does not know the difference. This, however, does not prevent Mme de Guermantes, after further long years of siege, finding evidence in her of great intelligence and culture.

But as soon as the Duchess begins to visit her frequently, all the charm which Mme de Cambremer has seen in her for so many years vanishes immediately, and she continues to receive her only as an act of politeness. Such is the satisfaction afforded by the realization of an ambition that has endured over half a lifetime and been pursued with an unerring zeal!

Or take as another example of futility, Mme de Gallardon, who lives only to proclaim from the housetops her kinship with her famous Guermantes cousins; who can neither think nor speak of anything that does not serve somehow to publish their relationship; yet whom the smartest of them will scarcely deign even to acknowledge! Or Mme de Saint-Euverte, who is so passionately anxious to maintain the position of her drawing-room (which, although it figures largely in the social columns of the Press and is visited, though only as an act of supreme condescension, by some of the smartest women, nevertheless is among the last in Paris) that she will pretend willingly not to have heard the most public and humiliating tirades of M. de Charlus, if only he can be persuaded to grace her next reception.

Or the Turkish ambassadress, another woman who divides her energies between an insatiable social ambition and the facile assimilation of unnecessary knowledge, and whose desire to appear socially successful is so overweening that, before she has been summoned to the Princesse de Guermantes' house, she goes to the most exaggerated lengths to conceal her admiration of that lady solely for fear lest her absence from her famous receptions should be attributed to the true fact that she has never received an invitation, rather than to the desirable assumption that she herself makes a practice of declining them.

Even at Oriane de Guermantes' exclusive dinners, the platitudes and inanities that have mysteriously acquired the reputation of brilliant conversation differ very little from those exchanged by the Mmes Cottard and Bontemps at Mme Swann's, save in the fact that they are of a more pretentious order. Indeed, despite the loftiness of their reputation, not only are the Guermantes and their set the epitome of stupidity, but very many of them lack even the saving grace of good manners. When, at the reception of the original Princesse de Guermantes, Mme d'Arpagon gets soaked to the skin by a jet of water from a fountain, the group of people near her greet the disaster with derisive laughter. And at the party arranged for Morel by M. de Charlus at the Verdurins', the insolence of the famous ladies who obey their beloved Palamède by honouring the "mistress" with their presence, would never be suffered by any of the well-bred middle-class women to whom they feel themselves so immensely superior. "Show me which is mother Verdurin; do you think I need speak to her? I do hope, at least, that she won't put my name in the paper to-morrow, nobody would ever speak to me again!" one of them says, perfectly well aware that her hostess can hear every word; while another inquires equally loudly, "Tell me, has there ever been a M. Verdurin?"

When they are not unpardonably ill-mannered, Proust's ladies of illustrious rank proclaim themselves by phrases of an equally futile and excessive cordiality. Such are the words, "She thinks you charming" which inevitably come, for Marcel, to signalize the species Royalty. He hears them first from Mme de Villeparisis after she has presented his grandmother and himself to the Princesse de Luxembourg, who, fatuously condescending, buys chocolates and cakes from the hawkers on the beach at Balbec to give to him to offer to his grandmother, for all the world as if they were animals in a cage. He hears it again, whispered in his ear by the Duc de Guermantes, just after he has been presented for the first time to the Princesse de Parme—that effusively amiable, and condescending lady who, "a scion of the noblest race, and endowed with the greatest fortune in the world (for, a daughter of the Prince de Parme, she had married a cousin of equal princelihood), sought always, in gratitude to her creator, to testify to her neighbour, however poor or lowly he might be, that she did not look down on him."

The whole machinery of the social sphere, together with the psychological laws that form its motive power, its pistons and its wheels, is revealed down to the minutest cog. It is not only external details that Proust describes—though this he does superbly—the way his people smile, the way they bow, the way they shake hands, their innumerable little tricks and oddities of speech and the fashion in which the men wear their monocles or the women dress their hair—but the peculiar inner foibles or justifications that produce their special species of snobbery. Thus Legrandin need never admit to himself that he is a snob, since he is always convinced that the duchesses he runs after lure him because of their beauty, their intelligence and their culture rather than by any peculiar eminence of their social position. M. de Bréauté, on the other hand, suffers from so different and inverted a species of snobbery that the general opinion is that he is quite the least snobbish person in society. "So that his reputation as an intellectual might survive his worldly success ... he would set out with ladies of fashion on long scientific expeditions at the height of the dancing season, and when a woman who was a snob, and consequently still without any definite position, began to go everywhere, he would put a savage obstinacy into his refusal to know her."

The complacency of the Verdurins is maintained by a completely different form of self-deception. In the La Raspelière days, the queen of their "little clan" is a *déclassé* Russian princess whom no one in society will accept. This drawback, however, is soon overcome by a form of mutual deception, so that, on the one hand, the Verdurins are able successfully to convince themselves that they are the only people that the Princesse Sherbatoff visits, not because theirs is the one drawing-room that is open to her, but because it is the only one that she finds amusing, while she reciprocates by adopting wholeheartedly the old fiction that the Verdurins really find the aristocracy insufferably boring and only make an exception in favour of herself on account of her remarkable intelligence.

In such a world it is not surprising to find that spontaneous good feeling has almost completely ceased to exist. When the Princesse Sherbatoff dies, although she and Mme Verdurin have been inseparable for years, the "mistress" announces, as a justification for not putting off one of her parties, that she simply cannot be a hypocrite, she never really liked the woman, and so she cannot now be expected to mourn her loss. While many of the formidable old dames who visit Mme de Villeparisis, like the famous "poacher in the wood" at Mme de Caillavet's, do so quite frankly in order to ferret out any new addition to her drawing-room that might prove welcome in their own.

But if there are hostesses who strive to consolidate their social position by enticing away the new "discoveries" of their rivals, there are equally those who pursue the same object by excluding their "dearest" friends. Such is Mme de Mortemart, who, having wilfully omitted to invite one to her latest party, greets her thus the following evening: "Dear Edith, I am so sorry about you, I did not really expect you last night, as I know that you are not very fond of parties of that sort which rather bore you. We should have been greatly honoured, all the same, by your company.... You know that you are always at home in our house; however, you were quite right, as it was a complete failure, like everything else that is got up at a moment's notice."

The abashed Edith, in this instance, is left speechless. But Mme de Villeparisis in similar circumstances is more than a match for her adversary. "My dear, speaking of Mme de Luynes reminds me of Yolande," one of her old rivals remarks to her at her afternoon "at home." "She came to see me yesterday evening, and if I had known you weren't engaged I'd have sent round to ask you to come. Mme Ristori turned up by chance, and recited some poems by Queen Carmen Sylva in the author's presence: it was too beautiful."

"I had no engagement," Mme de Villeparisis replies, "but I should not have come. I heard Ristori in her great days, she's a mere wreck now. Besides, I detest Carmen Sylva's poetry. Ristori came here once. The Duchess of Aosta brought her, to recite a canto of Dante's *Inferno*. In that sort of thing she's incomparable."

Of such is the fabric of social intercourse: and the dry humour and suave irony with which Proust describes it are superb. When he essays to reveal the more far-reaching social machinations, though his eye still remains detached, his tone assumes a slightly more acid inflection.

Typical of his most telling sketches in the comedy of manners is the episode of the Prince von Faffenheim-Munsterburg-Weinigen in pursuit of election as a Corresponding Member to the Academy of Moral and Political Sciences. Why this gentleman of grandiloquent name and elevated diplomatic position should be consumed with so ardent a desire for membership it would be a little difficult to explain. He is, however; and to his immense chagrin can count on support from no more than five members of that highly exclusive society. Aware, however, that M. de Norpois, whom he had known in Russia when at the same time they had both been the ambassadors of their respective countries, has considerable influence in this direction, he sets out to enlist his aid by endeavouring to place him under an obligation for which he can discreetly claim the payment of some reciprocal service. It is in vain, however, that he obtains for the Marquis certain high Russian decorations, and quotes his name with the most glowing enthusiasm in his articles on foreign politics. M. de Norpois remains sympathetic but non-committal. The Prince, therefore, surpasses himself in his efforts and arranges for his friend to receive the Cordon of St. Andrew: but again with no satisfactory result. Indefatigable, he embarks upon a series of further flattering references to his colleague in a new essay on foreign affairs for the *Revue des Deux Mondes*; but still he is aware that this will aid him but little in furthering his own cause. At last, acquainted with the Marquis's liaison with Mme de Villeparisis, and doubtless aware of that lady's somewhat declining position in the social scale, he plays his highest card. Informing M. de Norpois that his wife is planning a series of dinner parties for guests no less exalted than the King and Queen of England, he begs his colleague to use his influence to secure the presence of the Marquise at these humble festivities. Only then the Prince is aware that he has won the trick: for the Marquis, with suitable tact and diplomacy, assures him that even at the moment he is already fighting on his behalf.

Or consider the two brilliant marriages of convenience. With what triumph Mme de Cambremer-Legrandin must have assisted in sending out those invitations encrusted with the names of the most noble families of the aristocracy, which announced the marriage of her son to Mlle d'Oleron, the adopted daughter of the inimitable, the exclusive and the magnificent M. de Charlus! Of how much was she aware of her future daughter-in-law's origins? And even had she known that the girl's brilliant Guermantes title scarcely concealed the little dressmaker who had been deserted by Morel and had been ennobled by M. de Charlus partly out of spite for his late *protégé*, and partly on account of the unique role her uncle played in pandering to his depraved tastes; would it very much have dimmed her satisfaction in thus attaining the dizzy heights for which she had so often longed?

Probably no more so than Gilberte's Jewish blood counted against her when Mme de Marsantes decided to pursue this most desirable of heiresses for her son. Though notoriously anti-Semitic, and, much to Robert's disgust, professing the opinion that it would be shocking for Dreyfus to obtain a pardon even were he entirely innocent, Mme de Marsantes cannot resist the lure of Gilberte's enormous fortune. On this account she goes about loudly proclaiming Mlle de Forcheville's virtues, and declaring how charming a wife she would make for even the most exacting young man. So great is her enthusiasm that it gives the game away to one of her rivals, who, desiring the rich prize for her own son, is loud in proclaiming what a terrible misalliance it would be were Robert de Saint-Loup to marry a Swann. Temporarily abashed, Mme de Marsantes therefore determines to console herself with the second heiress on the marriage market; although, alas, her dowry is but a quarter of Gilberte's. It transpires, however, that this young woman has just been snapped up: so, overcoming her scruples, Mme de Marsantes makes Mlle de Forcheville a definite offer on behalf of her son, and announces their engagement before there can be any further chance of losing the desired quarry.

Such are the ways and ambitions of the Guermantes and their circle—those illustrious Guermantes with their noble and romantic ancestors of whom Marcel used to dream so often as a boy, completely convinced of their greatness and chivalry and scarcely daring to hope that he would ever have the good fortune to meet them face to face!

CHAPTER III

THE characters of *À la Recherche du Temps Perdu* are built up, over a long period of years, in a series of impressions which are gradually consolidated until at last they stand out clearly with all the depth, the coherence and the innumerable unexpected inconsistencies of living models. Complex, wilful and, like us all, composed of a mass of incomprehensible contradictions, they are each of them formed, not only of gestures, mannerisms and idiosyncrasies of speech of a generality that places them in the category of a representative type; but of individual features so faithfully copied from living models, that although they are most of them composite figures, they attain at last an undeniable reality of their own, which is increased in certain cases by the fact that Proust has intentionally projected upon them various features which he could have known only from the deliberate study of himself. To quote his own words, "The man of genius can give birth to works which will not die, only by creating an image, not of the man he is, but of the examples of humanity that he carries within himself."

This extraordinary verisimilitude is again heightened by the manner in which each character is studied continually through different eyes. As, in any given circumstance, we can see only one aspect of a creature whose complexities are as manifold as the facets of a diamond, it is necessary to examine each person in many different positions and from many different points of view. We know Bergotte and his work, not only through the impressions that Marcel forms of him but through the various and accumulated impressions of Bloch, Dr. du Boulbon, Swann, M. de Norpois, Mme de Guermantes and several more; and de Charlus through those of

INTRODUCTION TO PROUST

Saint-Loup, Marcel's grandmother, the Verdurins, the Duchesse and the Princesse de Guermantes, Morel, Jupien's niece, Brichot, Swann, and a host of others. Thus when Marcel's grandmother first sees Jupien, she is astonished that, despite the humbleness of his position, he has all the airs of refinement and breeding of a man of education; while years later he appears to Marcel as a brothel-keeper who caters only for the most degenerate tastes.

In the same way, Mme Swann, in whose figure, to Marcel's youthful eyes, all feminine elegance and beauty are personified, is to his mother no more than a notorious woman of doubtful morals whom she does not care to know: while the Marquise de Villeparisis, before either of them has got to know her, looks like a "shabby old pew opener" or an "old trot," according to whether she is seen through the eyes of Odette or of Marcel. Furthermore, it is made admirably clear how all these subjective impressions are in a state of continual flux, as, for example, in the case of Swann, who praises or derides Mme Verdurin as the result of her favouring or hindering his liaison with Odette.

This method is applied to most of the principal characters in turn: and if, at one dinner, much space is given to M. de Norpois discussing the Swanns, at a following party there follows a complementary passage in which the Swanns pass judgment on M. de Norpois—a device by means of which there can be shown not only the various external aspects that contribute to the formation of personality but the many subjective factors which contribute to the formation of opinion.

It is fortunate that it is possible for us to study the extraordinary thought and care with which Proust assembled the material for his book, and then built up each detail of background or of character. From his correspondence we find that the famous "little phrase" in the Vinteuil sonata was carefully composed from separate bars of a sonata by Saint-Saëns, a prelude of Wagner, a sonata by César Franck and a ballade by Fauré. From various other indications in his own books and letters, and from our knowledge of his circle, it is quite possible to trace a similar method of formation in other aspects of his work, especially in those cases where a person or a name had impressed itself with unusual distinction upon his imagination.

The name Guermantes itself was taken from a château in Seine-et-Marne which belonged to the Comte de Paris, and was built, probably, by Paulin Prondre de Guermantes at the beginning of the eighteenth century; while the description of the mansion of the Princesse de Guermantes was derived from a book on the seventeenth-century mansions of Caen and Louvre. Many of the place-names are but slightly altered from the names of real places in another part of the country—as Balbec was obviously suggested by Bolbec—just as some of the more individual Christian names and diminutives were suggested by such unusual originals as Auriane,[1] the Gothic surname of the much-vaunted Montesquiou ancestors; Boson,[1] a Christian name of the Talleyrand family, and Gégé,[1] the intimate diminutive of Comte Joseph Primoli, a cousin of the Princesse Mathilde.

Returning to the characters, in a similar manner it can be discerned that Swann was built up from a combination of features, some of which were derived from Charles Haas, a friend of Montesquiou whose portrait exists in a group by Tissot in which, on the balcony of the Rue Royale club, he is depicted surrounded by Gallifet, Edmond de Polignac and Saint-Meurice, and some of whose traits must have been so faithfully copied, that Mme Strauss always used to refer to Proust's hero as Swann-Haas; from Charles Ephrussi, the curator of the library of the *Gazette des Beaux Arts*, with whom the author was well acquainted, and whose taste he much admired; and from the uncle with whom he used to

---

[1] From which came, of course, Oriane, Basin and the diminutives Mémé and Grigri.

stay so often, in his youth, at Auteuil, and who seems to have shared his own early admiration of Mme Laure Hayman.

We know, too, that Oriane de Guermantes' famous wit was modelled almost exclusively upon that of Mme Strauss, just as her beauty, her taste in clothes, her manner of dressing her hair, and various features of her character, were derived from, among others, the Comtesse Greffuhle and the Comtesse Adheaume de Chevigné: that several features in Mme Swann were derived from Closmenil and Mme Hayman: that the appearance and manners of Saint-Loup were suggested by Bertrand de Fénelon, besides various other of Proust's aristocratic friends: that Robert's affair with Rachel was based on the liaison of one of his friends with Louisa de Mornand: that much of Mme de Villeparisis' conversation was derived from that of Mme de Beaulaincourt, and that the style and good looks of the Duc de Guermantes were drawn from the Comte d'Hausonville, as the famous Courvoisier bow was copied from that gentleman's wife.

Even M. de Charlus, probably the most closely observed of all Proust's characters, becomes finally considerably more than a simple portrait of Montesquiou; just as Elstir is more than a portrait of Monet, or Bergotte of France, both of whom can be dimly discerned, though no more than Ruskin, or even Proust himself, in the novelist and the painter in whose work is synthesized the literary and artistic activity of the period.

Undoubtedly there are traces of de la Fosse in Morel, if no more than in the great beauty expressed in each of their faces while they are playing: and the famous rupture between the violinist and his patron was based, as we know, upon a very similar episode in life. But it would be erroneous to suppose that Morel is a portrait of the pianist, as it would be to imagine that Mme Verdurin is a portrait of Mme Aubernon or Mme Lemaire, or Mme Swann a portrait either of Mme de Caillavet or Mme de Loynes.

Certainly the characters in Proust's work are limited to such types as he himself was able to meet and study: but within this range they are as varied as they are numerous. Doctors, diplomats, professors, waiters and Jews, of all conditions are described as minutely and as succinctly as duchesses and princes; and the activities of the servants' hall serve just as much for literary material as does the life of the drawing-rooms above.

Indeed, the chief reason why the novel continues to hold the attention despite its colossal length and the triviality of so many of its characters is that each of these, irrespective of all standards of moral judgment, is portrayed with so great a wealth of accuracy, insight and humour that not for a moment can his authenticity be doubted; and his affairs, in consequence, command exactly the same interest as would those of some extraordinary new acquaintance who, though we may cordially dislike him, arouses in us none the less an inordinate and unquenchable curiosity.

There is a very significant story that one day Proust was taken by a friend to consult a celebrated palmist. Having given only the most cursory glance at the author's face and hands, the man is said to have remarked: "Why do *you* come to consult *me*? It is for you, rather, to tell me my character."

To Proust art meant the incessant sacrifice of sentiment to truth, and never, with any of his characters, would he allow himself to deviate in the slightest from the stern principle of his own formulation. When *À l'Ombre des Jeunes Filles en Fleur* was first published, several ardent admirers of Swann lamented to the author that he had now made his hero look almost ridiculous. Proust replied that of course he himself hated Swann to look ridiculous, and that, far more, he would prefer not to have to make him die; but that he was in no way free to go against truth and to veil the laws of character.

This, no doubt, was the predominant reason why he would

never attempt to introduce into his work any character with whom he was not utterly familiar. And for this reason, if it is unnecessary to stress the author's Jewish blood, it is also impossible to ignore it. With any man of the calibre of Proust, each fact of his heredity and environment is bound to impress itself eventually upon the features of his work. And just as, despite his great love of English literature and the many influences he derived from it, much of his novel would have been materially different had he been born English instead of French, so too, indubitably, although such speculations are always largely futile, but for the family circle of Auteuil and his many Jewish and half-Jewish friends, the choice of his characters must have been more limited. For in the same way that his long conversations with his father upon medicine, and his acquaintance with many of the Professor's friends, enabled him later to express a knowledge and a familiarity both with doctors and with medicine that otherwise must have been less complete, so his intimate knowledge of Jewish life and character made it possible for him to create a Swann, a Bloch, a Nissim Bernard and a Rachel in a manner which portrays, with all the power of a deep understanding, the intelligence, the culture, the talent, the breadth of mind and the warmth of heart so peculiarly blended with stupidity, vulgarity and ostentation in the different strata of that race.

With a different background, he could never have understood Bloch's own anti-Semitism, the revolt of the ambitious and intelligent but ill-bred young Jew from the vulgar and undistinguished section of the community to which he belongs, and from which, despite his almost reverent affection for his very mediocre father, he intends to disassociate himself completely as soon as possible; just as he could never have understood Swann's complicated reactions during the Dreyfus case, when, although he continues still to play a certain part in the life of the Faubourg St. Germain, he nevertheless reverts to an atavism which proves to be more powerful than any of the qualities he has assimilated.

But most of all he could never otherwise have understood the deep and abiding loneliness and separateness of the Jew, even when he is most successful and most courted: a tragic isolation which Proust likens to that of the invert, and which is caused, not by any essential difference in his nature, but by the lamentable fact that no matter how vast his wealth, how lofty his position, how great his talent or how blameless his life, he can never be sure that to-morrow he will not become a victim to the lowest forms of hysteria, malice and brutality of which human rabble is capable, or that even his most intimate friends will not eventually turn against him when it becomes more convenient for them to disclaim him than to face an antagonism that might ultimately include themselves.

Undoubtedly, too, Proust's passionate interest in the Dreyfus case was caused no less by his profound conviction of the prisoner's innocence than by the quite unmerited ostracism and vituperation which he saw directed against some of his Jewish acquaintances, and, possibly, even against certain members of his own family. In any case, this *cause célèbre* which played so great a part in the politics of the period of his young manhood, plays an equally important role in the panorama of social life unfolded in his novel: although, in the necessities of art, all his old ardent partisanship has given way to complete impartiality.

But here again he has utilized his subject to illustrate with dexterous skill, the completely irrelevant and transitory factors which serve to form both private and public opinion, and the impermanent quality of the successive criteria which dictate the standards and the habits of the fashionable world.

With the first wild outburst after Dreyfus's indictment, the Faubourg St. Germain, with very few exceptions, becomes almost militantly nationalist and anti-Semitic; but though this continues, in some cases, even after the prisoner is rehabilitated, it evaporates immediately some other crisis, such as the Great War, supplies new motive power for reactions; when Dreyfusism, no longer execrable, passes into a respectable oblivion, much in the way that a notable pacifist, while hysterically decried during a war, may become a highly respected figure soon after a decisive victory.

In nearly every case, it is manifest how the reasons which dictate either Dreyfusism or its opposite are the effects of completely subjective and ephemeral causes. Saint-Loup is violently Dreyfusard, to the intense disapproval of all his family, for as long as he remains in love with Rachel, who is a fervent intellectual; but when he no longer loves her, his former enthusiasm gives place to an almost complete indifference. The Duc de Guermantes, on the other hand, is intensely nationalist until he is charmed by a lady whose opinions are directly contrary to his own, when his views undergo a violent reaction, and he promptly espouses the cause of the revisionists. As this fact is largely the cause of his being defeated in the next presidential election of the Jockey Club, he promptly changes his tune again, to the extent of declaring publicly that all the Jews should have been driven out of France. And if the Prince and Princesse de Guermantes become secret Dreyfusards because they believe sincerely in the prisoner's innocence, Swann and Bloch support the cause very largely on account of their heredity; and Mme Verdurin simply because of her pretensions to intelligence and her avowed aversion from society; while Morel expresses the most bitter anti-Semitism for the very revealing reason that, through the help of Bloch, he has borrowed money from M. Nissim Bernard which he has not the slightest intention of repaying.

And now, having obtained some idea of their derivations

and the environment in which they move, let us turn our attention to some of the characters themselves.

Swann, who towers over the first half of the work, dies some considerable time before the end, when his predominant position is taken by his old friend M. de Charlus. The son of a wealthy Jewish stockbroker, with a distinguished and elegant bearing, his refinement, his good breeding, his style, his cultivated and genuine love of art and letters, together with his keen and ironic sense of humour and an extreme modesty, have combined to win for him an unassailable position in the highest society. While Marcel's family believe that the "princesses" he visits are in reality ladies of a very different order, he is indeed courted by the whole of the Faubourg St. Germain, and for years has been the greatest friend of the Princesse des Laumes.[1]

We see him first as the good country neighbour, walking over from his country estate of Tansonville to dine or to spend an evening with his old friends at Combray: giving them receipts for unusual dishes, sending Marcel photographs from Italy, or, to his great aunts, wine; and so reticent of his position in society that none of them have the remotest conception of his importance. We see him at the reception of Mme de Saint-Euverte, walking up the grand staircase with its splendid array of footmen in knee-breeches and powdered wigs, greeted by his old friends, capping the sallies of the Princesse des Laumes, introducing the young Mme de Cambremer to General de Froberville, listening to the Vinteuil sonata, and brooding over his unhappy love for Odette. We see him at the Verdurins, where, until he is cast forth, he is quite prepared to deceive himself into believing that, so long as she favours his affairs with Mme de Crécy, Mme Verdurin is a woman with the keenest intelligence and the warmest heart. We see him through every successive stage of his love affair, and we see him as Odette's husband, when, long after he has

[1] Oriane, who later becomes the Duchesse de Guermantes.

ceased to love her, he still takes a certain uxorious pride in her elegance, and makes frantic efforts on account of his daughter, to establish her in some sort of society. But as none of his old friends will receive his wife, he is forced to curry favour with every sort of vulgar mediocrity. Hence his abrupt transition from the distinguished gentleman who would gracefully refrain from mentioning his friendship with the Comte de Paris or the Prince of Wales, to the apparently senseless snob who, with a complacency as pathetic as it is ridiculous, embarrasses all his visitors with detailed accounts of all the nonentities who have received his wife.

It is now that, owing to his long intimacy with fashionable society and despite all his culture, Swann begins to find himself completely anchorless. Having assimilated all the superficial scepticism, the lack of belief in all ultimate standards, of the finished man of fashion, he drifts vaguely and hopelessly with no abiding place in any world. Maintaining a desultory friendship with his own circle, who still refuse to acknowledge his wife, and whom he can only visit alone; bored and out of place among the people who are beginning to cultivate Odette, the one great passion of his life is now his daughter, whom he ardently desires should be received by his own friends, and most of all by the Duchesse de Guermantes, who refuses persistently to grant him this satisfaction.

During the period of the Dreyfus case, his position becomes increasingly unfortunate. Firmly convinced of the victim's innocence, and fiercely partisan, he is distressed no less by the attitude of his friends than by that of his wife, who, despite his Jewish origin, is rapidly advancing in the social scale by reason of her nationalistic views. In vain he protests to her, even in public, for openly soliciting the friendship of notorious anti-Semites; the very unusualness of such admonitions merely seems to invest his wife with some mysterious interest and procure for her the reputation of being thoroughly "sound."

At the reception of the Princesse de Guermantes, where Swann appears for the last time, signs of the mortal illness of which he is soon to die are already evident in his face. Here, however, he has the pleasure of learning that both the Prince and the Princess, each in secret so as not to wound the feelings of the other, are praying for Dreyfus's release; though he doubts that he can live long enough to see either of the two things that would give him any great satisfaction—Dreyfus rehabilitated and Picquart made a colonel. At the same time, tempering his own convictions with those of the man of the world, Swann refrains from signing all petitions for a retrial, and, since he has no wish to be mixed up in the anti-militarist campaign, even wears his old military decorations.

But despite the fact that he has been "very fond of life and very fond of art," he dies, alas, disillusioned and disappointed before either of his two great desires can be granted, though both of them are fulfilled comparatively soon after his death.

The origins of Odette were very different from those of her second husband. Emerging, in her girlhood, from a somewhat dubious life with an Englishman at Nice, to whom her own mother was said to have sold her, we are offered only the vaguest glimpses into her early life; and she appears first in the book as the beautiful lady in pink, whom Marcel when still a child meets at his uncle Adolphe's; and who already, with her pearls, her anglicisms and her cigarettes from a Grand Duke, presents to his young eyes a picture of feminine charm and refinement far too gracious to belong to a woman "of that sort," even of the highest type. Married first to an old nobleman whom she ruins and then abandons, she takes a series of lovers, until eventually she is patronized by the Verdurins, where she is for long referred to by the enthusiastic "mistress" as her "little piece of perfection" and soon becomes one of the most faithful of the little clan.

She was first introduced to Swann by M. de Charlus, who, having met her after some theatrical performance in which she had played the part of Miss Sacropant—as which character, incidentally, she was shortly afterwards painted by Elstir—had taken her home to his flat, and was only too anxious to avoid her persistent advances by palming her off upon his friend. From the first she is one of those shallow and sentimental women who love to associate with people who talk about beauty, art, literature and the rest; and, since she herself is completely lacking in all discrimination and intelligence, is invariably impressed by pretentiousness, and appreciates superficial chatter about such things far more than any real acquaintance with them.

Swann, who has all the tastes that she professes to admire, when once she is assured of his protection, leaves her completely cold, simply because he very rarely speaks of them. Nevertheless, when once she is married to him, and, having ceased to love her, he no longer suffers on account of her unfaithfulness, she does not necessarily make him a bad wife. Having lived together already for so long, and being acquainted with each other's most trivial tastes and inclinations, they remain attached to each other by many ties of indulgent affection, and a thousand little habits with which each of them has grown thoroughly familiar. While Mme Swann, at last unhampered by lack of means, is able to create for herself a completely new style of beauty, so that for many years the variety, the elegance and the simplicity of her clothes, together with the splendid ease and distinguished grace with which she wears them, make her one of the most notable and admired figures of the Allée des Acacias.

Good-natured, alluring, superstitious and futilely ambitious, she is determined to emulate the "mistress" and to form a drawing-room of her own. At first she meets with but little success, and her visitors consist merely of married men whose wives invariably happen to be too ill to accompany them, of members of the mediocre bureaucracy so assiduously beguiled by the now fatuous Swann, and of a few of the old circle from Mme Verdurin's. With the latter herself, since Swann still professes to find her odious, there has been a definite schism, the two ladies now paying each other formal calls only about once a year. Indeed, the situation when Mme Swann sets herself to lure from Mme Verdurin some of her most faithful, and goes even so far as to picture herself as a sort of modern Lespinasse taking from the contemporary Mme du Deffand several of her most attractive men, is almost parallel to that which arose between Mme Aubernon and Mme de Caillavet after the defection of Anatole France.

With the growing fame of Bergotte, who is still a constant visitor to the Swanns', the importance of Odette's drawing-room begins, slowly but steadily, to increase. Equipped with various little phrases which have come to her, through her husband, from the highest society; with an artistic jargon and the trick of "ejaculating" her phrases and "leading" the conversation, which she has acquired from Mme Verdurin, added to the fact that it is with her a religious law always to be at home to receive visitors at exactly the same hour late every afternoon; she gradually rises—partly owing to the growing admiration for Bergotte, who, though dying, has suddenly plunged almost from obscurity to an unbounded popularity, but largely through her position in several of the most exclusive anti-Semitic women's leagues into which she has managed to get herself admitted during the nationalist campaign—to receiving, first, some of the smarter intellectuals of the Faubourg St. Germain, who consider it fashionable to include so literary a hostess among their acquaintances; then, some of their more adventurous women friends, until, by the time her daughter is left an enormous fortune, thus bringing in the most stiff-necked in acknowledging Odette, there flock to her receptions many of the royalties and duchesses that even the most established hostesses find difficulty in enticing to their houses.

When her husband dies, to everyone's immense astonishment, Mme Swann mourns him for months with the greatest sincerity; and to the end of her days she continues to say of him, "Poor Charles, he was so intelligent, so seductive—exactly the sort of man I like." But this does not prevent her, shortly afterwards, from marrying that old lover and Swann's rival—the Comte de Forcheville.

With her daughter's marriage, some time later, to Robert de Saint-Loup, Odette's drawing-room at last becomes firmly established as one of the most brilliant in Paris, and long after she is widowed once more, she continues to maintain her traditional reputation for elegance and luxury by supporting her waning beauty with a series of magnificent jewels given her by her son-in-law out of gratitude for her services in persuading Gilberte to keep him plentifully supplied with money.

Her fame and position reach their peak when finally she becomes the mistress of the Duc de Guermantes, who serves her much in the capacity of a second Bergotte, by acting as a bait to lure towards her certain arch snobs who still would not have visited her without so irresistible an attraction.

Her beauty, however, serves her longer than her intellect; and at last, decayed and broken, she can no longer refrain from muttering aloud her inmost thoughts and feelings, so that, among her daughter's acquaintances, she earns for herself the reputation of being slightly off her head.

Neither riches nor environment nor social position have the power to change Odette's essential nature, and, the eternal whore, she takes the same part, in but slightly different scenes, until the end of her days when at last she is too feeble to play it any longer.

While Odette slowly rises from obscurity to social eminence so too by a completely different channel does Mme Verdurin.

From the first moment that we meet her, in the "mistress's" life there is but one ambition, one goal, one worship and one god—her "little clan," its welfare and its inviolability. For this all human feelings are ignored, all weaknesses forgiven—but only on condition that in no way will they lessen the adoration of the faithful. Yet despite all her self-deception, Mme Verdurin rises to social celebrity only indirectly through her own actions. In the days when Swann and Odette are of her circle, the very idea of society is anathema. What she desires and what she cultivates is a small nucleus of regular visitors, composed of no matter what mediocrities, so long as one or two of them have recognized aspirations towards the arts, over whom she can queen it unrivalled with all the dictatorial condescension of a benevolent patron. Measuring all things and all men by but one standard, the great virtue in her eyes is to be found in him whose conduct or career may help her to consolidate her position, as the greatest vice resides in him who may serve to weaken it.

Swann was excommunicated less on account of the heresy of his basic principles, than because of the danger that he might lure away Mme Verdurin's "little piece of perfection"; just as Elstir was allegedly dismissed because he did not invariably prove willing to lead the whole of his domestic life in public. The schism between Morel and de Charlus was effected not because Mme Verdurin had the slightest objection to the Baron's tastes, which, as she frequently averred, could hardly compromise *her*, but because she feared that ultimately he would lessen her own influence over the violinist, and thus imperil the homogeneity of the drawing-room that she valued as her life.

For similar reasons, on two separate occasions Mme Verdurin separates Brichot from his loves: and long after he has broken with Albertine, Marcel discovers that the "mistress" was planning a marriage for her with a young connection of her husband.

Mme Verdurin, as professedly republican as Mme Aubernon, and as hostile in principle to the presence at her evenings of pretty women, gives but few large parties; and when she does so, these, as with Mme Strauss, are alleged to be for the sole purpose of working off such "bores" as she is obliged to entertain. Instead, like Mme de Loynes, she has weekly dinners for her faithful, unparalleled in the fineness of the cooking and the magnificence of the appointments, at which each of her guests is treated with the same distinction as is Bergotte at Mme Swann's. Her drawing-room, like Madeleine Lemaire's, gradually becomes known as the "Temple of Music": and although the "mistress" has a genuine love of art, she is not above burying her face against the Princesse Sherbatoff's shoulder whenever a piece is being played, a gesture which serves the treble purpose of proclaiming her veneration for Vinteuil, displaying her affection for her friend, and concealing the somewhat distressing fact that during such performances she is prone frequently to drop off to sleep.

Habitually treating the unfortunate Saniette, with the collaboration of her husband, to the most cruel and unnecessary insolence, she nevertheless invariably melts towards him before he takes his leave, if only to make certain that he will not fail at her next evening. So anxious is she to attract new visitors to her house, that she endeavours to foster the competitive spirit in introducing their friends, amongst even her most recent guests. "You don't know little Mme de Longpont," Mme Verdurin remarks to Marcel on one of his visits to La Raspelière. "She is charming and so witty, not in the least a snob you will find, you will like her immensely. And she's going to bring a whole troupe of friends too.... We shall see which has the most influence, and brings the most people, Barbe de Longpont or you."

At the beginning of the Dreyfus case, Mme Verdurin follows the fashion and begins by professing the most virulent anti-Semitism. With the rise of the intellectuals, however, she begins to change her policy, and her drawing-room becomes an active centre for the revisionists. This *volte-face* serves her well by attracting new writers to her evenings, on account of their politics; and people go to her house after dinner to meet Picquart or Labori, just as, in actual fact, they used to meet at M. Charpentier's. During Zola's trial, indeed, Mme Verdurin is to be seen in court each day at the side of the novelist's wife: yet even this does not yet serve to further her secret social aspirations.

For while Mme Swann is steadily climbing on the ladder of nationalism, such few society women as call on Mme Verdurin are far too timid to fly in the face of fashionable opinion by acknowledging her in public. Her ascent is soon to begin, however, with the advent of the Russian Ballet. Then, seated night after night at her side in the stage box of the Princess Yourbeletieff, who has sponsored this magnificent blossoming of talent, she at last becomes known, if only by sight, to the society with whom the dancers have achieved their phenomenal success.

Henceforward she advances at an increasingly rapid pace. The number of "bores" in society begins to undergo a progressive diminution; and as, one by one, they begin to make advances to her, so Mme Verdurin suddenly becomes convinced both of their intelligence and their charm.

Neither death nor war must interfere with her famous evenings, and at the beginning of 1915, when men are very difficult to get, the exhortations that Mme Verdurin adopts to persuade them to go to her receptions are characteristic. "Sorrow is felt in the heart," she would say to some young man who had just lost his mother. "If you were to go to a ball, I should be the first to advise you not to, but here at my little Wednesdays, or in a box at the theatre, no one can be shocked. . . ."

Even as the Princesse de Guermantes, the "mistress"

remains true to her old ideals. If her milieu has changed, she herself remains the same, fairy godmother to artistic cliques and coteries to the last: and the final words we hear her utter are—"That's it, we'll form a group. I love the intelligence of youth, it so co-operates...."

Having ultimately arrived in society, however, both Mme Verdurin and Mme de Forcheville speak as if they had been there all their lives. "Verdurin? Oh yes, of course," says Odette, when she first hears the name mentioned in the Faubourg St. Germain: "I don't really know them, or rather, I know them without really knowing them, they are people I used to meet at other people's houses, years ago; they are quite nice.... Yes, I do seem to have heard a lot about them lately. Every now and then there are new people who arrive like that in society...." While the new Princesse de Guermantes might well have been born a scion of that illustrious family, according to her customary remarks upon Gilberte. "That's no new relationship for me," she broadcasts, "I knew the young woman's mother very well: why, she was my cousin Marsantes' great friend. It was at my house she met Gilberte's father. As to poor Saint-Loup, I used to know all his family, his uncle was once an intimate friend of mine at La Raspelière...."

And doubtless both ladies were able to persuade themselves that every word they uttered was completely true!

If the social graphs of Odette and the second Princesse de Guermantes describe ascending curves, that of the famous Oriane de Guermantes represents a descent to meet them. The Duchesse de Guermantes, even so, for years represents the highest peak of exclusive and fashionable society. Born into one of the most aristocratic families of Europe, Mme de Guermantes passed much of her early youth in the country, in an environment of deep culture which, years afterwards, made it possible for her to acquire the reputation, among other things, of being deeply intelligent, by the expedient device of quoting from time to time appropriate verses from Hugo or Lamartine that she had been forced to commit to memory in the schoolroom.

Having married, while very young, her fabulously wealthy and equally aristocratic cousin, the Prince des Laumes, she stepped almost at once into the position of queen of the most brilliant and, incidentally, the most futile society of the Faubourg St. Germain, among which she was courted alike for her beauty, her intelligence (presumably remarkable in this country of the blind) and most of all for her supreme gift of the Guermantes wit, which she always maintains is as extinct as the dodo in every member of the family save herself.

What Mme de Guermantes does possess, outstandingly, is the gift of acting, with discreet persistence, in the capacity of publicity agent for Mme de Guermantes. When she adopts an attitude of extreme modesty, such as she affects when, as an act of supreme condescension, she consents to put in an appearance for a few minutes at Mme de Saint-Euverte's (a woman whom she despises so heartily that years afterwards she asserts most vigorously that she has never even known her), it is only in order to create an effect, and certainly does not prevent her from looking down upon all her neighbours with her customary disdain: just as when she bursts frequently into peals of laughter, she does so deliberately in the belief that it both increases her beauty and advertises her wit.

Beautiful, elegant, with great taste and simplicity of dress; superficial, pretentious, inordinately vain and, in her own way, as great a snob as the most insignificant social climber, she manages nevertheless, for the greater part of her life, to retain her extraordinary reputation of possessing exactly the reverse of these latter qualities.

Although she always professes to have the deepest affection

for her "precious Charles" who, indeed, has been one of her most intimate friends for many years, this does not prevent her from boasting with inane self-satisfaction that she is one of the few people in society who have refused consistently to allow his wife and daughter to bow to her; or from publicly avoiding him during the Dreyfus case, with the most mean and petty cowardice, despite the unassailability of her position, for fear lest her friendship for him might in some way compromise her.

"It is quite true, I have no reason to conceal the fact that I did feel a sincere affection for Charles," Mme de Guermantes is wont to exclaim hypocritically whenever her husband inveighs publicly against Swann's Dreyfusism. And when, after his death, she consents at last, for a variety of reasons, to receive his daughter, she adopts the habit of referring to him with a no less patronizing duplicity. "I know quite well who he was, let me tell you," she informs Gilberte, speaking thus about the man whom the whole of society is well aware used to be her greatest friend: "He was a great friend of my mother-in-law, and besides, he was very intimate with my brother-in-law, Palamède."

Such wanton deceit, however, is one of the most persistent features of the Duchess's character; and desiring to appear to the world as a woman of unusual kindness of heart, she will make great public parade of consideration for her servants, while at the same time forcing upon them the most trivial and unnecessary occupations simply in order to prevent them from gratifying the innocuous pleasure of meeting their sweethearts.

Her reputation for possessing good taste is no less spurious than her reputation for intelligence and benevolence; but as she follows the fashions slightly less closely than the rest of her circle, it becomes a matter for great comment and admiration. It is true that she was one of the first women in so exalted a social position to buy Elstir's paintings: but then, she did so only on the advice of Swann, and always professes to dislike his work, until it becomes famous; when she immediately protests that from the first she has been one of his greatest admirers. Until his reputation becomes firmly established, the portrait that Elstir painted of her is referred to in public alternatively as "a ghastly thing" or "quite good" simply according to whether her friends happen to mention it or she wishes to acquaint them of its existence.

Similarly vacillating is her professed taste for furniture of the Empire style. At the period of Mme de Saint-Euverte's party, she roundly declares it to be horrible, devastating and smug: interesting historically, perhaps, but only suitable to be relegated to the attics. Years later, when, at the dinner party at which Marcel is present, the Princesse de Parme affects to be ravished by one of her Empire pieces, Mme de Guermantes pretends that she has always adored the style, even when it was not in fashion; and for some years exordiums on its merits form part of her public repertoire. During the War, however, she has changed her mind again and vehemently declares how greatly she has always detested it.

Having acquired the reputation, also, for great originality and daring, and for soundly despising the sheeplike stupidity of society, the Duchess frequently makes a point of staggering the whole of the Faubourg St. Germain by refusing to honour with her presence some ministerial ball which it is taken for granted she will attend; or by going away for a cruise in the height of the season when all the most exclusive people are striving desperately to get her to go to their houses. But at the same time she often desires passionately to know some woman whom she confidently pronounces to be charming, for no other reason than that the said lady has displayed not the slightest inclination to be introduced to her.

Even Mme de Guermantes' famous wit is not always devoid of insolence, and in her later years it develops into a sort of feeble plagiarism of herself. At its best, however, it is both apt and succinct, and as we know from the author, illustrates many of the famous sayings of Mme Strauss.[1]

"People do say of your M. Swann that he is not the sort of man you can have in the house. Is that true?" she is once asked by some pushing lady. "Why, you of all people should know that it is true," Oriane replies, "for you must have asked him a hundred times, and he's never been to your house once."

"What, were there no famous authors there? You astonish me!" she cries on another occasion. "Why, I saw all sorts of impossible people."

In the days before Mme de Guermantes has discovered Mme de Cambremer's intellectual charms, and delights in holding that lady up to ridicule, the latter is likened to a "great gramnivorous creature" sent to call upon her by the Duke. "She stayed a solid hour: I thought I should go mad" the Duchess declares to her enraptured audience. "But I began by thinking it was she who was mad when I saw a person I didn't know come browsing into the room looking exactly like a cow. . . ." Embroidering this theme in response to an appreciation it is a little difficult not to consider somewhat excessive, she concludes characteristically: "But this massed attack had been prepared for by long-range artillery fire, according to all the rules of war. For I don't know how long before, I was bombarded with her cards; I used to find them lying all over the house like prospectuses. I couldn't think what they were supposed to be advertising. You saw nothing in the house but "Marquis and Marquise de Cambremer," with some address or other which I've forgotten; you may be quite sure nothing will ever take me there."

Sometimes too, Mme de Guermantes has greatness thrust upon her, and there is an amusing story, of dubious authen-

[1] "All that is witty in this book comes from you," Proust wrote to Mme Strauss, when he sent her one of the first copies of *Le Côté de Guermantes*.

ticity, told of her, that the young Hereditary Duke of Luxembourg had once said to her: "I expect everyone to get up when my wife passes," to which she replied, completely ignoring the fact that the lady was always considered the very pattern of propriety: "Get up when your wife passes, do they? Well, that's a change from her grandmother's day. She expected the gentlemen to lie down."

Bored in time by her own fame, and desirous of making her life more interesting, the Duchess gradually begins to cultivate the society of actresses and music-hall stars, until she slips slowly from her old peak of social supremacy, and eventually the smart young women of succeeding generations are astonished if ever they learn of her former unique position. At last, querulous, exhausted, slightly *déclassée*, just as, in the old days, was her aunt Mme de Villeparisis, she is exiled from her own estate of Guermantes, where Mme de Forcheville has been firmly established as its mistress by the Duke.

The Duc de Guermantes used to be unfaithful to his wife from the earliest days of their married life. And though for many years one of his favourite gratifications is to bask in the reflected glory of her reputation, he never appears to consider her as anything save a suitable appanage of his own pre-eminent position. One of the premier dukes of France, and inordinately rich, his thin veneer of breeding and refinement is scarcely sufficient to conceal the colossal vanity and self-esteem that is rarely restrained from expressing itself to his social inferiors by means of the most insolent, the most wounding and the most unnecessary insults. As ignorant as he is stupid, like Mme Aubernon he keeps a book filled with aphorisms that he habitually consults before dinner parties, and later trots out with much complacence whenever a suitable opportunity occurs: and his suave and noble good looks mask his essential and trivial vulgarity as little as his affected cordiality conceals his innate and over-weening self-satisfaction.

Exhibiting his wife in public with an assiduous zeal, he treats her in private with a brutal callousness that is exceeded only by his persistent inconstancy. Though when appearing at her side in company, he faithfully prepares the audience to receive her latest witticisms, which, only after continual requests, she consents to repeat; or else never ceases to punctuate all conversation upon the nobility with his favourite interjection, "But she's Oriane's cousin"; he behaves to her, when they are alone, with a tyrannical meanness that serves him ultimately as a form of moral blackmail. For by withholding money from her whenever she refuses to accede to his wishes, the Duke compels her to receive, one after another, the mistresses he is constantly replacing, and then encourages her publicly to humiliate them as soon as he has found yet a new one.

Even the presence of death has no power either to subdue the Duc de Guermantes' sense of self-importance or to prevent the gratification of his desires. When Marcel's grandmother lies dying, and his august neighbour calls ostensibly to offer his condolences, the one object in that gentleman's mind seems to be the determination to show his condescension by shaking hands, and getting himself introduced to everyone, no matter how inconvenient may be these inappropriate attentions. On another occasion, when they bring the Duke news of a cousin's death just as he is about to taste the delights of a masked ball where he hopes to meet his latest mistress, "They exaggerate," he cries to the relations who come to announce the tragedy; and sends for his carriage before they can make him give up his adventure.

"I can tell you that his conduct towards ourselves has been beyond words," he tells General de Froberville, when they are on the subject of Swann's Dreyfusism. "Introduced into society in the past by ourselves and the Duc de Chartres, they tell me that now he is openly a Dreyfusard. I should never have believed it of him, an epicure, a man of practical judgment, a collector who goes in for old books, a member of the Jockey; a man who enjoys the respect of all who know him, who knows all the good addresses and used to send us the best port wine you could wish to drink, a dilettante, the father of a family. Oh! I have been greatly deceived. I do not complain for myself, I am only an old fool whose opinion counts for nothing, mere rag tag and bobtail; but if only for Oriane's sake, he ought to have openly disavowed the Jews and the partisans of the man Dreyfus."

Even when, at last, old and ill, he is reduced by suffering to the ruins of his former self, the Duke continues to humiliate his wife, whom now he treats in public with all the savage cruelty that formerly he at least attempted to conceal.

The Duke's brother, the Baron de Charlus, at once the most complex, the most powerful and essentially the most tragic figure in the book, both equals and exceeds the extraordinary personage who served in so many aspects as his model. An intimate friend of Swann, on whose behalf many for years he used to escort Odette everywhere, while aiding her, at the same time, to deceive her lover with several different men, he dominates the book from the first pages of *Sodome et Gomorrhe*. Affecting, in his prime, an excessive virility in complete contradiction to his real nature, he would express the most bitter disgust at the faintest shadow of effeminacy, just as, later, he used to attempt to mask his true inclinations by an exaggerated admiration of the most fashionable beauties of the day. His passion for exclusiveness surpasses that of even the most proud members of his own family, and for years he practises the most insolent snobbery as a fine art, priding himself with a savage satisfaction upon the huge number of people in society that he will never permit to be introduced to him. Thus, having obtained from his earliest youth an almost legendary reputation both for smartness and good taste, he lords it over the fashionable world with the same rigorous passion as Montesquiou.

The first time that Marcel meets him at Balbec, the Baron quotes the most charming passages of La Bruyère, and displays a sensibility so unusual in a man that Marcel's grandmother is both astonished and delighted. As he exchanges this manner, when he sees Marcel later, for a strange attitude which rapidly alternates between an aggressive insolence and the most sympathetic consideration, Marcel is deeply puzzled as to his character; until, long afterwards, he witnesses the Baron's extraordinary meeting with Jupien, and is amazed by the unusual likeness of his face when in repose, despite all his much vaunted masculinity, to that of a woman. Only then he realizes that "M. de Charlus not only looked like a woman, he was one. He belonged to that race of beings, less paradoxical than they appear, whose ideal is manly because their temperament is feminine, and who in their life resemble only in appearance the rest of men; there where each of us carries, inscribed in those eyes through which he beholds everything in the universe, a human outline on the surface of the pupil, for them it is not that of a nymph but of a youth."

As a young man, indeed, the Baron used to devote most of his leisure to such artistic pursuits as painting fans or composing pieces for the piano, until the realization of his inmost desires caused him to substitute externally for such methods of self expression everything that he considered to be most their opposite, and he adopted a rigorous leaning to such Spartan activities as long cross-country tramps, and bathing in ice-cold streams.

Studiously conservative in his manner of dress, but displaying, nevertheless, in the superlative taste devoted to the most trivial details, signs of the fine discrimination that he endeavours all but to conceal; his physical appearance, at once magnificent and repellent, seems eternally to suggest the mystery and tragedy of an enigma which separates him from the rest of his sex and is no less a malady than a misfortune.

Only slightly less witty than Montesquiou, M. de Charlus shares all that gentleman's ferocious and delirious pride, both in the pre-eminence of his social position and in his illustrious ancestry; and with the same propensity for feuds and quarrels, his invective frequently reaches a pitch of maniacal fury which is quite fantastic.

"I can see that you know no more about flowers than you do about styles," he cries to Marcel, on his first visit, with a shrill scream of rage, when the young man chooses a seat other than the precise one that has been offered him. "You can't even tell me what you are sitting on. You offer your hindquarters to a Directory Chauffeuse as to a Louis XIV bergère. One of these days you'll be mistaking Mme de Villeparisis' knees for the seat of the rear, and a fine mess you'll make of things then...." And later, when he has worked himself up into one of his incomprehensible passions, "Do you suppose that it is within your power to insult me? You evidently are not aware to whom you are speaking. Do you imagine that the envenomed spittle of five hundred little gentlemen of your type, heaped one upon the other, would succeed in slobbering so much as the tips of my august toes?"

This incredible insolence, expressed with his unique and characteristic venom, is used unsparingly at the slightest provocation. His invective against Bloch's parents, and the Jews in general, reaches a pitch of macabre and demoniacal fury which is nothing less than an expression of lunacy. While at the reception of the Princesse de Guermantes, where Mme de Saint-Euverte is busy enticing possible guests to her own forthcoming party, the Baron has no hesitation in relieving himself of one of his repulsive diatribes against her almost under her very nose. "Would you believe it, this impertinent young man asked me just now, without any sign of the modesty that makes us keep such expeditions private, if I was going to Mme de Saint-Euverte's; which is to say, I suppose, if I was suffering from the colic. I should endeavour in any case to relieve myself in some more comfortable place than the house of a person who, if my memory serves me, was celebrating her centenary when first I began to go about town, though not, of course, to her house. And yet who could be more interesting to listen to? What a host of historic memories, seen and lived through in the days of the first Empire and Restoration, and secret history too, which would certainly have nothing of the 'saint' about it, but must have been decidedly 'verdant' if we are to judge by the amount of kick still left in the old trot's shanks. What would prevent me from questioning her about these passionate times would be my olfactory organ. The proximity of the lady is enough. I say to myself at once: Oh, good lord, someone has broken the lid of my cesspool, when it is simply the Marquise opening her mouth to emit some invitation. And you can understand that if I had the misfortune to go to her house, the cesspool would be magnified into a formidable sewage cart. She bears a mystic name, though, which has always made me think with jubilation, although she has long since passed the date of her jubilee, of that stupid line of poetry called deliquescent: 'Ah, green, how green my soul was on that day. . . .' But I require a cleaner sort of verdure. They tell me the indefatigable old street-walker gives garden parties, I should describe them as invitations to explore the sewers. . . ."

Such excesses of vituperation are poured out with equal relish upon enemies, relations or former friends: and the Comtesse Molé, whom for years the Baron has escorted everywhere in public, just as formerly he used to escort Odette, never, at receptions, leaving her side for a single moment, is treated, finally, to a series of the most vile and scandalous diatribes, which he gets Morel to publish anonymously, about her morals.

The whole course of M. de Charlus's degeneration is painted with a dispassionate power in which pity, mystery and terror are extraordinarily blended. His conversation, in which formerly the faintest references to his own particular vice was always rigorously suppressed, becomes more and more imbued with remarks which cannot fail to reveal his habits, until, ostrich-like, he never ceases to discuss the subject of inversion, while optimistically believing that his acquaintances will remain convinced that his interest is purely theoretical.

His passion for Morel, an interlude between innumerable relations of a far lower order, gives place to the most perverse excesses; and at length, followed about in the streets by the blackmailing mendicants whom formerly he has stalked, it remains no longer possible for him to conceal the vice which, like some implacable disease, has by now corroded his entire being.

Even when he is struck down with blindness, nothing can prevent him from striving to find some means of satisfying his by now incorrigible tastes. But time lays low even M. de Charlus's pride, and at last we see the man who would not so much as rise from his seat to greet a Mme Cottard, no longer in possession of all his faculties, and bowing low, even to Mme de Saint-Euverte, with a tragic and assiduous deference.

The Prince de Guermantes, on the other hand, although addicted to much the same vices as M. de Charlus, is nevertheless a far greater gentleman than either of his cousins. Despite the antiquated rigidity of his aristocratic prejudices, and the stiff formality of his wife's receptions, which are replete with much of the boring etiquette of some minor Bavarian court, both of which, indeed, are a subject of open mockery to the Duke and Duchess, his reserved but simple manners are altogether devoid of the aggressive insolence of M. de Charlus, or the more subtly affected man-to-man condescension of the Duke.

The only other Guermantes man who has even normally good manners is Robert de Saint-Loup; and he, beneath the stiff and acquired formality with which he performs such conventional civilities as shaking hands, displays an innate and exceptional courtesy which is far more a matter of the heart than of any question of habit or imitation. So smart as to be almost daringly well dressed, strikingly handsome, with his fresh complexion, his blue eyes and his golden hair, Saint-Loup, in his youth, combines all the charm of good breeding with a passion for the things of the mind, which causes him to seek the company of intellectuals or even revolutionaries rather than any of the fashionable contemporaries of his own station. Drawn to Marcel chiefly on account of an inordinate admiration for his intelligence and culture, he loves to display these to his young companions on military service so that he can bask in a reflected glory: but though for a long time the friendship between them appears to be very close, it is essentially superficial if only by reason of the fact that Saint-Loup's love of letters, just as, later, his Dreyfusism, is largely the result of his relationship with Rachel, and very soon deserts him once he has ceased to be infatuated with her.

When, years later, Saint-Loup is married to Gilberte, who, once she has succeeded in getting the Faubourg St. Germain to accept her, promptly loses all interest in it and ceases to visit all those people whom, formerly, she has most desired to know, he willingly falls in with her taste for a quiet and comfortable life spent largely at home, and finds his greatest pleasures in secretly following in his uncle's footsteps.

To the end of his life, however, Saint-Loup retains a certain breadth of vision as a result of the principles he has imbibed in youth; and although, before he is killed in the war, he is decorated for bravery, he never ceases to praise the courage of the Germans or to view the conflict from that large and tolerant point of view which deplores the insanity of a narrow and excessive patriotism.

With the publication of *Le Côté de Guermantes*, Proust was accused from all sides of being a snob, presumably on account of the exalted social position of so many of the characters in the book, and Marcel's frankly expressed desire to meet them. To attribute snobbishness to any author for producing a gallery of such brilliant and comprehensive aristocratic portraits as those of the Guermantes is, of course, mere incompetent folly: while to continue to do so to Proust, now that his work can be assessed in its entirety, would be to show an incapacity for judgment exceeded only by a vulgar and irrelevant malice.

By now it should be more than obvious that the Guermantes simply served their author as literary material, and that the innate and futile stupidity of all their ideas and ambitions are no less persistently, because tacitly, compared with the more natural and wholesome standards of Marcel's mother and grandmother, who, even when they adhere most rigidly to the somewhat stiff and conventional outlook of their youth, have no hesitation in calling a prince of the blood common when he gives evidence of being so, or of finding signs of true nobility and breeding in the most unexpected quarters. For just as Proust found in his own mother an innate simplicity and goodness infinitely preferable to any brilliance to be discovered in the fashionable beauties to whom, before he knew them, distance had lent so powerful an enchantment, so Marcel's grandmother and mother, both of whom were largely drawn from Mme Proust, continually serve as foils, by their attitude and conduct, to the false values and the pretentious vanity of the women of the

Faubourg St. Germain. Only slightly distinguishable one from the other, since they resemble each other so closely in their almost deliberate self-effacement and the unobtrusive but whole-hearted devotion which they bestow unstintedly upon all those whom they love, these two women, the very archetype of the woman of worth lauded in the Proverbs, whose price is above rubies, embody all those qualities of true nobility and unspoiled virtue which, to the end of his life, Proust most admired. And in the huge desert of pretentiousness, stupidity and vice that the author set himself to portray, he alights upon the rare actions of simple goodness which occasionally reveal themselves to him, with all the spontaneous enthusiasm of a child.

In order to appreciate the impersonal but very deep interest that Proust had in all types of humanity, completely regardless of their position or their class, it is only necessary to consider the great space that is devoted to the servant Françoise, who is one of the most closely studied and finished portraits in the book.

Capable, faithful and conscientious, but with all the latent avarice and callousness of the peasant, from the beginning Françoise deliberately refuses to adopt with visitors any particular manner that might serve to ingratiate herself with them, since she is quite aware that she is far too well established with her mistress for her position to be undermined by any adverse criticism from without.

Intensely devoted to her own family, and determined by her own exertions to establish its fortunes upon a solid foundation of success, she will willingly force herself, at times of crisis, to the most unremitting labour, but less out of consideration for her employers than from fear of the fact that, with any additional help, she might at once run the risk of finding some worthless rival admitted too freely to the good opinion of her mistress; and even, at last, of usurping her own position.

When Marcel's "aunt" Leonie lives shut up in her one room at Combray, Françoise refuses to allow any other servant to enter her room for the purpose of performing even the most humble task; and in her last illness, so attached has she by now become to her, she refuses to leave her for a moment, until she is dead.

Although an excellent cook, and immeasurably proud of the fact that, as Marcel's mother pleasantly reports to her, M. de Norpois has glowingly referred to her as "a chef of the first order," Françoise is never too proud to perform the duties of a general maid; and is delighted to take advantage of her privileged position to convey to Marcel, when he is infatuated with the Duchesse de Guermantes, how all that lady's servants are talking about the way he is annoying her with his attentions.

Her private code of conventions is as implacable as that of the most aristocratic spinster. In the hotel at Balbec, where she begins by ringing the bell at all hours and for the most trifling reasons, she not only ceases to do so for herself, when once she has made friends with one of the kitchen staff, but, ever fearful of the possibility of disturbing her new acquaintance while at the servants' dinner, even refuses to do so at the request of her employers. And when, on another occasion, she leaves the hotel at the end of the season without saying good-bye to the housekeeper, she insists upon returning to the hotel, although thereby causing Marcel great inconvenience, in order not to show herself lacking in the performance of what she considers to be not only a necessary civility but even an unavoidable obligation.

With an extravagant respect for wealth, which she has come to regard almost as the external expression of inner virtue, Françoise is invariably afflicted with an insatiable curiosity regarding the amount of the tips which her employers give to others; and just as, at Combray, she used to be devoured with desire to know the value of the coins which her mistress every week used to press secretly into Eulalie's hands, so, many years later, when Marcel is grown up, no matter into what distant corner of the room he repairs when offering a tip, Françoise will always manage to find some trivial reason for approaching to perform her ill-disguised investigations.

Although she will never express herself in so many words, she takes a keen enjoyment in conveying to her employers her own knowledge and opinions of their activities, particularly if these are in any way derogatory; and she will not only read Marcel's correspondence almost as a matter of habit, but, in cases where he may have some particular cause for concealment, will even leave the offending letter in some conspicuous position in order that he shall not fail to be aware that she has done so.

When Marcel's grandmother is dying, Françoise looks after her with a characteristic devotion in which there is blended a callous stupidity and a morbid curiosity in her various symptoms that is not altogether devoid of cruelty. This almost stony indifference to human suffering near her, is opposed by a large and lachrymose pity for any tragedy sufficiently spectacular and remote to touch her imagination; and she will weep bitterly for such sorrows of the most distant strangers as, could she view them nearer, would leave her indifferent and unmoved. Insatiably curious, although she persistently refuses to acquaint herself with the usage of the telephone, or even to answer its ring, she will make a point of lingering about the room whenever a private conversation is in progress; and with great determination evolves an oblique yet infallible method for eliciting all such information that she dare not ask outright.

Her various characteristics and opinions, indeed, are no less individual than generic; and everyone who becomes acquainted with her will recognize her immediately as the embodiment of a universal type.

. . . . .

It is this peculiar blending of typical characteristics with purely individual features which gives so many of Proust's characters their extraordinary reality and significance; added to the fact that despite their many contradictions, they nevertheless retain in every case a substratum of consistency in all their actions. Nowhere throughout the whole of the book, is there a single man or woman who is but the personification of a phrase, a mood, an attitude, a virtue or a vice.

Frequently, it is true, by exhibiting the same traits in two or more characters, the author is able to illustrate the generality of certain psychological laws, as when Bloch and Andrée, not unlike the Turkish Ambassadress, at different periods both invent slanderous stories about certain people they imagine despise them, and then, when once they discover the contrary to be the case, immediately rush to the other extreme of loudly singing their praises. Similarly, M. Verdurin's chief function as husband is to protect his wife's "sensitiveness," just as the Duc de Guermantes' is to protect his wife's "generosity"—though in each case these qualities are purely fictitious. Yet Bloch and Andrée, as M. Verdurin and M. de Guermantes, are always quite distinct and separate personalities.

The Simonets, with their annoyance if anyone spells their name with a double N, and their pride in their single consonant as though it conferred on them some supreme distinction; Bloch's father, who "knows people without knowing them" and Andrée's mother who, because she is acquainted with certain people's names and addresses, calls this having "known them all her life," like Mme Swann and Mme Cottard discussing clothes, are all further manifestations of a purely general significance: but such foibles are seldom shown unallied to those complementary traits of individual character which correspond to them.

Thus Swann is capable of the greatest delicacy, as of the most obtuse vulgarity; and Mme de Guermantes callously refuses to use her influence to get her nephew, when he is in love with Rachel, brought back from Tunis, though when he dies, she weeps for him for a week. Similarly, the Verdurins habitually treat Saniette with the most unnecessary cruelty, yet when he loses all his money they endow him secretly with a modest income to support him for the remainder of his days; while M. de Charlus, a very monster of insolence and pride, mourns for his dead wife with a prolonged and genuine sorrow. Even Morel, who, despite his great talent and his extraordinary physical beauty, oscillates between bouts of neurasthenia and the most bestial depravity, is not without his moments of kindness; and though, one minute he is insulting his fiancée with callous ferocity, the next he is to be found sitting on the kerb of a neighbouring street weeping bitterly with remorse and self-disgust.

Indeed, none of Proust's characters, in the words of Mrs. Hushabye, have their "vices and virtues in sets." In the manner of all living "they have them anyhow, all mixed up."

CHAPTER IV

THROUGHOUT the whole of *À la Recherche du Temps Perdu*, interpenetrating the life of the drawing-rooms, reciprocally influencing and nourishing it, is depicted the world of art and its creators. Each of the major arts—literature, music, painting and the drama, is represented by the work and by the personality of, respectively, Bergotte, Vinteuil, Elstir and Berma. And despite, in most cases, the failure and the disappointment of their private lives, their contribution to the work in general and to Marcel's development in particular, is immense.

Bergotte himself, the Bergotte whom Marcel for years had pictured as a venerable and godlike old man with a head of snowy hair and infinite understanding, proves to be a somewhat pathetic creature, common looking, malicious and of evil reputation, who, despite the fine quality of his work and a small number of deeply enthusiastic admirers, attains but little popular success until he is almost dying, when he plays the lion for Mme Swann, at whose house he has been a distinguished guest for many years; and his sick room is invaded almost continuously by the new admirers that his latest works, vastly inferior to those which have gone before, have won for him.

Vinteuil, the composer, is even more unfortunate—indeed a man of music "grown grey with notes and nothing else to say." Poor and obscure until the hour of his death, the whole of his being which is not given to his compositions is devoted with a pathetic passion to his motherless daughter, the scandal of whose Sapphic attachments is said ultimately to have driven him to his grave.

While Berma, who has worn herself out by her ceaseless

devotion to the stage, becomes at last a moribund and embittered old woman, treated with almost inhuman indifference by the daughter she adores and for whose sake, in order to keep her well supplied with luxuries, she is killing herself by continuing to play the most arduous and exhausting parts long after she has lost the physical strength necessary to perform them.

But suffering, for Proust, is one of the first requirements—the inevitable nourishment—of the artist's life. For it is only when his whole being is in a state of agitation and many hidden springs of action are therefore flung to the surface, that he can experience, observe, study and understand fully those invariable laws which govern human life.

Elstir, of them all, alone has any real dignity as a human being: and he is one of the few fine characters in the book. Having spent the whole of his youth in artistic coteries, and been, for years, one of the most familiar intimates of the Verdurins, at whose evenings he used to contribute to the general entertainment, not only with impassioned harangues upon art, but by means of the most wildly embarrassing practical jokes, he breaks at last with his old friends, ostensibly because Mme Verdurin tries to separate him from his wife, but in reality because he has outgrown all the sterile pretensions of the "little clan" and wishes henceforward to devote himself unhampered to the development of his ideas and of his work. A man of exquisite taste, of great intellectual power and of deep generosity, he is one of the great pioneers of impressionism, and his art, no less than his life, is characteristically expressive of his fierce and persistent striving after truth.

Once more, by means of the passage of time, Proust shows how their respective works, considered at first, like Rachel's manner of reciting, to be either meaningless, affected, wildly revolutionary or frankly ludicrous, become gradually assimilated into the general consciousness of the period.

INTRODUCTION TO PROUST

The books of Bergotte, admired first chiefly by such self-conscious aspiring young intellectuals as Bloch, suddenly flower into an Indian Summer of popularity, and give rise to a whole host of pale imitations, which, though obviously reminiscent of the master's characteristic style and vocabulary, nevertheless lack completely the essential quality of his work. For Bergotte's foremost aim in writing—like Ruskin's, like Proust's—was to pierce below appearances, and so reveal the element of truth inherent in all phenomena; for which reason the importance of his work lies rather in the veracity of the scenes reflected than in any intrinsic merit in the scenes themselves: a fact of which the school to which he gave rise appears to be completely unaware.

Similarly, the music of Vinteuil, neglected for years and appreciated, for a long time, only by a few "advanced" melomaniacs, becomes heard with increasing frequency and gradually receives a wide appreciation, thanks, not only to the Verdurins, with whom the musician has become almost a cult, but, paradoxically enough, thanks also to the prolonged and tender care with which his last works have been transcribed from an almost illegible series of torn and dirty scraps, and preserved by the daughter and her friend who desecrated his memory.

Whilst Elstir, whose pictures for years are mildly ridiculed by the Cottards, and classed bluntly as vulgar by M. de Guermantes, gradually gains the prestige of a master, until at last he is acclaimed almost unanimously as one of the greatest painters of the century.

In the Proustian approach to art, this slow process from a position of obscurity and even of ridicule or aversion, to general appreciation, is not only necessary but inevitable. For the hall mark and the measure of true talent lie precisely in its difference from popular imitations, and its value is proportionate to the originality of the aspect that it affords in a sincere approach to truth. Thus all great art is bound, by the very nature of things, to be misunderstood at first, not only by reason of its novelty but because it demands from the reader, the audience or the spectator a completely new and unaccustomed effort of attention, judgment and understanding.

As all these faculties require education, it is obviously impossible for the general public to arrive at the spontaneous appreciation of a work whose main feature appears, superficially, to lie in the very difference from every form to which it is compared. The sudden shock of being placed, naked of all habitual associations, in a strange new world, is at first so startling that the reaction it provokes appears to be the most acute distaste. This becomes converted into satisfaction only when the language of this new world has been mastered; and arouses increasing respect the more generally it becomes assimilated into the accepted vocabulary of the day.

It must be understood that in the sphere of art, Proust is never concerned with those purely superficial works which, masquerading as "great," are no more than the spurious and mediocre travesties that the undiscriminating majority are always willing to accept as an easy substitute for something that they are unable either to appreciate or to understand. Art, for Proust, is raised infinitely above the most elegant social pleasures of those drawing-rooms which profess to exist for the sole purpose of pursuing her. It is the great bridge by which man can occasionally glimpse and even gain entrance to a supraterrestrial and secret world which usually is inaccessible to him.[1]

All this is best, and with remarkable subtlety and power,

---

[1] There can be little doubt that Ruskin influenced enormously Proust's attitude to the value and meaning of art; and his consistent contention that great artists are never concerned with superficial reproduction, and that the function of true art is to reveal aspects of Deity was fully accepted by Proust as the basis for all his own theories and convictions. This does not mean to say that Proust deliberately borrowed these ideas: but that, feeling them intuitively to be true, they aided him in the formulation of his own.

illustrated through the music of Vinteuil, which forms an extraordinary link between the inner lives of Swann and of Marcel, and the purely superficial activities of the drawing-rooms they frequent. When Swann first hears the "little phrase" of the sonata for violin and piano, ignorant not only of the name of the composer but even of the name of the work in which it occurs, it gives him the taste of a beauty so keen and strange that it seems even to offer him a renewal of his lost youth. Later, however, when it is played frequently at the Verdurins', it becomes to him so inseparable from his love for Odette, that when he hears it yet again at Mme de Saint-Euverte's, it seems to express for him the very essence of all his emotion and his suffering. As time passes, his reactions to it become even more subjective, and are formed rather by his habit of memory and desire than by any emotion which the "little phrase" originally evoked; until at last, all that it recalls are those calm and moonlit nights in the Bois, when he listened to it so often with the Verdurins, and Odette at his side.

At the same time, years later, when Mme Swann plays it on the piano in her drawing-room, and Marcel hears it for the first time, save for its strangeness it barely registers in his consciousness. Only long afterwards, when he seems to hear it echoed in the septet given at the Verdurins', does he feel that it offers him the possibility of complete and noble happiness infinitely superior to any of the spurious pleasures he has already known. Like certain other of the most deep and mysterious of his impressions, which he has never been able to make yield up the full significance of their latent beauty, it seems to beckon him to those remote and elusive regions in which he feels that he will be able alone to realize his true life. He concludes, therefore, that a work of art must contain a far deeper significance, a far fuller meaning, than can ever be discovered in an artist's life. For just as Vinteuil, in common with every other great musician, seems to him to have sought in each new work to recapture and to recreate the wonderful lost harmonies of some half-forgotten home, so every true artist is for ever striving to reach a lost country that he dimly remembers, but from which the routine of his life seems to have completely separated him. This hidden goal, with all the truth, the significance, the profound and elusive beauty of a different state of consciousness dimly discerned but rarely realized, is the source from which flow the only waves of true reality, however faint, that ever reach us —the only intimations of immortality that we can ever know.

But though this reality is a state that remains for ever constant, men nevertheless are very different, so that each separate artist, no matter whether he be painter, writer or musician, can open for us, by his unique and individual approach, some completely new aspect, of which, without his help, we should have remained ignorant and unaware. Not only is this paradise lost the artist's one true inspiration, it is, no less, our own ultimate goal, so that a work which serves even to recall to us its existence is infinitely to be preferred to any purely social or sensual pleasure. The truths that art, in no matter what form, seeks to realize, are invariable; but so vast, so complex and so far removed from our habitual life, that every new facet that can be expressed to us is like the revelation of a hidden world.

But if the inspiration of art, as will be elaborated later, is always the result of a contact, no matter how transient, between the artist and some objective reality infinitely greater than himself, art itself, of necessity, must be in a state of continual flux. For the orientation of the world is never constant, and as each new generation assimilates into its general outlook, albeit unconsciously, the most staggering theories and discoveries of the decades immediately before its own, so it becomes necessary for the artist not only to enrich his work by every available means, but to express himself in an idiom which, no matter how characteristic or unique, is expressive, nevertheless, of the particular attitude and approach of his contemporaries. Thus every genius is the child, no less than the father, of his age.

Applying these principles to Proust himself, it is not difficult to understand why the innovations which he brought to the novel are far more easily assimilated to-day than ever they could have been when first his work appeared. Even during his lifetime, like Bergotte, he had his imitators and his followers, but it needed time for the drama of the inner world, and the whole field of psychological activity, to become as much the accepted material of the novel as was, formerly, the simpler field of external action.

CHAPTER V

GILBERTE and Albertine, Marcel's two great loves, are the most elusive characters in the whole of his experience, since his very infatuation makes it impossible for him to consider them with the same objectivity as those other women to whom he is less, or not at all, attached.

Gilberte he never knows well until long after he has ceased to love her and she is married to Robert de Saint-Loup. Even so, there are certain traits in her character which persist throughout the whole of their acquaintanceship. As a child, despite all her demonstrative affection for the father who adores her, Gilberte insists upon going to a concert much against his wishes, inventing the reason, to justify herself, that she does not wish to allow any merely conventional attitude to rob her governess of one of her few rare pleasures; just as, when she becomes Mlle de Forcheville, she outrages his memory by attempting even to conceal the fact that she was born Swann and her father was a Jew. In the same way, while still a girl, she makes great pretensions to disdaining the position of the political mediocrities whom her father inveigles, with such arduous persistence, into visiting Odette; while many years later, when her husband is dead, she professes loudly to disdain all the Guermantes, not excluding the Duchess, although for years it was her greatest ambition to be received by her. For as with Mme Cambremer-Legrandin, the Guermantes milieu attracts her only so long as she feels herself excluded from it, and when once it has become her customary environment, she willingly relinquishes it for the society of such ordinary middle-class women as Andrée, who eventually becomes her greatest friend.

The character of Albertine is even more elusive; and for the reader, no less than the writer, she remains a deep enigma. Attractive, charming and intelligent, we see her subtly transformed from the boisterous young hoyden of the Balbec promenade to the smart, alluring, cultured and companionable young woman into whom she blossoms later as Marcel's mistress. But as we can view her only through his eyes, her real independent self we never know.

When Marcel first hears of her at Mme Swann's, where Mme Bontemps proudly regales the company with an example of her niece's wit—a retort of a somewhat vulgar and precocious pertness which, it must be admitted, differs in essence but little from some of the less brilliant efforts of Mme de Guermantes, Albertine has already attained the reputation of being likely to grow up rather "fast." Indeed, the first time he sees her on the front at Balbec, her appearance and manners are such that he takes her for the juvenile mistress of some trick cyclist. But this stage of youthful exuberance soon passes, and the girlish stupidities natural to her age gradually give way to an innate intelligence.

In most of her relations with him, Albertine treats her lover with an affectionate consideration which makes it somewhat difficult to believe in the truth of his suspicions: but the tragedy is that once these have become implanted deeply in Marcel's mind, he feels that he can never hope to keep her by very reason of his inability to offer her, or even to conceive, the pleasures that he feels she most urgently desires. In consequence his most terrible paroxysms of jealousy are aroused by her most casual glance at, or even the presence in the same room of, another woman whom he believes to share her secret tastes. No matter that, even when he sends Françoise to fetch her unexpectedly from the theatre, because he discovers that Léa is performing there, Albertine returns without delay, sending ahead of her a messenger with a most charming and spontaneously affectionate note to allay his anxiety. He can only see in her somewhat childish and probably quite innocuous deceptions, signs of the deepest duplicity and guilt.

Admittedly Albertine deceives him over innumerable trivial details, but considering the alarming results of some of her most harmless admissions, and the frenzied cross-examinations to which she is continually subjected, this is scarcely a matter for surprise. Certainly, no matter what her tastes, her life with Marcel could have brought her but little happiness; and it is not improbable that she was quite simply a normal and healthy young girl who, bored by being left so frequently to herself, naturally hoped that one day her lover would marry her, and who left him simply because his innumerable jealousies and deceits ultimately proved unbearable; and the whole position was spoiling her chances of getting married to anyone else.

Poor Albertine; never, while she is living with him, allowed to go out without some more or less unwelcome chaperone; modelling her literary theories upon his own, which she admires immensely; imbibing all his ideas on art and music; acquiring from Elstir an exquisite taste in all matters of dress and decoration; and, without prospects or fortune, patiently awaiting a day when Marcel may at last decide to make her his wife. Such, probably, is the very ordinary truth about her. Why else should she, so popular and attractive, and with so many other wealthy friends, have placed herself in the invidious position of living indefinitely, and during their absence, in his parents' flat, continually watched over and spied upon as though she were the inmate of a harem? Why else should she have offered to come back to him as soon as she learned that he truly desired her return?

It is true that Marcel never seeks to justify his actions and describes his most intimate reactions, in the interest of truth, with the same detachment as if they were the symptoms of a malady: even so, there comes a time when his tortures become merely exasperating, and our sympathy is all for his reluctant prisoner. Both of them victims of their own natures, and of the forces created by their separate environments, they turn a love affair which offers the most charming possibilities of companionship, the most moving passages of tenderness, into a fantastic duel of lies, evasions and mutual recriminations. The volume which deals with their life together contains some of the most moving passages in romantic literature, and the pages in which Marcel watches his sleeping mistress is imbued with all the sensitiveness, tenderness and beauty of lyric poetry. But Proust was too honest not to reveal in equal detail the opposite aspects of emotion; and if Marcel loves, at moments, with the capacity of a Romeo, he also suffers all the tortures of Othello, and probably with as little reason.

The essential tragedy of their relations is the result of a complicated combination of general psychological laws and of specific personal associations which have become, in time, as powerful and as automatic as the most carefully conditioned reflexes. While Proust is probably indebted to Stendhal more than to any other writer for his theories on love, indubitably it was through self-observation that he corroborated those conclusions which place him in the category of the most uncompromising realists. Throughout the whole of his work he sought to illustrate and to develop the causes which result ultimately in the idea of romantic love proving to be a complete chimera. It was not so much that Proust believed that a successful and fully reciprocal love affair was utterly impossible, as that he realized that such a thing depends upon the fortuitous conjunction of so many exceptional factors as to make it, from the point of view of the illustration of general laws, sufficiently rare as to be considered irrelevant. Too well he realized that identical emotions are felt simultaneously in the hearts of lovers as rarely as genuine sympathy is experienced in the hearts of friends. Both of them may, in turn, feel passionate, friendly, tender, indifferent, thoughtful, grave or gay: but since each of these moods in one party usually appears in company of the most opposite in the other, consistent harmony is a happy accident that borders almost upon the miraculous. Thus all the love affairs in his novel are either tragic or disastrous.

Friendship, for Proust, as we have seen, was, in its last analysis, a very spurious and frivolous pleasure. It is impossible for the most philosophic of men to live entirely to himself, and even the most persistent efforts of creative energy require relaxation. Therefore it was necessary for him to have friends. But for Proust, as for his Marcel, friendship could serve as a pleasant relaxation only when he had ceased to believe in its ultimate value, and finally rejected the implication that it enables us to communicate and to exchange our deepest ideas, and so to advance in understanding. Rather it seemed to him, by forcing us to relinquish a life at the centre of our being for a vague existence upon its periphery, it causes us to dissipate our ideas, our personality and our energy in a series of excursions which are not only profitless, but wasteful. Since it is almost impossible for mutual confidence and sympathy to be both simultaneous and reciprocal, we can gain in conversation little save the complacent and unhealthy sense of being supported by the approval and admiration of another personality, with whom to try to share our inmost thoughts and feelings is a form of harmless lunacy not dissimilar from talking to the furniture. Friendship, therefore, is best regarded as a form of self-indulgence acceptable only when, consciously or unconsciously, a human being wishes temporarily to escape from the bondage of his own individuality.

But if, for Proust, the reality of friendship is little but a myth, how purely mythical is the reality of love! For love, in the Proustian scheme, is fundamentally a subjective manifestation of which the essential components are imagination and desire; and the lover is drawn irresistibly, less by any real person than by some wholly illusory figure in his own mind. Thus, for Proust, the only difference between normal and homosexual love lies in the brain, whereon, instead of a figure of a nymph, the invert has ingrained the ineradicable features of a young man.

Projecting upon the personality of his mistress a force of attraction which has its being within himself, the lover persists in imbuing both her character and her person with a series of attributes which have no correspondence with the woman she is. Even the most intelligent of men remains in ignorance as to the real nature of the creature who has enslaved him, since the very intensity of his passion blinds him to all impersonal vision, and causes him persistently to conceal her features with a veil that he alone is incapable of penetrating. Swann is reduced to a state bordering upon imbecility when he is infatuated with Odette, and for a long time believes in a virtue the very suggestion of which would have produced an outburst of ridicule in any man who was not in love with her: while Marcel, before Albertine's most trivial actions, finds himself faced with a series of enigmas more difficult to interpret than any propounded by the most evasive oracle.

Passionate love is considered as a transitory desire crystallized by uncertainty and nourished continuously by jealousy or doubt; and absence is one of the most necessary conditions of its maintenance, since this alone affords full play to the imagination. What otherwise could make Saint-Loup find such beauty in the Rachel who, to Marcel, was merely a very ordinary girl whom he had been offered in a brothel for a few francs: could make Marcel almost take his life over a young woman whom all his friends consider unworthy of him: could make M. de Charlus temporarily lose his head over some utterly unattractive tram conductor, or Swann suffer for so many years over a woman who, to Bloch, was no more than an attractive whore who gave herself to him gratuitously in a train?

Any woman, no matter how commonplace or devoid of beauty, has the power to subjugate us completely when once we have permitted ourselves to project upon her all those desires and dreams which we persist in believing can be satisfied by union with another soul. Albertine for Marcel (or Odette for Swann) is Maya, the eternally unobtainable, the eternally desired. Let her once be possessed without danger of loss, and all her magic leaves her, like a plucked flower that fades, or a pebble stolen from the sea. Only when she is elusive, uncertain and arouses his jealousy can she excite simultaneously the maximum of passion and desire.

We place little value upon what we possess and seek always that which is beyond our reach: so the faintest prospect of disappointment, the merest suspicion of a rival, is quite sufficient to transform a latent physical attraction into the most passionate love. And because such love demands complete possession, it is doomed inevitably to suffering and frustration. For ultimate possession implies a complete authority over time and space, over every moment of the past and future, over every point upon the earth that the beloved ever has or ever will occupy. An impossibility, of course: so that infatuation can produce only a continuous series of violent inner disturbances, and peace remains unattainable, even after consummation; since each satisfaction is followed immediately by the birth of a renewed desire. More painful still, the lover is completely impotent; for to emphasize, or even to admit, his passion, is merely to defeat his own ends by arousing in the object of his desires boredom and vexation, and, should he persist, even aversion and disgust.

Having realized that Mme de Guermantes only withheld her friendship from him so long as he persisted in pestering her with unwelcome attentions, Marcel, as soon as he is deeply in love with Albertine, determines to deceive her as to the state of his emotions, and affects an almost wounding indifference when most he is lacerated with jealousy, for fear lest the very vehemence of his passion should arouse her indifference, or even turn her from him.

The whole precarious and tragic quality of his relations with Albertine is dependent upon a synthesis of the various foregoing ideas. No sooner is his jealousy temporarily assuaged than he begins at once to feel how irksome is his mistress's continual proximity, and to realize not only how it continually demands his living on the surface rather than in the depths of his being; but even prevents him from indulging a whole series of casual desires in which she can play no part. But as soon as his suspicions are aroused anew, and jealousy reborn, he is at once tormented by the prospect of being dispossessed, and Albertine becomes the one creature on earth indispensable to his happiness.

For if his love is born of carnal desire, nevertheless it requires continual anxiety to maintain its life; and since he is unaware of any rival, this continual anxiety is supplied for him, just as, in part, it was for Swann, by his ineradicable suspicion of his mistress's Sapphic tastes. No matter that these suspicions may have had but the most trivial foundation: jealousy and suspicion are quite sufficient to induce the most acute and terrible suffering.

Long after Albertine's death, Marcel still tries to discover the truth about her tastes: but he is never able to do so. Though he collects a huge mass of evidence, none of it can be considered decisive, since the various people who supply it are, for one reason or another, equally untrustworthy, and may have their own reasons for wishing to deceive him. Until at last the subject ceases to hold any interest for him, and he is forced to realize that he has grown so indifferent that even could Albertine return to him from the dead, it would no longer afford him the slightest satisfaction.

For all love, no matter how passionate and persistent, must eventually die. It must die because man is composed of an innumerable congregation of states, desires, ideas, emotions and memories, which he sheds continually as a snake its skin or a tree its leaves, only to substitute for them in the course of time, others so completely different that eventually he ceases to be the same person. The Proustian character is a being without any definite and persistent ego; a creature who, within the sheath of his own body, harbours a whole kingdom of men, each of whom has his own private interests and desires, and continually vanishes or reappears in accordance with the accidental stimulus of the moment. He is composed, moreover, not only of this legion of subsidiary men, but of the gradual accretion of the whole series of his different states, one of which is piled upon another in a purely temporary and accidental order that is liable to be disturbed violently at any moment, and so produce the most unexpected cataclysms.

Thus the working of man's love or jealousy can never be understood so long as they are considered as the permanent and unchanging expression of an individual. Only when it is realized that, just as he is composed of a continuous series of successive men, so are his apparently consistent emotions constructed from a mass of smaller and ephemeral emotions which create an illusion of unity simply by reason of their close proximity, can the transience of all human feelings be explained.

Indeed, the man at length changes so completely that in the end the being who loved and suffered is no more, even though a new man within the same body may be loving and suffering over some completely different woman, as did Marcel first with Gilberte and later with Albertine. For if the object continually differs, desire itself persists: but this desire is something completely new, with little or no memory and knowledge of the old. And because the essential causes reside in himself alone, love, no matter how painful, must always remain incurable; a malady of continual recurrence for which there can be no cure save the inevitable operation of the laws of time.

In the words of Pascal: "We change and are no longer the same persons. . . . He no longer loves the woman whom he loved ten years ago. I quite believe it. She is no longer the same, nor is he. . . ."

CHAPTER VI

IT was Proust himself who first referred to his books as novels of the unconscious. Deeply aware of the new theories in the philosophy and psychology of his own day, and well acquainted with the work of Freud and of Bergson, the latter, indeed, being married to a cousin of his mother, he wished to demonstrate through the means of his own characters certain ideas, which, although undoubtedly influenced by these two men, had undergone his usual prolonged tests of verification; and, transformed to meet the requirements of his own conclusions, and assimilated into the general body of his thought, form certain of the basic themes and part of the essential structure of his work.

With Proust, it is first of all necessary to understand, the idea of the unconscious is inseparable from his theories of memory and habit, since it is these, even more than imagination, accumulating in force with the passing of the years, that divorce us most completely from the real world.

What we usually call memory is, for Proust, a completely uncontrolled and uncontrollable series of images of the past; flat, colourless and without life, which, like the cinematograph of imagination, is governed automatically by habit, and offers but a very weak, inaccurate and superficial recollection of the past. The images both of people and places which this automatic memory incessantly reproduces, independently of all reason or desire, correspond to the moments they pretend to recreate as little as the purely fictitious qualities with which we imbue unknown names coincide with the real places or people that such names actually represent; since the very habit that has preserved them robs them simultaneously, just as it robs all our other impressions, of their deepest meaning and vitality. But buried in our unconscious, in those hidden regions where is stored miraculously the whole of our past life that we have no definite means of reaching, there lie other memories—rich, vibrant and authentic' which reveal themselves to us but rarely, and then only through the agency of some fortuitous and accidental association. That is why sensations, and particularly, for Proust, the sensations of taste and smell, seem to conceal within themselves some deep and elusive secret of our lives that we can never evoke by any deliberate effort of our intelligence or our will. For it was by their aid alone that he was able to resavour the sweetness and charm of the whole of the childhood he had forgotten, as when, coming home late one dreary winter afternoon, he was given unexpectedly a piece of madeleine dipped in tea, like that which his "aunt" Leonie used to give him in the glorious distant days at Combray. Such memories, instinct with life and undiluted, undistorted, because so long forgotten, can never be regained by any deliberate effort; and alone have the power of bringing back, with the poignancy of tears, the essence of a past from which, without their aid, we should be severed completely until the day of our death. Evoked only, as if by magic, through the accidental recurrence of some feature connected with the original impression —the scent of lilac, the crackling of fire, the freshness of rain —such memories can even revive in us the being who, living then, has seemed to us long dead, and cause him miraculously to live again.

It is thus that there is created within us the "intermittences of the heart"—those pauses in the emotional life caused by the refusal of the feelings to be aroused either by colourless memories or facts, while they spring with a deep and instantaneous response to recollections which are keen and living. For this reason, also, we are widely separated from the world of direct causes, and our most bitter joys and griefs have but little correspondence with the external sources from which they have arisen. We suffer, not when we lose someone whom we love, but when our emotions at last receive the full impression of our bereavement. When Marcel's grandmother dies, emotionally he is scarcely aware of the fact. Only long afterwards, on his second visit to Balbec, when the movement of bending down to take off his boots evokes for him a living memory of her presence as she used to perform this action for him, is he desolately aware of the full significance of his loss. The real drama and development of our lives is quite subjective, and the reactions which most move us are only indirectly connected with an exterior cause.

Our emotional life undergoes long and involuntary pauses, because our most significant memories are concealed from us in the submerged recesses of the unconscious, and we have no means of recalling them at will.

But if authentic memory, by reason of its dependence upon chance, can but seldom revive for us the most living moments of our past, at least its rarity is instrumental in enabling us at last to escape from suffering. In time we forget everything, regardless of its relative value, and Marcel recovers at last from the loss of Albertine, even when his limbs retain a separate memory of her of their own, and a sensation of his arms or legs will recall to him a dim remembrance of the days when they sometimes fell asleep together, simply through his incapacity to recall either her features or her personality.

Authentic memory, however, as opposed to automatic memory, is not only our only means of recapturing the past, but the one and only instrument by which we can measure the processes of time, which only become fully apparent to us with the juxtaposition of two moments widely separated by the years but simultaneously perceived. For the past is always present within us, and separated from our consciousness only by our inability to resurrect it; just as we are usually severed from reality by the automatism that continually substitutes a screen of indifferent and unnecessary images for the objects and impressions which in consequence they exclude.

But if this automatic functioning of memory is one of our greatest barriers to direct perception, no less so is the equally automatic functioning of the imagination. Indeed, Proust's ideas on imagination are influenced by his appreciation of Pascal almost as much as are some of his ideas on love. Throughout the whole of *À la Recherche du Temps Perdu*, imagination, never once used in the Ruskinian sense as the "highest intellectual power of man," is shown as a persistent faculty that colours independently of intention or desire, everything that it approaches.

In accordance with a psychological law common to all mankind, Marcel follows a path in which each new aspect of the life unfolding about him is imbued with a glamour which his imagination alone imparts to it. With every phenomenon that attracts him, he is forced at last to realize that the power for so long exerted upon him resides, not in the names, the places, the books or the women to whom he is irresistibly drawn, but in the fictitious qualities and associations with which his own imagination has endowed them, and which have no connection with the objects of his attention. It is thus that we spend the greater part of our lives, seeking in things outside ourselves some indefinable but compelling satisfaction which our own subjective ideas have attributed to them; and but rarely realize that the causes of disillusion reside within ourselves, or that our imagination has accomplished nothing save the severing of the mind from the realities which face it, and the substitution of yet another barrier between ourselves and the world.

But imagination not only prevents us from perceiving things as they are; it may equally arouse in us the most vehement emotions over sufferings that we picture to ourselves. Pity, sympathy or indignation are evoked by invented features which we ascribe to the tragedies of others, just as malice and hatred may be caused by some intellectual ideal that affords an inner justification for deeds that from without seem to be the expression of the most callous wickedness.

Imagination, indeed, deceives us continually in nearly all our judgments, no matter whether these are of others or of ourselves; and only the most persistent and determined observation can enable us to assess impartially our own emotions and reactions. This self-deception is the more subtle because it depends usually upon some element of truth. Whereas most of our motives are complicated, rather than face the bitter knowledge of our own littleness, we involuntarily choose only to recognize the secondary and not unpleasant aspect which we substitute quite unconsciously for the less creditable primary one. We say to ourselves "how sweet she was" when all we mean is "I liked kissing her," and justify all our least respectable actions with similar phrases that enable us to live comfortably in continual ignorance of the true working of our passions. It is clear, when we admit this, that the reasons we ascribe to our actions, and quite sincerely believe to be responsible for them, are very different from the motives from which our actions spring.

When Robert de Saint-Loup inveighs bitterly against the viciousness of the men who make advances to Rachel, firmly convinced that they are the most depraved voluptuaries, he is unable to see that their conduct is in no way dissimilar to his own: just as Bloch prefers to call the unnecessary curiosity he displays in Saint-Loup's financial affairs a "Balzacian interest."

The picture that we have of ourselves differs very widely from that which others form of us, since the motives which are unmistakable to a detached observer are almost invariably hidden from ourselves. All these primary motives remain in the unconscious, that is to say, in some region of the mind of which we are not aware, less because we have no control over them than because we have neither the courage nor the desire to reach down to them. Our conception of ourselves, as our conception of the world, is distorted by a series of deceits, prejudices, habitual preconceived ideas and irrational beliefs, which permit us always to remain in ignorance of truth, and even to maintain the most ludicrous convictions when we are confronted by their actual disproof. We live in a personal and subjective world that very rarely comes in contact with the world of facts. Even our most spontaneous reactions, are occasioned less by actuality than by the modification of our perceptions. All the time Marcel is growing up, his beloved grandmother is growing old: but this he never perceives. Because he sees her every day, he never really looks at her, and the visual image that his eyes retain is immediately exchanged for the habitual image which her name invariably rushes automatically to his mind. And as, for years, living with her on terms of the greatest intimacy, he has never really seen her, it is a terrible shock to him when one day he suddenly realizes that she has grown ugly and withered. She must have been just as ugly and withered weeks, months, even years before: but he never suffered at the realization, simply because he never noticed it. And thus it is with everything. The external world has existence for us in direct ratio to the breadth and intensity of our impressions, and ideas have meaning only to the extent that we assimilate them. Apart from our own perceptions and our own understanding, we can possess nothing; and beauty, whether it resides in nature or in art, is only ours when we can appreciate its significance. It is our awareness of our surroundings which charges them with life; our lack of consciousness which makes richness and colour vanish from our world.

Therefore our greatest enemy, because the greatest destroyer of our true life, is habit. For habit not only controls all our reactions—and particularly such psychological reflexes as imagination and memory—but it accustoms us so quickly to the details of our life, performs for us so accurately, without our will or knowledge, the series of trivial actions which forms our day, that by reducing the work of our senses to a minimum and permitting the deliberate use of our faculties to lie dormant, it causes us at last to dispense with using them at all. Our memories, recurring by means of an involuntary automatism, become robbed of their inner richness, as our eyes take in with a blind indifference the customary objects upon which they fall. Our minds become cluttered up with stale images and lifeless knowledge, until there is formed around us an impermeable shell that shuts us off completely from the world. Crystallized, at last, in an almost blind, insentient and impervious combination of reflexes and reactions, all real life in us becomes extinguished, and thus we are separated for ever from the spontaneous happiness we knew in childhood.

CHAPTER VII

IT is by means of the gradual accumulation of such realizations that Marcel's understanding develops, throughout the whole of his history, towards the final experience which reveals to him the reality for which he has always been searching, and which determines him at last to start to write the book that he has longed to produce ever since his boyhood, but for which, hitherto, he has never been able to find sufficient inspiration. This revelation, which is described in the magnificent third chapter of *Le Temps Retrouvé*, forms the climax for which the most careful preparation has been made in each separate aspect of the preceding volumes, and is the consummation both of his life and of the book.

Shades of the prison house begin to close about the growing boy almost as soon as he can read, when deliberately he seeks to lose himself in an imaginary existence of his own; until the celestial light of childhood becomes obscured completely by the screen of pictures that he superimposes upon the life about him, his most vivid impressions are obscured, and the man at length becomes obsessed with nostalgia for the "lost lilac and the lost sea voices" of his youth. By imagining absent pleasures, he forsakes the happiness he has, and in his progress through the various stages of adolescence, youth and early manhood, creates for himself a series of dreams, the fulfilment of each of which he is confident would procure for him the ultimate and essential beauty for which he has never ceased to crave.

But no sooner does he attain one or another of his desires, than he finds it lacking in all the expected magic which was the illusory bloom laid upon it by his imagination. He im-

INTRODUCTION TO PROUST

bues the names of places, of people and of things with an unattainable beauty, and is forced in consequence, to learn, through an implacable and inevitable series of disillusions, that his most powerful desires have been for spurious satisfactions which correspond to no reality. Everything is disappointing—Berma in *Phèdre*, the church at Balbec, even Bergotte himself. His love for Gilberte and Albertine brings him little but suffering, and his friendship for the Guermantes boredom and distaste. Only the music of Vinteuil, by helping him to penetrate into himself, seems continually to promise him the taste of a fulfilment that dimly he senses he has both known and forgotten, and for which he has never ceased to long. At last even nature herself ceases to move him,[1] women offer him little but the possibility of a fleeting pleasure no different from that which h has enjoyed a dozen times before, and the life of the mind but a sterile lucidity that is far removed from all that he has lost. Even the value of literature, in which he has believed implicitly since his childhood, loses its former significance, and he begins to doubt whether it is worth while for him to continue to sacrifice his leisure to a profession in which he no longer believes, less because he doubts his own talent than because it appears to him unworthy as an ideal. Magic and mystery have vanished from the world.

It is in such a mood that he goes to the final reception of the Princesse de Guermantes, hoping to find there some faces that will recall for him his childhood. For buried in the past—in lost time—lies his real and essential happiness, and his deepest instinct is to find some means by which he can recapture it. His nostalgia and longing to find the real world —his true life—have now reached the pathos and the passion of that famous cry of Catherine Linton: "I'm tired of being enclosed here. I'm wearying to escape into that glorious

[1] Compare with Ruskin's "The deadliest of all things to me is my loss of faith in Nature", and who, at times, even went so far as to assert that Nature had "deteriorated" within living memory.

world, and to be there always: not seeing it dimly through tears, and yearning for it through the walls of an aching heart; but really with it and in it. . . ."

Only now there occurs the final miracle. On several occasions in the past—when he ate his sop of madeleine dipped in tea—when once, out driving with Mme de Villeparisis near Balbec, his attention was captured by a line of trees that seemed imbued with a mysterious and inexplicable significance which he was completely at a loss to understand—he has been filled with a wonderful sense of joy and peace for which there seemed no conceivable reason. Finally, by means of three successive incidents, apparently completely trivial, he suddenly attains a state of illumination infinitely deeper than any that he has experienced before.

In crossing the courtyard, he accidentally stumbles across two unevenly placed paving stones, which not only recall to him the sensation that he experienced when walking over just such another uneven surface in the Baptistry of St. Mark, and reproduce for him the whole essence of the Venice that formerly he had been unable to recapture through the series of colourless snapshots that are all his memory can bring to mind, but produce in him the same deep sense of happiness which he experienced long ago when he ate the madeleine. A moment later, in the ante-room, where he waits while they are finishing a musical performance, the noise of a spoon knocking against a plate, so similar to the sound of a hammer on the wheel of a carriage, brings back with an equal intensity the moment, with every detail of the impressions it contained, in which he heard it; while yet a third sensation—the wiping of his lips with a stiff napkin when he has finished taking some refreshment in the library—recalls with similar vividness the Balbec that he saw from his window, when, on the day of his first arrival he dried himself with a towel of similar texture. But these three resurrections of the past, which suddenly recapture for him the lost time that he has longed so passionately to regain, contain for him infinitely more than their separate moments of days which are no more. They produce in him a temporary change of consciousness in which suddenly he sees the whole of life from a completely different point of view; in which his eyes are not only intoxicated with a sense of azure, and his being invaded with a new vitality and satisfaction, but in which the thought of death no longer has the power to touch him, and the idea of his own personality becomes so unreal that it no longer seems even to exist. Immediately he is aware that here, at last, he has found his true life; the only state which is ultimately to be desired, the ecstasy which real art is ceaselessly attempting to transmit, the one inspiration for the book which it once more seems worth while to begin. The immense long littleness of life is both obliterated and transcended, and he is fully sensible of the beauty and the wonder that have eluded him for so long.

Convinced now that there exists a reality quite independent of our usual existence, he is determined to understand the meaning and the value of his experience, and so to formulate his ultimate conclusions in some abiding form.

The real world, he understands at last, is always saturated in beauty; but usually we remain unaware of it because we substitute within ourselves arbitrary interpretations for impressions that we do not understand, or else base our opinion of the weariness and boredom of life upon a series of sterile perceptions that are devoid of beauty and vitality simply because of our own obtuseness. Every moment in which we have been deeply aware, every moment in which our perceptions have been clear, intense, authentic, is stamped indelibly and for ever with the details of each form and sensation of which the experience was composed; and the recurrence of any similar form or sensation can superimpose that memory upon the present, and so cause the past to live again. Now if, at the moment of this resurrection, instead of obliterating the present we can continue to be aware of it: if we can retain all the sense of our own identity, and at the same time live fully in that moment which we had for long believed to be no more, then, and only then, we are at last in full possession of lost time, and have reached in ourselves the inmost essence of our being, far removed from that superficial personality that usually we consider to be ourself. The whole of our time is stored in the series of authentic memories in our unconscious, and our true life is only possible when we are no longer separated from them. Only then the essence in us which is unchanging, and therefore independent of time's laws, can reach the surface—the part of our being which was aware of that past, and lives still—the part of ourselves which in consequence is timeless, and can thus contact a reality which is impervious to change.

It is this part of ourselves, usually so deeply overlaid by the accumulated weight of our customary imagination, memories, intellectual theories and habits, that alone has the capacity to receive deep and rich impressions, and to experience, to appreciate our true life. At such moments, when imagination is precluded by an awareness of the past, which is joined, at the same time, to a sense of our present existence, then at last we know reality, a moment of time in its pure essence, the only experience which can nourish and delight that essential man in us who is at last awake and liberated from time's usual order. Raised if only for a short time, above that plateau of a dead past and an imaginary future which is our only usual sense of life, our consciousness is concerned exclusively with its immediate experience, and we are splendidly immune from the accustomed tedium and usual fears that are the inevitable concomitant of things transitory.

The lost time, therefore, which hitherto Marcel has believed could be regained only by some fortuitous accident of authentic memory, is, in fact, both supratemporal and supra-terrestrial, existing in a dimension far removed from that in which we usually pass our lives, and an aspect of the reality which can be attained only by a change of consciousness. Although this changed state of consciousness is, with Marcel, rare, accidental, and only of very short duration, yet it is the one experience, he is convinced, that illuminates the apparent chaos and futility of life and is worthy to form the foundation of the work of art that it has given him the renewed desire to create.

That this state approaches very closely certain experiences which have been classed in certain literature among the mystical, it cannot be denied.[1] For this reason, several of the most sympathetic of Proust's commentators have had no hesitation in pronouncing him a mystic.[2] A somewhat excessive term to apply to any man who, even if he has experienced an authentic heightening of consciousness, has only done so occasionally and by accident. The main conditions of Proust's experiences—providing that in this instance, as it seems reasonable to suppose, the essential features of Marcel's revelation are autobiographical—are that they were fortuitous, accidental, of very short duration, and invariably evoked by external associations; while the mystic's life is governed by the conscious and deliberate efforts that enable him at length to produce such experiences for himself, and, ultimately, to control them. But this in no way impairs the validity or the significance of the final illumination itself, although it would seem sometimes to be obscured somewhat unnecessarily by Proust's determination to express it in original terms.

How, is his next problem, can he translate this experience into a literary equivalent that will convey the different series of ideas and laws which alone have permitted him to com-

[1] See *The Varieties of Religious Experience*, by William James. *Cosmic Consciousness*, by Dr. Bucke, etc.
[2] See *Marcel Proust: sa révélation psychologique*, par Dandieu; *L'Amitié de Proust*, par Cattui.

prehend it? Only, it seems, by penetrating as deeply as possible into his mind and emotions, by subjecting the whole of his past to the most intense and ruthless scrutiny, so that his intelligence can fully illuminate the laws and motives which must have governed his existence, but which, hitherto, have remained both unconscious and unexplored. His duty at last becomes clear and pressing: to recreate the whole of his life in a permanent form built up from those transcendental truths which alone can enable him to interpret it; and by becoming at once the scientist and his own guinea pig, to establish through detached observation, and so assert, the psychological laws which govern all our reactions, but which we persistently disregard in favour of some more flattering and palatable fiction.

Intuition as opposed to logical reason, can be his sole criterion, and the value and significance of each experience measured only by the depth and validity of the impressions it evokes. Our real life, Marcel now believes, is consistently concealed from us, and art is the one channel by which it may be revealed. So-called realism is useless to him as a medium of expression, since it deliberately confines itself to the description of external forms, and is concerned only with the photography of a superficial inner life that we have grown so accustomed to accept that we mistake all our subjective justifications for an objectivity from which they are immeasurably far removed. Such realism is as devoid of beauty as it is of truth; for beauty is revealed, not by external symbols, but only by that penetration which can pierce through the world of appearance. The function of the writer is to interpret the series of experiences and impressions of which his own life has been formed, by recapturing the reality which recedes from him persistently the more he finds himself circumscribed within the walls formed by the subjective ideas and prejudices which usually are falsely ennobled with the name of knowledge. In the realm of psychology, he must force himself to pierce the hide of complacency, deceit and the immense capacity of imitation which obscures his real self, and lay bare, with the ruthlessness of a surgeon, those stark and unsympathetic springs of action which the majority would doubtless infinitely prefer should remain hidden. This requires relentless courage. It implies a deliberate acceptance of suffering, and means stripping himself of his most cherished illusions, revealing his unconscious, no less than his intentional lies, of accepting the fact that love is no more than a mixture of desire and imagination, and exposing the inmost sanctuary of self-love, cowardice and hypocrisy.

The idea of time, he then decides, must serve him in a dual capacity. It must be employed to portray the fourth dimension of man, his "long body," of which the being we see is but a cross section; and it must be shown as the vast and relentless force that drives him ever further from the source of all inspiration, all beauty and all truth, until at last it severs him from the reality which lies buried in his most poignant memories.

Thus has Proust formulated for us the "metaphysical" aspects of his own work in an exposition which triumphantly weaves into a final pattern the separate threads of his various themes, and is a masterpiece of subtlety and skill in its continuous counterpoint on the opposite yet reciprocal aspects of his theory of time.

Le Temps Retrouvé is both the key and the cornerstone of the whole edifice of Proustian thought, a consummation which is equally an end and a beginning, and describes the full circle that is the outward form of the book's construction. Perhaps the most typical and expressive of its author's genius, it pushes the development of philosophical speculation and psychological analysis to a point far beyond that which any other novelist has yet attained. And in its complete generosity of spirit, it places Proust's conscience as an artist, together with his talent, in the highest rank.

INTRODUCTION TO PROUST

From the hour of his mother's death, Proust gave the best of himself, the whole of himself, to his work. He lived for it, and there can be little doubt that, by supplying an incentive deeper even than that of reason, it helped to prolong his life. And it stands, no less than as a history of the social life of his period, as a portrait of himself. Those who wish to discover the real Proust, will find him not only in the ideas, the impressions, the experiences and the conclusions of his Marcel; they will find him in the Dreyfusard Swann who loves Vermeer and the Pascal *Pensées* no less than the writings of Saint-Simon, in the M. de Charlus, who quotes La Bruyère, and explains that he tries to understand everything and to condemn nothing, just as they will find him, the writer, in certain aspects of Bergotte. But most of all they will find him in the Elstir, who, having spent his youth in artistic coteries, eventually isolates himself from the world in order that his talent may grow and flower unhampered, yet who, despite his deep love of solitude, would willingly give the whole of himself to anyone that he felt might understand him.

CHAPTER VIII

À la Recherche du Temps Perdu, however, is by no means a faultless book. Undoubtedly it is too long: not only hundreds of words but hundreds of pages too long. It is true that the various circumstances which made impossible publication in the manner that the author at first desired, permitted him later to make considerable amplifications to his work; but it is also true that all such elaborations were not equally necessary. By excessive diffusion, the original form of the novel was subjected to a terrific strain; and by altering the scale without sufficiently reinforcing the actual structure, its shape became so obscured that for a long time it seemed to be meandering and insignificant.

It was inevitable that during Proust's lifetime it should be generally imagined that his book, however original in style and method, was a perfectly straightforward autobiographical novel composed of a series of haphazard and quite unrelated memories of his past life; and much as he himself deplored the fact, there was nothing he could do but try to possess his soul in patience until the whole of the work should be published; an event, alas, that he was never to live to see. The fact that he died before he was able to correct and revise the last three parts of his novel was as great a tragedy for his work as it was for the author. *Albertine Disparue* and *Le Temps Retrouvé*, in particular, are marred by an occasional sketchiness and uncertainty that is far less apparent in any of the previous volumes; and despite the immense labour that it must have cost his literary executors—Jacques Rivière and Robert Proust—to prepare his manuscript for the press, errors so astonishing remain in the text that they give the impression that the development of the book was never fully planned.

In *Albertine Disparue*, for example, there is a passage stating that Saint-Loup is to keep his wife continuously supplied with offspring, when in the succeeding volume he leaves but one daughter; just as it is stated that Gilberte is eventually to become the Duchesse de Guermantes, an event which certainly never happens during the course of our acquaintance with her, and is, presumably, some error left from the original version, in which, of course, her husband could not have been killed in the War.

Similarly, in *Le Temps Retrouvé*, there are other passages which herald future developments that are never realized: there are identical phrases employed to describe the physical results of the same vice shared by Legrandin and Saint-Loup: Oriane de Guermantes is supplied with the completely new name of Marie-Sosthènes, and even in the remarkable dissertation upon time, there are curious obscurities and redundancies, to the extent that in some cases the same passage has been inserted twice, with the variation of but a few words, and only a few pages between each version.

Moreover, the method by which the whole book was amplified has created a certain sense of unreality regarding several of the most important details. As a considerable part of the first and third chapters of *Le Temps Retrouvé* must have been completed round about 1912, and the long chapter dealing with the War not until several years later, we find many of the major characters at the Princesse de Guermantes' party, despite the evidences of age announced, still remarkably young after the lapse of time which has intervened since their last appearance. We know that the "little clan" was in full swing, and that Swann was in love with an Odette no longer in her first youth, before Marcel's birth. So that even allowing that the latter is intended to be a few years younger than Proust himself—he could not be much more, since we know that he is a young man entering society at the beginning of the Dreyfus case—this means that the "mistress" is still giving huge crushes, and Mme de Forcheville taking lovers, when both these ladies must be very nearly seventy. But if this is barely credible, hardly more so is the external aspect of the deeply intimate life which Marcel leads with Albertine beneath his parents' roof, while his mother is called away conveniently to Combray to nurse a relative who remains ill for an unconscionably long time, and his father disappears from the narrative altogether.[1] Even as early as the first volume of *À l'Ombre des Jeunes Filles en Fleur* there are vague and inexplicable inconsistencies, as when Marcel's grandmother seems to live, now permanently with his parents, and now in a separate establishment of her own; and in the hotel at Balbec Marcel reads of Albertine's arrival with her parents, when subsequently she appears to be an orphan more or less in the care of her aunt, Mme Bontemps.

In addition, throughout the whole of the work there are to be found long and redundant passages which could add little of value to any novel. The famous introduction to *Sodome et Gomorrhe*, is, although a remarkable innovation, indispensable to the development of the work, and a treatise of great power and understanding. But it is difficult to find any adequate justification for the lengthy expositions of military tactics, or Brichot's endless dissertations upon the meaning of the place-names about Balbec. The sum of many such digressions, when it does little to advance the portrayal of character or the development of the action, merely serves to weaken the cumulative effect of a work which was composed with the most detailed and passionate care. Yet despite all its diffuseness, it is amazing how the subtle and persistent interlocking of episodes never weakens. Not only is the moment when

[1] It is almost certain that Proust's affair with "Albertine," whoever she was, terminated shortly before the war. Many long passages would therefore have been interpolated later which explains, though it does not excuse, this strange uncertainty.

Albertine announces to Marcel her knowledge of Mlle Vinteuil prepared for thousands of pages before, when as a child, he looks through the window of Montjouvain; and the climax in *Albertine Disparue*, when he receives Gilberte's telegram and imagines that it comes from Albertine, anticipated already in the early days of *À l'Ombre des Jeunes Filles en Fleur*, when Gilberte writes to him for the first time, and, owing to her ornate and pretentious calligraphy, he finds the utmost difficulty in deciphering her signature; but nearly every fresh episode in the book at once develops some past theme, and simultaneously introduces a new one. With what ingenious skill the introduction to *Sodome et Gomorrhe* is foreshadowed in the conversation about the fertilization of her plant at Mme de Guermantes' dinner party, or M. de Vagoubert is first discussed by M. de Norpois, and the full significance of certain implications demonstrated only much later, when he is shown at the Princesse de Guermantes' in conversation with M. de Charlus.

Nevertheless, here and there, and particularly in *Albertine Disparue*, there are wellnigh interminable passages so excruciatingly boring that it is an undeniable tribute to the fascination of the book as a whole that we ever succeed in ploughing our way through them at all. There are so many minor characters, also, who have little definite significance, that the very inclusion of their names merely increases the reader's difficulty in registering such others, whose number is already vast, as perform a very necessary part in the development of the exposition. Yet others recur under different names, such as Mme d'Orvillers and the Princesse de Nassau; both of these ladies, if not actually the same, being so similar as to serve little or no purpose by their dual representation.

Indeed, the greatest weaknesses of the book are the expression of precisely the same qualities that contrived to produce its extraordinary power, and are consequently inseparable from it. For Proust was so determined to give everything that he possessed, so determined to express himself with ultimate freedom and completeness, so determined that nothing that might add to the value of his work should be omitted, that he could not restrain himself from saying everything too frequently, too persistently and too much. Every idea, every psychological law, every theme that he utilized to express the truths he desired to illustrate, is repeated again and again; applied now to this character and now to that, stressed and overstressed with so consistent an emphasis that the result appears, sometimes, one of such deadly and hopeless monotony that it becomes almost unbearable. Every painful throb of jealousy and desire that is experienced by Swann for Odette is felt again by Marcel for Gilberte, and then superlatively and for the third time, by Marcel for Albertine. While this skilfully illustrates the fact that we learn never through our knowledge of the suffering of others but only, ultimately, through our own; and that the path by which we come to understand the truth of ideas which hitherto we have admitted only theoretically, and as platitudes, is essentially the same for each one of us: nevertheless, by lack of contrast, it tends ultimately to diffuse its force by reason of its very persistence.

Similarly it may be quite reasonably asserted that too many of Proust's characters turn out to be inverted. Whereas no legitimate objection can be taken to the choice of this phenomenon as literary material, and his treatment of the subject is, in every sense, beyond reproach, it adds nothing to the value of his contribution that he has made this weakness so ubiquitous. Certainly in the biblical Sodom there was found, ultimately, to be no man untainted; and doubtless in the idle and decadent society of which Proust treats, the vice was almost unimaginably widespread. Even so, it is quite unnecessary that such minor characters as Legrandin, Theodore, the Prince de Guermantes and M. Nissim Bernard should be added to the number of those whose ways have been quite adequately exposed through the observation of de Charlus, Vagoubert, Chatellerault and Saint-Loup.

Moreover the book is limited by the very environment of its characters; but then, as Proust himself was at such pains to explain, the author is as little free to choose his characters as a man is to select his parents. His true function is that of an interpreter, and for his work to have value, he must restrict himself to depicting such people as the circumstances and the manner of his own life have enabled him both to know and to understand. For in penetrating to a sufficient depth, in any group, the same fundamental laws which ultimately govern human nature can be laid bare.

It is true also that most of Proust's characters are drawn from a rich, aristocratic and idle society that has little to do but dabble ineffectively in the arts, fritter away its time at magnificently pretentious and unspeakably boring parties, pursue its sexual desires as though copulation were the ultimate goal of all existence, and suffer those emotional tortures which are very much the luxury of the man of leisure with too little to do. But it is useless to protest that they do not illustrate a manner of life and an attitude of mind which are changeless and universal. Some of the glory may have already departed from the Faubourg St. Germain, just as it has departed from Babylon and Rome; but even if the Guermantes themselves are now outmoded, their exact equivalents can still be found in many a mansion of contemporary London and New York. Indeed, the Guermantes with all their pride, their snobbery, their perversions and their essential worthlessness and vulgarity are typical figures because they correspond to recurring features which are inherent in mankind. Thus the general picture of Proustian society, as of his individual characters, is just as much a representation of phenomena which are eternal, as it is of any historic period that can be captured between the numerals of two successive dates. Proust's foremost intention was to strip his own world of all its hypocrisies and pretentions: that he has done so with the power and the bitterness of a Swift can scarcely be denied.

It is frequently observed of Proust that he is the supreme example of a novelist without discrimination. In reality it would be far more accurate to say that his work suffers from an embarrassment of riches. Certainly there are some long digressions that might well have been deleted; but lack of discrimination in this sense is but a minor technical weakness. Evidently it is not a psychological one. For it is almost wholly in his quite extraordinarily sensitive intellectual and emotional sense of discrimination that the whole value and significance of his work resides. But this discrimination is manifest not in the actual choice of his material, but in the persistent contrast between spurious, relative and ultimate values, and the sources and intensity of various impressions. The princely parties of the Guermantes are described in such punctilious detail, not because Proust considers them as important as the vivid and joyful impressions of his childhood, but because this is the supreme method by which he can show the ignorance, arrogance, complacence and stupidity which are the greatest barriers to our true life, and demonstrate his final proposition that the depth, validity and power of our most valuable impressions are quite independent of any worldly grandeur.

It is for a similar reason that drama, with Proust, is concerned far more deeply with inner realization and illumination than with any external action. Many of the most important events in the book take place as in a play, off stage, and are sketched in quite roughly in a few lines, as, in the theatre, a minor character may divulge a major tragedy in a short speech. This is not to say that Proust cannot write dramatically in the accepted sense—for the scene in which Mme Verdurin incites Morel to quarrel with M. de Charlus has a naked power and a pathos that is almost

Shakespearian—but that, for him, the most intense drama lies in the sudden juxtaposition of two impressions which, simultaneously compared, produce a powerful emotional realization of the persistent but unperceived changes which have taken place between them. Thus probably the most powerful and the most poignant moment in the book is where, shortly after having spoken to her over the telephone from Doncières, where he has been staying with Saint-Loup, Marcel arrives home unexpectedly to find her asleep in a chair, and realizes that the face which is alive in his memory, and which habit has prevented him for years from seeing as it really is, exists no more, and it is manifest to him with a sudden and painful shock that his adored, handsome and noble grandmother has become a weary, doddering and ugly old woman. In the same way the essential tragedy in the history of Marcel's passion for Albertine lies, not in the moment when she tells him of her friendship for Mlle Vinteuil, not in the moment when he learns that she has left him, nor yet even in the moment when he is informed of her death: but rather in that terrible moment years later, when he is compelled to admit to himself that the man in him who loved her exists no more, and that the possibility of meeting her again fills him less with indifference than with aversion.

These moments of concealed drama, which depend for their value not upon any external action but upon the sudden realization of change, occur at irregular intervals throughout the book, repeated with increasing frequency until, in *Le Temps Retrouvé*, they form the basis of all the author's philosophical conclusions, and their plaint reaches the fervour of a prophetic monody. All is vanity, is the heartfelt and persistent cry, as M. de Charlus, old and broken, bows low before Mme de Saint-Euverte, as Mme de Forcheville, fading and half witted, is cruelly insulted by her daughter's guests, as the last wishes of the moribund Berma are callously ignored by her daughter, as Legrandin, now the Comte de Méséglise, drags his decaying body through the Princesse de Guermantes' drawing-room, and Gilberte, the seductive and elusive nymph of the Champs Élysées, is no longer recognizable in a stout and middle-aged woman who is rapidly developing a double chin. Time, imperceptible but relentless, is not only the supreme master but the great destroyer: and Marcel's search for reality, for the state of noble and celestial happiness which he dimly senses to be foreshadowed in art and music, is therefore realized for him only at moments when the whole scale of his usual values is reversed and he has attained to a state of being which, though fugitive, is his only true life, since it alone can offer him a satisfaction undimmed and unalloyed by the usual laws of time.

For this reason it was necessary for Proust to evolve his individual technique, and to construct his novel in a manner which appears at first sight to be far more revolutionary than actually it is. Its complexity, indeed, like the flexibility and complexity of his style, is an essential feature, since only through such means could he incorporate successfully his long dissertations on social behaviour, and his elaborate essays on æsthetics and psychology. His book is the essential and inevitable creation of a highly cultured, powerful and comprehensive mind that, being unable to modify its expression to conform to any recognized and customary mould, was forced to produce its own peculiar form, at once hybrid and synthetic, which would incorporate the many and diverse aspects of his material. For *À la Recherche du Temps Perdu* is no more a pure novel than it is pure autobiography, pure psychology or pure philosophy. Incorporating every aspect of the author's physical, emotional and intellectual life, it portrays probably a more vivid and a more comprehensive picture of a growing and developing consciousness and personality than any other novel that has yet appeared.

Its method of detached objectivity, even when it appears to be most subjective, is applied as much to the unfolding of

Marcel's inner life as it is to the description of the life about him. For realism, to Proust, meant an exact reconstruction of the inner essence, rather than of the outer aspect, of his authentic impressions. It is for this reason that he deliberately substitutes for a photographic reproduction a form of representation that most truly permits him to describe accurately his most valued perceptions. Unlike Elstir, the quintessence of the impressionist school of painting, he rarely seeks to describe the outward aspect of things as they appear to the eyes rather than to the intelligence. Nor ever once, like Balzac, does he assemble with minute accuracy the interior of a room. But by recreating the beam of sunlight that spilled upon the floor, the scent of lilac in the air, or the musty smell of old books, he can convey a sense of vividness and depth that any amount of detailed description is powerless to evoke. Aware by experience and experiment that our most living memories are composed of the sum of sensations that are connected with the visual impression, he seeks to reproduce in these all the inner richness of mystery and beauty which gave them their significance. His childhood days at Combray are spread clearly before the eyes, not because we can see the style and position of the furniture in Marcel's room, but because we can smell the polish on the floor, hear the sound of church bells that drifts in through the window, and see the figures traced by light and shadow upon the walls: for with the simple description of a barrel organ tune and a column of dust, Proust can evoke the whole atmosphere, both of a room and of a mood. But if his method can thus, to a certain extent, be termed expressionistic, it also reveals a certain aspect of surrealism, since the sensations—the subtle and fleeting moments that he seeks to capture—bear upon their outward form the purely subjective associations with which they happen, at that moment, to be linked. These images and associations are recaptured and transmitted through phrases of a strangely original and unexpected beauty. The famous madeleine, for example, is "richly sensual beneath its severe, religious folds," and Gilberte's face, when she is sullen, recalls to Marcel "those dreary beaches where the sea, ebbing far out, wearies one with its faint shimmering, everywhere the same, fixed in an immutable and low horizon."

His style, despite all the complexity of those interminable sentences, deeply influenced by his admiration and appreciation of the prose of Ruskin,—"that mighty and majestic prose ... so fervid and so fiery coloured in its noble eloquence, so rich in its elaborate symphonic music, so sure and certain, at its best, in subtle choice of word and epithet"—is a triumph of flexibility and expressive skill. Clear, curt and suave when he is ironic, it can be brilliantly acid, tenderly poetic; sombrely powerful or lyrical with the most gentle and most moving beauty. In the final chapters of *Le Temps Retrouvé*, there are long passages which, with their subtle intricate rhythms and their mournful, plangent cadences, are as pregnant with the melancholy prescience of mortality as any lamentation of Ecclesiastes. Enriched by his remarkable and comprehensive culture, by his deep love and understanding of classical literature, of music and of painting, the whole work displays a wealth of similes derived with an equal aptness and facility from biology, from physics, from botany, from medicine, or from mathematics, that never ceases to astonish and delight.

As for the characteristic and elliptical form of the sentences themselves, despite their occasional obscurity, the habit of assimilating them without difficulty is very soon acquired. And while undoubtedly Proust will always remain caviare to the general, the great sensitiveness and variety of his prose is alone sufficient to keep his name alive so long as a civilization remains that can appreciate an exceptional culture, and value literature as an art. But style, with Proust, as with all the great writers, is never more than the means to an end, and at no time, as for example, with the Henry James with whom he has so much in common, does it overstep its position in the narrative to violate the laws of character. All Proust's people speak in their own way with their own phrases, or with the phrases of their respective sets, and never in the involuted and complicated phrases of the author.

In conclusion, it must be emphasized how inconspicuous, almost irrelevant indeed, Proust's faults become in comparison with the superb success and ingenuity with which so many supplementary themes are continually interwoven and continuously developed until they are combined at last in the incomparable final chapter. This alone would make it impossible to deny Proust's right to claim his place amongst the greatest novelists of the world. Essentially different from those others from whom, nevertheless, he has derived those qualities of depth and solidity which place him, despite his various innovations, in the direct line of the great tradition, his subtlety and power so far exceed his obvious deficiencies that he can well stand with Tolstoy, Dostoievsky, Balzac, Stendhal and Thackeray, with all of whom he has so much in common.

To those who seek in the novel a form of diversion or an opiate such as is offered by the cinema or the radio, Proust has nothing to say. But to those others for whom literature, as every other branch of art, of science, of philosophy and of religion, is a recognized approach towards understanding the mystery and beauty of the world, his work will afford a quite extraordinary amount of suggestive and interesting material. For he put into it every observation, every realization, every emotion and every painfully acquired truth that was the harvest of a life of deep isolation and physical suffering. With the courage of the scientist who, in the course of his experiments, never flinches from inoculating himself with a virus that might easily cause his death, he lays bare every tremor of the nerves, every aspect, no matter how base or callous, of his own motives, in the interest, not of fiction, but of science and of truth. Thus he has lifted the novel out of the realm of fiction altogether. His book is no arbitrary portrayal of life, but the lives of himself and of his circle, penetrated to the most obscure and inaccessible depths that he could reach. No other novelist has ever been so little concerned with entertainment or distraction. His work contains humour, poetry, drama, passion and tragedy: all the irony, the triviality, the beauty and the disillusion of human life. But nowhere does he make the slightest concession to imagination.

At a first attempt, the prospect of toiling through the seven[1] long parts of *À la Recherche du Temps Perdu* may appear to be formidable and even distasteful. But once set ourselves to do so, and, when we have reached the end, it is probable that our most powerful sensation will be that never again—at least until many years are past and we can re-read the book with something of our original appreciation and excitement—shall we find any novel that compares with it in its impressive wealth of insight and understanding. Its verisimilitude and its veracity are amazing. In this lies its greatest strength. For, in the words of Ruskin, "Wheresoever the search after truth begins, there life begins;" of Goethe, "The first and last thing required of genius is the love of truth."

---

[1] As they are now divided.

BIBLIOGRAPHY

The works of Marcel Proust, published by *la Nouvelle Revue Française*:

À la Recherche du Temps Perdu:—
  Du Côté de chez Swann: two volumes
  À l'Ombre des Jeunes Filles en Fleur: three volumes
  Le Côté de Guermantes: three volumes
  Sodome et Gomorrhe: two volumes
  La Prisonnière: two volumes
  Albertine Disparue: one volume
  Le Temps Retrouvé: one volume

  Chroniques: one volume
  Pastiches et Mélanges: one volume
  Les Plaisirs et les Jours: one volume

La Bible d'Amiens by John Ruskin, translated and with notes and preface by Marcel Proust, published by *la Mercure de France*.

Sésamé et Lys, by John Ruskin, translated and with notes and preface by Marcel Proust, published by *la Mercure de France*.

The novels only have been superbly translated into English by C. K. Scott-Moncrieff, with the final volume by Stephen Hudson, and issued, under the general title of *Remembrance of Things Past*, by Chatto & Windus, as follows:

  Swann's Way: two volumes
  Within a Budding Grove: two volumes
  The Guermantes Way: two volumes
  Cities of the Plain: two volumes
  The Captive: one volume
  The Sweet Cheat Gone: one volume
  Time Regained: one volume

BIBLIOGRAPHY

The Letters of Marcel Proust:

Correspondance Générale, published by Librairie Plon
1. *Lettres à Robert de Montesquiou*
2. *Lettres à la Comtesse de Noailles*
3. *Lettres à M. et Mme Sidney Schiff, Paul Souday, Jacques-Émile Blanche, etc.*
4. *Lettres à Pierre Lavallée, F. L. Voudoyer, Robert de Flers, Mme Gaston de Caillavet, B. de Salignac-Fénelon, Robert Dreyfus, etc.*
5. *Lettres à Walter Berry, Louisa de Mornand, Mme Laure Hayman, Mme Sheikevitch, etc.*
6. *Lettres à Mme Strauss*

Lettres à Robert de Billy (Lettres et conversations). R. de Billy

Autour de soixante lettres de Marcel Proust (à Lucien Daudet) published by *la N.R.F.* in the series, *Les Cahiers Marcel Proust*

Lettres à la N.R.F. published by *la N.R.F.* in the series, *Les Cahiers Marcel Proust*

Lettres à Louis de Robert (Comment débuta Marcel Proust) par L. de Robert, published by *la N.R.F.*

Lettres à René Blum, Bernard Grasset et Louis Brun, par L. Pierre-Quint, published by Kra.

BIBLIOGRAPHY

Important French works on Proust:

Marcel Proust: Sa vie, son oeuvre	Léon Pierre-Quint
Marcel Proust à 17 ans	Robert Dreyfus
Souvenirs sur Marcel Proust	Robert Dreyfus
Marcel Proust: lettres et conversations	R. de Billy
Comment débuta Marcel Proust	L. de Robert
Au bal avec Marcel Proust	Princesse Marthe Bibesco
L'Amitié de Proust	Georges Cattui
Marcel Proust: sa révélation psychologique	A. Dandieu
Proust, Gide, Valéry	Paul Souday
Hommage à Marcel Proust	Various Writers
Répertoire d'À la Recherche du Temps Perdu	Charles Daudet
Répertoire des thèmes de Marcel Proust	Raoul Celly
Introduction à la correspondance de Proust	Pierre Raphael

Important works upon the literary and social life of his period, in which references to Proust occur:

Les Pas Effacés, Mémoires: three volumes	Robert de Montesquiou
Souvenirs d'un Temps Disparu	Marie Sheikevitch
Robert de Montesquiou et Marcel Proust	E. de Clermont-Tonnerre
Le Salon de Mme Arman de Caillavet	Jean-Maurice Pouquet
Souvenirs de la Vie Mondaine	Abel Hermant

For a historical survey of the period, and a history of the Dreyfus Case:

La Troisième République	David Robert
The Dreyfus Case	Charpentier

INDEX

Acacias, Allée des (see *Bois*)
Action Française, 150
Adolphe (*Marcel's uncle*), 175, 200, 238
Affaire Lemoine, 125, 149
Agostinelli, 124, 126, 139
Aimé, 189, 194, 208
Albaret, Céleste, 139, 140, 145, 155, 162, 165, 166
Albaret, Odilon, 139
Albertine, 187, 191, 192, 196, 198, 199, 200, 201, 202, 203, 205, 206, 207, 208, 209, 210, 242, 271, 272, 273, 274, 276, 277, 278, 279, 283, 289, 299, 300, 301, 304
Albertine Disparue, 164, 165, 169; synopsis, 206–10, 297, 298, 300
Albuféra, Marquis d', 101, 137, 149, 152, 159
Amiens, The Bible of, 107
Amphion (*country house of the Brancovans*), 111
Andrée, 191, 199, 202, 206, 207, 262, 271
Annunzio, Gabrielle d', 35, 135
Antoine, 36
Arabian Nights, The, 18
Arlesienne L', 29
Arpajon, Mme d', 222
Artagnan d', 57
Aubernon, Mme, 33, 34, 35, 37, 39, 40, 41, 42, 43, 56, 72, 91, 216, 217, 231, 240, 243, 250
Aurelius, Marcus, 116
Aurore, L', 90, 114
Auteuil, 18, 19, 21, 23, 24, 231

Bach, 75
Baignères, Mme, 28, 66
Baignères, Jacques, 26, 72
Baignères, Paul, 85
Balbec, 175, 183, 189, 192, 198, 208, 210, 219, 230, 253, 260, 272, 283, 289, 290, 299
Ballet, Russian, 130, 135, 138, 244
Balzac, 72, 125, 306, 308
Banquet, Le, 51, 77, 85, 96, 147

Barbusse, Henri, 50, 150, 151
Barrès, Maurice, 43, 91, 92, 103
Barrès, Mme, 61
Bartet, Mme, 56, 62
Beaulaincourt, Comtesse de, 68, 231
Becque, 36
Beethoven, 75, 135
Belgium, Queen of, 55
Beraud, Jean, 87
Bergotte, 109, 128, 176, 183, 184, 187, 195, 198, 217, 228, 231, 240, 241, 243, 264, 266, 270, 289, 296
Bergson, 164, 281
Berma, La, 176, 183, 184, 186, 264, 289, 304
Bernard, M. Nissim, 233, 235, 301
Bernhardt, Sarah, 27, 55, 57, 60
Berry, Walter, 146, 151, 152
Bibesco, Prince Antoine, 98, 99, 100, 102, 131, 132, 149
Bibesco, Prince Emmanuel, 98, 99, 100, 102, 141
Billy, Robert de, 45, 47, 53
Bizet, 29
Bizet, Jacques, 26, 27, 50, 51, 72, 85, 137
Blanche, Jacques Émile, 19, 66, 85, 103, 136, 142, 164
Bloch, 176, 188, 190, 192, 194, 211, 228, 233, 235, 262, 266, 276, 285
Blum, Léon, 50
Blum, Réné, 101, 133, 145
Bois, the, 53, 54, 153, 185, 189, 239, 268
Boisdeffre, General, 95
Boldini, 58
Bontemps, Mme, 187, 192, 207, 210, 217, 222, 272, 299
Borda, Gustave de, 87
Botticelli, 180
Boulbon, Dr. Du, 195, 228
Boulenger, Jacques, 157
Bourget, Paul, 54
Brancovan, Princesse Bassaraba de, 102
Bréauté, M. de, 223

INDEX

Brichot, 180, 200, 203, 229, 242, 299
Brunschwicq, Léon, 21, 26, 45, 97
Bruyère, La, 52, 253, 296
Burne-Jones, Sir Edward, 42
Byron, 154

Cabourg, 23, 115, 124, 126, 139, 147
Caillavet, Mme Arman de, 33, 37, 39, 40, 41, 42, 43, 45, 46, 50, 59, 91, 217, 224, 231, 240
Caillavet, M. Arman de, 38, 91
Caillavet, Gaston de, 45, 46, 47, 48, 50, 55, 97, 141, 147
Caillavet, Mme Gaston de, 59
Calmette, Gaston, 96, 123, 124, 133, 136
Cambremer, Dowager Marquise de, 199
Cambremer-Legrandin, Marquise de, 175, 199, 220, 221, 226, 236, 249, 271
Cambremer, Marquis de, 209
Capion (country house of Mme A. de Caillavet), 38
Captive, The (see *La Prisonnière*); synopsis, 202–6
Caraman-Chimay, Princesse Alexandre de, 102, 116
Carmen, 29
Carolus-Duran, 129
Caucheval, Professor, 25
Champs Élysées, The, 20, 21, 24, 26, 183, 184, 185, 186, 187, 195, 305
Charlus, Baron Palamède de, 159, 177, 182, 190, 194, 195, 197, 200, 202, 203, 204, 205, 209, 210, 211, 216, 221, 222, 226, 228, 231, 239, 242; character, 252–6, 257, 263, 276, 300, 302, 303, 304
Charpentier, 60, 93, 244
Chartres, 16
Chatellerault, Duc de, 302
Chauve-Souris, 57
Chef des Odeurs Suaves, 57
Chénier, 62
Chevigné, Comtesse Adhéaume de, 51, 54, 55, 149, 231
Cities of the Plain (see *Sodome et Gomorrhe*); synopsis, 197–202
Clermont-Tonnerre, Princesse de, 123, 149
Closmenil, 27, 231
Cocteau, Jean, 135
Cœur Volant (country house of Mme Aubernon), 37
Combray, 171, 174, 175, 176, 190, 208, 236, 260, 282, 299, 306
Comœdia, 136

Condorcet, Lycée, 21, 23, 45, 50, 85
Conférence Parlementaire de la Rue, Serpente, 52
Conte de Noel, 51
Contre l'Obscurité, 96
Copeau, Jacques, 131
Coppet (country house of Mme d'Haussonville), 65
Coppée, 43
Coquelin, 55
Côté de Guermantes, Le, 138, 156, 157; Synopsis, 192–7, 258
Cottard, 179, 186, 187, 195, 199, 200, 266
Cottard, Mme, 187, 217, 222, 256, 262
Coucher de la Mort, La, 62
Crécy, Comte de, 126
Crécy, Odette de (see *Odette*)
Croix de Bois, La, 155
Croniques, 51
Curies, The, 42

Darlu, Professor, 26, 91
Daudet, Alphonse, 66, 96
Daudet, Mme, 66
Daudet, Léon, 66, 150, 153, 154, 157, 160
Daudet, Lucien, 66, 71, 76, 103, 136
Dauphin, The, 57
David, 61
David à Dgéas, de, 142
Debussy, 220
Deffand, Mme du, 33, 240
Derby, Lord, 162
Detaille, 43
Détourbet (maiden name of Mme de Loynes), 41
Diaghileff, 126
Diane de Lys, 36
Dickens, 18
Dieu Bleu, Le, 126
Diner en Ville, Un, 83
Diologues, Plato's, 26
Dobson, Austin, 80
Doll's House, The, 36
Dominique (pseudonym of Proust), 109
Doncières, 190, 193, 304
Dorgèles, 154
Dostoievsky, 72, 142, 308
Dreyfus Case, The, 88–95, 114, 194, 198, 233, 234, 237, 243, 247, 299
Dreyfus, Captain, 88, 115, 198, 199, 227, 234, 238
Dreyfus, Mme, 95
Dreyfus, Robert, 21, 50, 85, 86, 97, 137, 151, 153, 160
Dumas, fils, 36, 37, 39, 40, 41

INDEX

Duncan, Isadora, 159
Duras, Duchesse de, 204
Duse, 57
Dyck, Van, 53

Éblouissements, Les, 124
Echo de Paris, L', 136
Einstein, 164
Eliot, George, 96
Elstir, 179, 191, 192, 196, 231, 239, 242, 247, 248, 264, 265, 266, 273, 296, 306
Ephrussi, Charles, 104, 230
Esquisse Après Madame . . . , 51
Essais, Les, 130
Esseintes, Des, 57
Esterhazy, 89
Étranger, L', 82
Eugénie, Empress, 66, 95
Eulalie, 175, 261

Faffenheim-Munsterburg-Weinigen, Prince von, 225-6
Fasquelle, 133, 144
Faguet, 125
Fauré, 123, 230
Félix-Faure, Antoinette and Lucie, 21
Fénelon, Comte Bertrand de Salignac, 98, 100, 141, 231
Feu, Le, 150
Feuillet, Octave, 36
Figaro, Le, 38, 90, 91, 96, 109, 123, 124, 125, 131, 136, 145, 150, 151
Fin de la Jalousie, La, 83, 84
Flaubert, 43, 68, 125
Flers, Robert de, 26, 47, 50, 53, 55, 97, 147, 151, 160
Forain, 30, 43, 55, 85, 92
Forcheville, Comte de, 180, 181, 182, 241
Forcheville, Comtesse de (see Odette)
Forcheville, Mlle de (see Gilberte)
Fosse, de la, 61, 62, 231
Fragments de Comédie Italienne, 83
France, Anatole, 37, 39, 40, 41, 42, 43, 46, 55, 58, 80, 81, 103, 110, 217, 231, 240
François le Champi, 174
Françoise, 173, 175, 183, 185, 186, 193, 199, 203, 206; character 259-61, 272
Franck, César, 229
Freud, 281
Froberville, General de, 236, 251

Gallardon, Marquise de, 221
Gallifet, Général Marquis de, 230

Gandara, La, 58
Ganderax, 51, 103
Gaucher, Professor, 25
Gaulois Le, 96
Gautier, Théophile, 18, 57
Gazette des Beaux-Arts, 230
Germany, Empress of, 55
Gide, André, 131, 143
Gilberte, née Swann, becomes (1) *Mlle de Forcheville*, and (2) *Marquise de Saint-Loup*, 176, 177, 184, 185, 186, 187, 188, 189, 198, 208, 209, 210, 211, 216, 219, 226, 227, 237, 241, 247, 257, 271, 279, 289, 298, 300, 301, 305
Gisèle, 191, 192
Goëthe, 309
Goncourts, The, 60, 68, 125
Gonse, General, 89
Gothic Cathedrals, 99
Grand'mère, Une, 124
Grandmother, Marcel's, 176, 189, 190, 195, 198, 208, 229, 251, 253, 258, 261, 283, 286, 299, 304
Grand Prix, 164
Grasset, Bernard, 133, 134, 137, 144
Greffulhe, Comtesse, 33, 61, 65, 135, 149, 216, 231
Gregh, Fernand, 19, 50, 51
Guermantes, Basin Duc de, 193, 197, 211, 219, 222, 231, 235, 241; character 250-2, 257, 262, 266, 301
Guermantes, Oriane Duchesse de, 51, 83, 177, 181, 182, 190, 192, 193, 195, 196, 202, 208, 209, 211, 216, 217, 219, 220, 221, 222, 224, 228, 229, 231, 236, 237; character, 245-50, 257, 262, 272, 277, 298, 300
Guermantes, Paulin Prondre de, 146, 230
Guermantes, Prince de, 198, 211, 219, 235, 238, 256, 300
Guermantes, Princesse de, 193, 216, 217, 220, 221, 222, 229, 230, 235, 238, 254
Guermantes, 2nd Princesse de (see Verdurin)
Guermantes Way, The (see *Le Côté de Guermantes*) synopsis, 192-7
Guerne, Comtesse de, 65, 103
Guiche, Duc de, 101, 149, 152

Haas, Charles, 230
Hahn, Reynaldo, 55, 56, 72, 80, 103, 116, 126, 160

315

INDEX

Halèvy, 29
Halèvy, Daniel, 26, 27, 45, 50
Halèvy, Ludovic, 36, 125
Hamlet, 27
Hanotaux, Gabriel, 88
Hari, Mata, 42
Harvey, Gladys, 54
Hausonville, Comte d', 231
Hausonville, Comtesse d', 55, 65, 231
Hayman, Mme Laure, 54, 158, 217, 231
Heath, Willy, 53, 80
Hébrard, Adrien, 136, 148
Helleu, 58
Henry IV of France, 57
Henry, Lt.-Col., 95
Hoche, Avenue, 39, 41, 45, 47, 91
Hogarth, 216
Hohenzollern, William II of, 90, 94
Horatio (pseudonym of Proust), 109
Hugo, 21
Huysmans, 57

Ibsen, 36, 51
Illiers, 15, 17, 18, 23, 45, 100, 161
Imitation of Christ, The, 76, 82
Imitations, Proust's, 73, 125, 126
Impressions de Route en Automobile, 124
"In-the-Soup" (see Octave)
Irreligion d'État, L', 52

Jallifier, 24
James, Henry, 308
Jansen, 135, 152
Jean Christophe, 130
John Gabriel Borkman, 36
Journal, Le, 90
Journées de Lecture, 124
Jupien, 193, 197, 202, 210, 211, 229, 253
Jupien's niece, 193, 197, 202, 205, 209, 226, 229

Labori, 115, 244
Laprévotte, Mlle, 183
Laszlo, de, 58
Lauriers sont Coupés, Les, 85
Lauris, George de, 101
Laumes, des Prince and Princesse (see Duc and Duchesse de Guermantes)
Lavallée, Pierre, 26, 71, 72
Léa, 203, 272
Leblois, 89
Legion of Honour, 164
Legrandin, 175, 194, 211, 220, 223, 298, 301, 304

Lemaire, Mlle Suzette, 116
Lemaire, Mme Madeleine, 54, 55, 56, 59, 72, 80, 132, 216, 217, 231, 243
Lemaître, Jules, 27, 36, 37, 39, 41, 42, 43, 55
Leonie, Marcel's "Great-Aunt," 174, 176, 183, 188, 260, 282
Lespinasse, Mlle de, 33, 240
Linton, Catherine, 289
Lisle, Leconte de, 21
Liszt, 98
Lorrain, Jean, 87
Loti, 57
Louis XIV, 57
Loynes, Comte de, 41
Loynes, Comtesse de, 33, 41, 42, 91, 217, 231, 243
Lundi, 27
Luxembourg, Hereditary Grand Duke of, 250
Luxembourg, Princesse de, 222
Lytton, Lord, 30

Macaulay, 70
Mallarmé, 18, 57
Marcel, 84, 171–4, 183–212, 216, 218, 219, 222, 227, 228, 229, 236, 238, 242, 243, 251, 253, 254, 257, 258, 260, 261, 264, 268, 271, 272, 273, 274, 275, 276, 277, 278, 279, 283, 284, 286, 288, 292, 294, 296, 298, 299, 300, 301, 304, 305, 306
Mariage à la Mode, 216
Marsantes, Mme de, 194, 226, 227
Massenet, 55
Mathilde, Princesse, 30, 55, 66, 67, 68, 95, 217, 230
Maugny, Comtesse de, 142
Maupassant, de, 43
Mélancolique Villégiature de Mme de Breyves, 83
Meline, 94
Mercier, General, 88
Mercure de France, 106, 132
Merimée, 68
Méséglise, Comte de (see Legrandin), 304
Messina, Square de, 36, 39
Meyer, Arthur, 30
Meyerbeer, 220
Michelet, 125
Modern Painters, 180
Molé, Comtesse, 255
Mondanité et Mélomanie de Bouvard et Pécuchet, 83
Monet, 93, 231
Monnot, Professor, 49

INDEX

Montaigne, 52
Montesquiou, Abbé de, 57
Montesquiou, François de, 57
Montesquiou, Comte Robert de, 56–63, 68, 76, 102, 103, 109, 110, 135, 149, 152, 159, 160, 230, 231, 253, 254
Montjouvain, 177, 202, 300
Montluc, Blaise de, 57
Morand, Paul, 163
Morel, 200, 202, 203, 204, 205, 209, 210, 211, 216, 220, 222, 226, 229, 231, 235, 242, 256, 263, 303
Mornand, Louisa de, 231
Mort de Baldassare Silvande, 81
Mortemart, Mme de, 224
Mother, Marcel's, 171, 172, 173, 174, 185, 201, 202, 229, 258, 266, 299
Mounet-Sully, 55
Musset, de, 21

Nassau, Princesse de, 300
Nêne, 163
Nerville, Mme de, 34
Neuilly, 48
Nietzsche, 51
Noailles, Comtesse de, 102, 104, 109, 120, 124, 128, 149, 156, 164
Norpois, Marquis de, 186, 190, 194, 208, 225, 228, 229, 260, 300
Nouvelle Revue Française, La, 131, 132, 143, 144, 145

Octave, 191, 210
Odette, de Crécy, becomes (1) Mme Swann, and (2) Comtesse de Forcheville, 134, 158, 178, 180, 181, 182, 183, 185, 186, 187, 188, 199, 202, 208, 211, 215, 216, 217, 219, 229, 231, 236; character, 238–41, 242, 243, 245, 250, 252, 255, 262, 264, 268, 272, 276, 277, 298, 299, 301, 304
Oleron, Mlle d' (see Jupien's niece)
Olivier, 149
Ollendorf, 133
Ombre des Jeunes Filles en Fleur, A l', 145, 150, 156, 163, 164; synopsis, 186–92, 232, 299, 300
Orvillers, Princesse d', 300

Paris, Comte de, 230, 237
Parisienne, 36
Parme, Princesse de, 217, 222, 223, 248
Pascal, 52, 97, 218, 280, 284, 296
Pastiches et Mélanges, 150
Pater, Walter, 96

Pavillon des Muses, 61, 62, 63, 110
Pecheurs des Perles, les, 29
Pèlerinages Ruskiniens, 96
Pensées (Pascals), 97
Phèdre, 186, 289
Picquart, 89, 93, 115, 238, 244
Pierrebourg, Baronne de, 33
Plaisirs et les Jours, Les, 51, 80–5, 96, 108
Plato, 26
Polignac, Prince and Princesse de, 65
Portraits de Peintres, 72
Poulet, 162
Presse, La, 96
Primoli, Comte Joseph, 230
Prisonnière, La, 81, 83, 169, 170; synopsis, 202–6
Prix Goncourt, 150, 153, 154, 159, 163, 164, 169
Proust, Mme, 16, 20, 72, 104, 107, 111, 112, 258
Proust, Professor Adrien, 15, 20, 77, 105, 106
Proust, Robert, 16, 19, 77, 106, 141, 149, 161, 166, 297

Rachel, 188, 190, 193, 194, 195, 210, 211, 231, 233, 235, 257, 263, 265, 276, 285
Racine, 21
Radziwill, Prince, 101
Rake's Progress, The, 216
Rebours, A, 57
Récamier, 33, 65
Recherche du Temps Perdu, A la, 133, 170; synopsis, 171–212, 213, 215, 228, 264, 284, 297, 305, 309
Red Lily, The, 48
Régnier, Henri de, 103, 125
Regrets, Rêveries Couleur du Temps, 83
Reichenberg, 62
Reiter, Eugene, 51
Réjane, 36, 55, 152
Remembrance of Things Past (see *A la Recherche du Temps Perdu*), 164; synopsis, 171–212
Renan, 36, 125
Renoir, 93
Rentrée Litteraire, Une, 151
Revue Blanche, 96
Revue Bleue, 25
Revue de Seconde, 27
Revue des Deux Mondes, 51, 226
Revue Lilas, 27
Revue Verte, 27
Ribot, 116
Risler, 123

INDEX

Ritz Hotel, 123, 146, 155, 157, 158, 165, 169, 210
Rivebelle, 191
Rivière, Jacques, 131, 143, 297
Robert, Louis de, 93, 94, 130, 133, 135
Rochefoucauld, Gabriel, Duc de la, 19, 66, 103, 149
Rochefoucauld, La, 52, 218
Rodin, 58
Rohan, Duchesse de, 60
Roman d'un Malade, 130
Rosamonde, 191
Rose, Palais, 110
Rostand, 57, 136
Rothschild, Baronne Alphonse de, 66
Rubinstein, Ida, 135
Ruskin, 64, 96, 99, 100, 107, 108, 109, 133, 155, 160, 161, 180, 231, 266, 267, 284, 289, 307, 309

Sainte-Beuve, 41, 68, 125
Saint-Euverte, Marquise de, 182, 215, 221, 236, 246, 248, 254, 255, 256, 268, 304
Saint-Loup-en-Bray, Robert, Marquis de, 100, 159, 191, 192, 193, 194, 195, 196, 198, 201, 207, 209, 216, 217, 219, 228, 231, 235, 241, 245, 257, 271, 276, 285, 298, 302, 304
Saint-Loup, Marquise de (see Gilberte)
Saint-Saens, 55, 229
Saint-Simon, 52, 57, 125, 149, 296
Salle, Louis de la, 21, 26, 50, 97, 141
Sand, Georges, 18
Sandherr, Col., 88
Saniette, 179, 200, 243, 263
Sardou, 36
Sazerat, 175, 208, 209
Scénario, 84
Scheurer-Kestner, 89–90
Schiff, Mr. and Mrs. Sidney, 157–69
Schlumberger, Jean, 131
Schopenhauer, 51, 117
Sentiments Filiaux d'un Parricide, 124
Sesame and Lilies, 116, 124
Sévigné, Mme de, 123
Sheikevitch, Mme, 129, 135, 136, 146, 148
Sherbatoff, Princesse, 200, 223, 224, 243
"Ski," 200
Sodome et Gomorrhe, 111, 126, 159, 160, 161, 163, 169, 170; synopsis, 197–202, 252, 299, 300
Sorel, Professor Albert, 50
Souday, Paul, 136, 137, 157
Stendhal, 72, 274, 308

Stermaria, Mlle de, becomes Mme de, 189, 196
Strauss, Mme, 28, 29, 30, 33, 36, 50, 51, 55, 66, 85, 91, 114, 123, 128, 133, 135, 136, 152, 216, 230, 231, 243, 249
Swann, Charles, 84, 134, 172, 176, 177, 178, 179, 181, 182, 185, 186, 198, 199, 200, 202, 203, 215, 216, 227, 228, 229, 232, 233, 235; character, 236–8, 239, 240, 241, 244, 247, 249, 251, 252, 262, 276, 277, 278, 296, 298, 301
Swann, Mme (see Odette)
Swann (*du Côté de Chez*), 28, 81, 83, 108, 116, 130, 134, 136, 137, 138, 143, 145, 146, 149, 150, 159; synopsis, 171–86
Swann, Gilberte (see Gilberte)
Swann's Way (see above), synopsis, 171–86
Sweden, King of, 55
Sweet Cheat gone, The (see *Albertine Disparue*), synopsis, 206–10
Swift, 303
Swinburne, 51

Tansonville, 177, 210, 236
Temps, Le, 51, 90, 136, 137, 148
Temps Retrouvé, Le, 82, 108, 138, 163, 169; synopsis, 202–6, 288, 295, 297, 298; Pt. 2, Chap. 7, 304, 307
Tendres Stocks, 163
Thackeray, 308
Théodorc, 301
Three Musketeers, The, 57
Time Regained (see *Le Temps Retrouvé*), synopsis, 202–6
Tinan, Jean de, 21
Tissot, 230
Titles (choice of), 133–4
Tolstoy, 72, 142, 308
Trariaux, Gabriel, 26
Trombert, Mme, 217
Troubetskoy, 58
Trouville, 23, 72, 115
Turkish Ambassadress, The, 221, 262

Uzès, Duchesse d', 55

Vagoubert, Marquis de, 300, 302
Vaudoyer, Jean-Louis, 130, 135
Verdurin, M., 204, 262
Verdurin, Mme, 170, 180, 181, 183, 199, 201, 203, 204, 205, 210, 211, 215, 216, 217, 219, 220, 222, 223, 229, 231, 235, 236, 238, 240;

INDEX

Verdurin, Mme (cont.)
   character, 241–5, 263, 265, 266, 268, 289, 298, 303, 305
Verlaine, 57
Vermeer, 128, 296
Victoria, Queen, 94
Village, 36
Villeparisis, Marquise de, 37, 176, 189, 190, 192, 193, 194, 196, 208, 209, 216, 217, 222, 224, 225, 226, 229, 231, 250, 254, 290
Vinteuil, 176, 177, 201, 243, 264, 266, 304
Vinteuil, Mlle, 177, 201, 203, 205, 266, 300
Vinteuil's Septet, 203
Vinteuil's Sonata, 179, 182, 187, 229, 236, 268, 289
Violante, ou la Mondanité, 51, 82

Wagner, 75, 98, 142, 229
Wagram, Princesse de, 65
Wales, Prince of, 237
Wales, Princess of, 55
Weber's (restaurant), 74, 147
Weil (family), 16
Werner, Sir Jules, 125
Whistler, 58, 59, 62
Wilde, Oscar, 80
Within a Budding Grove (see *A l'Ombre des Jeunes Filles en Fleur*), synopsis, 186–92

Yourbeletieff, Princesse, 244
Ytturi, 62, 103, 149

Zola, 90, 91, 94, 114, 115, 130, 244